Redesigning the Firm

Redesigning the Firm

EDITED BY

EDWARD H. BOWMAN
and BRUCE M. KOGUT

New York   Oxford
OXFORD UNIVERSITY PRESS
1995

Oxford University Press

Oxford   New York
Athens   Auckland   Bangkok   Bombay
Calcutta   Cape Town   Dar es Salaam   Delhi
Florence   Hong Kong   Istanbul   Karachi
Kuala Lumpur   Madras   Madrid   Melbourne
Mexico City   Nairobi   Paris   Singapore
Taipei   Tokyo   Toronto

and associated companies in
Berlin   Ibadan

Library of Congress Cataloging-in-Publication Data
Redesigning the firm / edited by Edward Bowman and Bruce Kogut.
p. cm.   ISBN 0–19–508710–0
1. Industrial management.   2. Industrial organization.
I. Bowman, Edward H.   II. Kogut, Bruce Mitchel.
HD31.R436 1995
658.4′06—dc20   —dc20
[658.5′62]   94–38971

1 3 5 7 9 8 6 4 2

Printed in the United States of America
on acid-free paper

To Ann and Monika

Foreword

The modern business firm is undergoing a period of rapid transformation in response to rapid changes in its competitive environment. Vertical structures of the past are tilting into more horizontal organizations. Hierarchies are being interlaced with teams. Business process re-engineering is cutting across functions to remold the organization.

This book draws together the insights of leading researchers in diverse disciplines at the Wharton School and of senior executives at some of the most innovative of today's firms to provide insight into the kinds of the organizations that will compete effectively in markets today and tomorrow. The Wharton School is in a unique position to undertake such a project. Wharton has powerful functional breadth, with leading experts in eleven departments—including management, public policy, accounting, marketing, operations, and finance. The intellectual depth of these departments are joined and focused by a network of more than twenty research centers. The project that led to this book was organized by one of these centers, the Reginald H. Jones Center, under the able guidance of center director Dr. Edward H. Bowman, a leading researcher on the modern corporation and the concerns of top management, and Dr. Bruce Kogut, now co-director of the center.

In addition to its faculty expertise, Wharton benefits from the involvement of hundreds of senior executives who serve on the boards of our research centers. These business leaders help test new conceptual frameworks and insights in the crucible of management experience. Among the most active of these executives is Reginald Jones, a distinguished Wharton alumnus and chairman emeritus of General Electric, who lent support to this project.

This work also reflects Wharton's longstanding role as the leader of thought in management, research, and education. As the world's first school of management, we consider it both our tradition and responsibility to continually extend the leading edge of management practice and education.

This spirit of innovation is reflected in the development of our new MBA curriculum over the past few years. Wharton was among the first of the leading business schools to grapple with the emerging demands for leadership in the twenty-first century. In creating our new curriculum, Wharton began with a careful assessment of emerging management needs through interviews with hundreds of senior executives. We then developed a blueprint for a program to meet those needs and then redesigned and restructured our own organization to be able to deliver that program.

A key emphasis of the new curriculum is interdisciplinary perspectives. Our faculty members are organized into teams to coordinate their teaching across twenty programs. Marketing, statistics, and operations professors, for example, collaborate on teaching a core course. Other faculty members work together to examine issues such as entrepreneurship and geopolitics.

This book reflects our understanding that the world is not organized in the same way as the departments of a business school. Modern organizations are increasingly seeking a cross-functional approach to solving business problems. The chapters in this volume were constructed to emphasize an interdisciplinary approach to problem solving. Faculty members from diverse departments were commissioned to work as teams to examine key areas of organizational transformation. Each chapter, then, is a synthesis of more than one perspective.

This volume also reflects our strong belief that neither management scholars and teachers nor practitioners can afford to operate in a vacuum. Wharton is deeply concerned to ensure that there is a high-value impact to our research, both via the classroom and in the field. Each year we sponsor a series of "Impact Conferences" to gather together business, government, and academic leaders to grapple with critical business challenges. This book, with involvement of senior executives in its design and execution, reflects this focus on real-world implications. It offers the broad perspectives of academic experts integrated with the view of experienced executives.

The Wharton School is very pleased to present this book to managers. We hope that it will provide insights and direction to those who are engaged in redesigning their firms. We also hope that this work will encourage further forays by faculty researchers in all institutions into the valuable and productive arena of interdisciplinary research.

Thomas Gerrity
Dean, The Wharton School
University of Pennsylvania

About This Book

This book is the outcome of an experiment that surprised us all. It began with a discussion between the two editors immediately after the Wharton School had completed a major revision of its curriculum. The primary mission of the Wharton School is to educate future managers for a world that is rapidly changing. Our old curriculum had failed to keep pace with this change and, through the combined efforts of many of its faculty, the School had put into place a new and more flexible curriculum that reflected the kind of world in which managers would find themselves competing.

But teaching managers is only part of what a business school does. It also conducts research that sheds light on a myriad of factors that can make for business success or failure. Much of this research is reported in scholarly journals, where most managers never see it. Some finds its way into popular business press. But too little of it gets translated into usable form for the managers who have to make the hard decisions on a daily basis. That is what this book is about.

The contributors to this volume had participated in the curriculum changes at Wharton that had begun under Dean Russ Palmer and that had been further developed and implemented under Dean Tom Gerrity. Academic institutions are not accustomed to radical structural change, and, indeed, the reach exceeded the grasp, and some of the initial ideas were modified. But the curriculum had changed, and while few would believe that this process followed some principle of optimality, the outcome has not been far away from the objectives established in the beginning.

The one doubt that persisted concerned whether the change in curriculum could be sustained due to the strong functional orientation of research at Wharton. Even more dubious was the idea that these changes might affect the nature of research by opening up new avenues of cooperation among the faculty.

Changing curriculum makes sense as an expression of Wharton's commitment to train the managerial work force of this and the next decades. Yet, research is defined by the academic community, which remains deeply divided by discipline and function.

It is unlikely that this book, and the joint chapters, would have been written in the absence of the experience in redesigning the curriculum. Without the background of cross-departmental meetings and the creation of cross-functional teaching, our task of persuading busy faculty to divert their attention to work outside their specialty would have been more difficult.

We made the following proposition. We went to various faculty members whose research showed an interest in firms, managers, and policy and proposed that they write a paper with a colleague from another discipline on a simple topic: "designing the firm." We asked them to describe the leading practices in an aspect of design close to their proven research interests.

In some cases, we matched people on the basis of ongoing projects, or incipient projects; in other cases, we asked a colleague to name someone with whom to work; in a few cases, we chose the team based on what we knew of their work. We sold the project as being fun, with the output directed toward a sophisticated managerial audience.

The first meeting was held in May 1992 to discuss objectives. October 9th was set as a workshop date, where we would present early versions of the work and hear the comments of managers. We decided to seek the reaction and advice of the business community early in the writing process.

We had several meetings during the summer to discuss some of the papers and ideas. The attendance was remarkable for the summer, the discussion was first rate, and it was clear that the enterprise was already successful. Indeed, if this project has had a shortcoming, it is that as we shifted from process to product, we could not continue, for the present, with these innovative meetings.

The evening of October 8th and the sessions on October 9th were exhausting. Nine papers were presented and discussed. There was lively debate, and the comments of the managers were instructive and frank. The revision of the chapters owes much to the quality of this advice. We thank the many managers who gave us their time and advice as commentators.

Philadelphia   E. B., B. K.
October 1994

Acknowledgments

We would like to acknowledge the participation of the other seventeen authors to this book and our five academic colleagues who chaired the sessions. Almost 15 percent of the Wharton faculty were involved in this book, and we are very thankful for their enthusiasm and help. Getting this book to print was not a difficult process. In our many discussions, we frequently relied upon the judgment of Michael Useem, to whom we owe a special nod of graditude.

This endeavor received the strong financial and moral backing of Tony Santomero, the Deputy Dean for Academic Affairs, and Dean Tom Gerrity. The Reginald H. Jones Center of the Wharton School, directed by Ned Bowman, provided the bulk of the financial support. Reginald Jones gave the opening remarks to the conference and spent the next day with us. Though his was not the only voice, he surely tipped the decision to adopt the "Re" before the "Designing" in the title.

We benefited from the fine support of our Public Relations office, especially from Chris Hardwick. Editorial advice was superbly provided by Alan Alter. Susan McMullen, Coordinator of the Reginald Jones Center, has given major support to both the arrangement of the Conference and the production of the book.

We have also had the pleasure of working with excellent editors at the New York office of the Oxford University Press. Mary Sutherland, who had helped us in a previous endeavor, added to the persuasion to go with Oxford. Herb Addison's contribution to the conception and editing of the book cannot be underestimated.

A good deal of this book was redesigned while the editors were on sabbatical. We would like to thank our hosts during this period: MIT and Harvard were the safe havens for Ned; the Centre de Recherche en Gestion at the Ecole Polytechnique in Paris provided a reflective ambiance for Bruce. We were both away from Wharton, but one of us was closer. No matter what the talk about the shrinking of time and space, the editors, Ned in particular, learned that proximity matters.

We promised that this book would not require much extra work, as we were to stay close to what we had already researched. Of course, it turned out that we fibbed. Cooperation with new colleagues from different fields required effort; it also opened up new vistas. It is not our fault if we could not resist expanding into new areas. That is kind of what this project was all about. And we thank our colleagues for their professionalism and grace.

Contents

III Form, Space, and Time

IV Summary

Participants

Wharton School Contributors

Franklin Allen
Department of Finance and
    Economics

Erin Anderson
Department of Marketing

Elizabeth E. Bailey
Department of Public Policy and
    Management

Edward H. Bowman
Director, Reginald H. Jones Center
Department of Management

Morris A. Cohen
Department of Operations and
    Information Management (OPIM)
Co-Director, Manufacturing and Lo-
    gistics Center

George S. Day
Department of Marketing
Director, Huntsman Center for
    Global Competition and Innova-
    tion

Deborah Dougherty
McGill University
Faculty of Management

John Farley
Director, Joseph H. Lauder Institute
    of Management and International
    Studies
Department of Marketing

Marshall Fisher
Department of Operations and
    Information Management
Co-Director, Manufacturing and
    Logistics Center

Christopher D. Ittner
Department of Accounting

Anjani Jain
Department of Operations and
    Information Management
Associate Director, Wharton
    Graduate Division

John Kimberly
Department of Management
Department of Health Care System

Steve Kobrin
William H. Wurster Professor of
    Management
Director, Wurster Center for Inter-
    national Studies

Bruce Kogut
Department of Management

John Paul MacDuffie
Department of Management

Toshihiro Nishiguchi
Department of Management

Weijian Shan
J.P. Morgan

Peter D. Sherer
Department of Management

Michael Useem
Department of Management
Department of Sociology

Industry Discussants

Daryl Brewster
Manager
Campbell Soup Company

John J. Burke
Vice President, Manufacturing
Unisys Corporation

Raymond Bromark
Deputy Vice Chairman
Price Waterhouse

Blaine Davis
Corporate Vice President AT&T
Strategic and Market Planning

Arthur L. Glenn
Vice President,
Strategic Systems
GE Aerospace

Denis Hamilton
Director, Quality Management
    Customer Satisfaction
Johnson & Johnson Quality Institute

David Pierson
Principal
Towers-Perrin

Barry Rand
Executive Vice President
Xerox Corporation

Session Coordinators

Janice Bellace
Vice Dean and Director, Wharton
    Undergraduate Division
Professor of Legal Studies and
    Management

William F. Hamilton
Ralph Landau Professor of Manage-
    ment and Technology

Paul R. Kleindorfer
Universal Furniture Professor
Professor of Decision Sciences and
    Economics

Howard Perlmutter
Professor of Social Architecture and
    Management

Anthony M. Santomero
Deputy Dean, The Wharton School
Richard King Mellon Professor of
    Finance

Participants

James C. Allison
Division Manager
International Strategy and Planning
AT&T

Robert Bernstock
Vice President, Soup Sector
Campbell Soup Company

Martin J. Brill
Vice President
Reliance Group Holdings, Inc.

John J. Burke
Vice President, Manufacturing
Unisys Corporation

Martin Coyne
Vice President
Healthcare Strategic Marketing
  Health Group
Eastman Kodak Co.

William Epstein
Director, Government Affair
Roy F. Weston, Inc.

Arthur L. Glenn
Vice President,
Strategic Systems
GE Aerospace

Mark Goldberg
Senior Vice President, Corporate
  Planning
Philip Morris

Eric Gordon
Vice President & Chief Financial
  Officer
Connaught Laboratories Inc.

Denis Hamilton
Director Quality Management
  Customer Satisfaction
Johnson & Johnson Quality
  Institute

Takashi Hatchoji
Chief Researcher
Hitachi Research Institute

Reginald H. Jones
Chairman Emeritus
General Electric Company

Gerald P. Kaplan
Business Strategy Consultant
IBM

Pierre Lescaut
Chief Executive Officer
L. K. Comstock

Carol Marino
Senior Director
Strategic Planning & Business
  Intelligence
Merck & Company Inc.

Alison McGrath Peirce
Director, Senior Management
  Programs
Wharton Executive Education
Aresty Institute

David Pierson
Principal
Towers-Perrin

Carl J. Schaefer
Vice President, Human Resources
ABB Power T&D Company

Roger R. Schnorbus
Executive Vice President
Mrs. Paul's Kitchens, Inc.

Beverly D. Sved
Business Strategy Consultant
IBM

Larry Swerling
Rohm & Haas Co.

George Van Gilder
Executive Vice President
Chubb & Son Inc.

F. M. Worthington
Division Manager
AT&T Corporate Development

William H. Wurster
The Wurster Group

Redesigning the Firm

1

Introduction: Redesigning the Firm

EDWARD BOWMAN AND BRUCE KOGUT

This book revolves around two ideas: the first appears center stage, the second is behind the scenes. The first idea is that fundamental changes occurring in advanced industrial societies have occasioned a revolutionary rethinking of the design of corporations and business. The second is that the business school, as one of the most important institutions for the formation of managers and for the advancement of business-related knowledge, is itself being transformed by wider social and economic changes.

The chapters in this book consequently represent two endeavors. The first is to present a wide range of insights into organizational redesign that will allow firms to compete into the next century. Nineteen experts examine the critical issues facing firms and, in chapters written for practicing managers, provide powerful tools for orchestrating change.

The second endeavor is to describe how the Wharton School at the University of Pennsylvania is changing in response to the same forces that are acting on business firms. It would be absurd if professors of management failed to understand that the need to redesign business organizations applies equally to business schools.

These chapters reveal how changes in the market and the competitive environment are forcing changes in the capabilities of firms. Speed, variety, and quality of production and service have emerged as vital factors in world competition, but they have not emerged like the gods of Ovid, who choose their own moments to appear on earth. They are organizational capabilities that resulted from a long-term historical evolution.

It is widely recognized that these capabilities rest upon the quality and competence of managers and workers. We take this fundamental recognition as our starting point and focus on the organizational design of human resources.

The following chapters formulate principles by which managers and workers organize to generate the new capabilities of the contemporary firm. To achieve variety of products at reasonable cost is a desired capability of many firms. The firms that succeed in achieving this goal are those that have developed new methods of organization, from cross-functional teams to flexible control system.

Be faster is easy advice, yet hard to implement because it demands a redesign of the organization. To create a capability of speed requires the redesign of supplier and buyer relationships. To be more flexible across borders requires the creation of a network of subsidiaries supported by information, budgeting, and transfer price systems. To increase variety necessitates not only investments in automated equipment, but the changes in the way work is measured and rewarded.

The following chapters look at these and other issues of redesign and capabilities. Some deal with how flexibility is motivated through accounting systems; others analyze the changing nature of a firm's boundaries with the external environment of suppliers, customers, governments, and shareholders. The analyses examine all levels of an organization, from the shop floor and multifunctional organization to its position as a member of a wider network of firms and public institutions.

Managers have found these issues to be startlingly difficult because they are complex and multifaceted. Research in business schools has frequently failed to address these issues for the same reasons. Academic business research is invariably the outcome of specialized functional divisions. But academics advise corporations to create cross-functional teams and to render the borders of the firm more permeable to the outside.

The contributors to this book have taken this medicine ourselves. The first written drafts of the chapters, by cross-functional authors, were exposed to the scrutiny of practicing managers. The drafts and the counsel of managers were discussed in a relatively small gathering of academics and executives. The results of this process are the nine chapters, plus a summary, that constitute this book.

Strategy by Introspection

We can understand the changes in corporations by peering at a mirror or through a window (Bowman 1995). The manager can ask what is it that we do well or should do better. Or, she can ask what is happening in the market and how do I better position my product vis-à-vis my competitors.

There is the sense these days that more managers prefer the mirror over the window. It is tempting to say that these trends represent no more than the fads of managerial ideology. After a decade of looking outward to financial markets and to the conditions of industry competition, the market for this endeavor is saturated. So what we are witnessing is the repackaging of advice to firms about what should be done inside their firms given by consulting firms and business professors.

We prefer the middle ground, where the question of how to vie in world markets is understood as a problem of the design of work and the choice of the markets in which to enter and compete. It is easy to dismiss the preoccupation with the mirror of design as no more than a fad during troubled times. At the turn of the last century, the Italian economist and sociologist Vilfredo Pareto suggested that ideologies rise and fall along with the business cycle. The current discussion of the humanization of the work place is no more, by this view, than a reflection of the harder economic conditions of this decade.

But it would be a serious mistake to believe that the current public discourse is simply a phase of an eternal cycle between looking inward and outward. To the contrary, we are witnessing an historic structural break in the practice of organization and management. These changes are no less revolutionary than the wave of innovations associated with the names of Frederick Taylor and Henry Ford in the beginning of this century.

The most remarkable fact in the economic history of this century has been the increasing concentration of production by the largest corporations in industrialized countries. It has been the sheer rapidity of this corporate growth that has spelled the limits of its continuation. The labor forces of corporations today are vastly more productive than before. The rising productivity of labor has outpaced the growth of the value of output by the largest firms. By this statement alone, the implications are clear. Large corporations require increasingly smaller work forces to maintain the high levels of productivity and service.

There is, we suspect, a more fundamental change occurring than simply the outpacing of big firm output by productivity growth. We are witnessing a major shift, in which the historical advantage of the large corporation is no longer assured. The uncertainty of markets, the importance of niches and innovations in increasingly more wealthy societies, the creation of new flexible technologies and telecommunication systems, and the growth of well-educated workers and managers have created a major break in the organization of work and its division among large and small firms.[1]

These observations are visible in the very simple data in Table 1.1 regarding the relationship among the employees, assets, and sales of the largest U.S. and global corporations. For the largest U.S. corporations listed in Fortune magazine, there has been an absolute drop in the number of employees for the largest 100 and 500 firms. Moreover, the growth in sales (measured in constant dollars) has dramatically fallen over the last decade, even though the value of total assets

TABLE 1.1.   Growth of Large Companies ($ Billions)

	Sales	Assets	Employees	Inflation Adjusted Sales	Inflation Adjusted Assets
Fortune 500 Industrials					
1955	$ 161	$ 122	8605	$ 529	$ 461
1960	205	176	9179	613	544
1970	464	432	14608	1180	1078
1980	1650	1175	15909	1875	1370
1990	2304	2416	12429	1933	1966
Fortune 100 Industrials					
1955	108	83	5460	354	313
1960	132	117	5632	395	361
1970	288	279	9110	733	696
1980	1115	767	8722	1267	894
1990	1645	1820	7888	1380	1481
Global 100 Industrials					
1956	49	32	3917	158	117
1960	63	60	5738	188	186
1970	182	196	9029	462	488
1980	1037	877	9877	1178	1034
1990	2148	2201	10721	1802	1791
Fortune 100 as percent of Fortune 500					
1955	67	68	63		
1960	64	66	61		
1970	62	65	62		
1980	68	65	55		
1990	71	75	63		
Global 100 as percent of Fortune 100					
1960	48	51	102		
1970	63	70	99		
1980	96	116	113		
1990	131	121	136		

Source: Fortune, various issues.
Notes: Sales adjusted using U.S. finished goods deflator (1982 = 100). Assets adjusted using U.S. capital equipment deflator (1982 = 100).

continued to grow (especially for the largest 100 firms). In the United States the sales of the largest corporations grew at a rate only 80 percent of the overall growth in manufacturing.[2] No wonder that there has been such an increase in shareholder revolt over the past decade!

The stagnation in sales may be due to the overall loss of competitiveness of U.S. large corporations. Indeed, during this period of time, the 100 greatest non-U.S. firms experienced declining, but still formidable sales and asset growth. We can compare their growth against the largest 100 U.S. corporations. Note, first, that the American 100 has grown faster than the overall 500. Still, the global 100 has greatly outpaced the largest American corporations, to the point where they show, on average, considerably larger assets, sales, and employees.

We should not deduce, however, that the old trend towards large corporations is continuing in the rest of the world. Part of the non-U.S. growth is due to the great expansion overseas during the 1980s. European and Japanese firms invested heavily in the United States, and Japanese firms also began, toward the end of the decade, to invest more agressively in Europe.

Moreover, there are large country differences. Japanese firms are, for example, dramatically smaller than their U.S. counterparts. In 1990, General Motors had 616,000 employees compared to Toyota's 96,849; IBM, 373,816 to Hitachi's 290,811; and Dupont 141,000 to Asahi Chemicals 14,920. The swollen global corporation is not a feature of Japanese capitalism.

In certain countries, the trends show a diminution in firm size. In France—which has one of the best performing economies over the past decade—small and medium enterprises are growing at a faster clip than their larger counterparts (INSEE 1993). The most dynamic sectors in the Italian economy are dominated by smaller firms. And even among developing countries, the diversified and dynamic small firm sector of Taiwan looks more promising than the large Korean chaebol group.

There are many ways to understand these changes. We accept the view that they indicate a revolutionary break with the design principles of mass production and economies of size. Competitive pressures are forcing large companies to redesign how work and management are organized in order to be more flexible, quicker, and market-oriented.

Of course, the nature of product markets and competition is of fundamental importance. No matter what the organization design, a brilliant computer company such as IBM was caught in a difficult strategic position due to the decline of demand for its principal mainframe market and the inroads made by ever-more powerful and smaller machines. Products and markets matter.

What compounds the difficulty of getting the strategy right, however, is that radical strategic change requires a redesign of the principles of organizing. But the new design is not clear. The wavering of IBM between spinning off affiliates but holding equity stakes or internally transforming the businesses is itself notable. Figuring out how to do new things is tremendously difficult in the absence of templates that can be borrowed from other corporate experiences.

What a firm wants to be capable of doing depends on how it does things. The "how" and "what" are inextricably linked (Kogut and Zander 1992; Bowman 1995). For many firms, the capabilities which they desire consist of the ability to deliver high variety and quality products and services quickly and flexibly to the market. "What" they desire to do forms the wish list of the capabilities to support their product and market strategies. However, the daunting question facing many firms is not what capabilities they should have, but how to acquire the organizing principles that generate these capabilities. Or, to use an old expression often used in connection with the transfer of U.S. techniques to countries around the globe, the heart of the matter lies in developing the appropriate "know-how."

In Table 1.2, we match a few fundamental organizing principles to the capabilities they generate. This list is hardly complete, but it provides insight into why we say that design is the terrain on which competition is fought. We believe that speed, cost competitiveness, and quality are three of the most important capabilities for competing in markets today.

Consider, first, the organizing principles underlying the capability to be quick to the market. There is a fairly large consensus that in the case of manufacturing firms, speed is generated by designing sytems in which customer demand pulls the product by reverberating down the value chain of assembly to components. These systems, often called *kanban* after their Japanese origin, are usually coupled with just-in-time (JIT) deliveries and low inventories.

Flexibility is a capability that is particularly important when the prices of materials are unknown. How convenient it would be for a multinational company to respond to a sudden increase in the value of the yen by decreasing the amount of components sourced from Japan. To create this capability, however, means that the global firm must be structured as a coordinated network of subsidiaries, that flexible transfer prices must be created, and that managers must be rewarded for taking advantage of unexpected changes in currency values.

Quality of product and service as a competitive objective has stumbled on the problem of complexity of delivery. To provide a menu of high-quality choices to the consumer has led to creating more autonomous teams of workers. Quality circles and team problem solving have been major work place innovations oriented toward improving the variety and reliability of products and services.

TABLE 1.2. Principles of Design and Capabilities

Organizing Principles	Capabilities
Just-in-time and Kanban	Speed
Multinational network	Quality
Multifunctional skills and autonomous teams	Operating flexibility

These capabilities pose issues of design and of the leadership and motivation to implement corporate change. If board and shareholder meetings have become more confrontational, it is because of the growing pressures to transform the corporation into a more competitive entity. The long-term decline in profits and market share for many corporations are bellwether signs that a radical redesign of the organization is required.

The Wharton School and Management Education

As surprising as it may seem, the linkage between *what* a firm does and *how* it does it has been neglected by academic research and remains an open terrain of inquiry. This neglect stems, no doubt, from the nature of how a school of business is itself organized. There is probably no organization more departmentalized and functionally organized than a university!

The way knowledge is organized in the university and in the business school constrains what can be taught and researched. Over the past years, a revolution in the structure or, if you will, the organizing principles of business education has been underway. The Wharton School itself has been a leader in this revolution by introducing a radically revised curriculum for its Master of Business Administration Program.

Yet, while changes in the curriculum have been made, or are in the process of being made, the thorniest problems are often posed by the implications for research. A great achievement of the modern university is the gains in knowledge made through research conducted by specialists. At the same time, because of its role in training and educating the managerial work force, the business school is caught between how to balance the virtues of specialization in research with the growing need to intermarry the functions.

What do these efforts to redesign the corporation mean for business schools? Imagine teaching a class of business students what French auto corporations should have done in 1980 to defend their home market against Toyota, Nissan, and Honda if Japanese car imports had not been limited by law to 3 percent of the market. How easy it is to suggest that they should have produced better cars and designed them faster for the market. The more difficult challenge is knowing how to redesign the organization to do so.

Business schools have not been at the cutting edge of these changes during the 1980s. The concepts of just-in-time inventory management, kanban systems, activity analysis, quality programs were picked up more quickly by leaders in industry than by academic researchers. It was only after 1985 that JIT systems, widely held to be a major Japanese innovation in minimizing inventory levels, truly entered the curriculum in operations courses at Wharton. By this time, some U.S. corporations had already invested considerable sums of money in recreating the supply networks in the United States that they had observed, or had experienced through their affiliates, in Japan.

Many say that the U.S. business school is a contributor to the decline of large corporations in the United States. The correlation looks damning; the country with the most developed system of business education in the world has slipped so rapidly from a position of economic leadership to a contender among many. There is no question that the United States by almost any economic measure is no longer the single leading nation.[3] And it has become common to place some of this blame on its business education institutions.

And why not? Almost one out of four students in U.S. colleges and universities today majors in business. In 1957, one out of five U.S. students matriculated in a business school. Since then, the number of business schools has grown five-fold.

The clever answer to these concerns has been that there is no problem. The correlation is easily dismissed as spurious. A class in statistics often begins with the story of how, in the 1800s, the peasants in Russia noted an association between cholera and the arrival of physicians, leading to their deep suspicion that modern medicine was responsible for the epidemics. Certainly, the business school bears no responsibility for the health of the American economy.

We are not so sure. Of course, the decline in the relative positioning of the United States was almost foreordained, as its stature in the world economy after World War II was the result of the destruction of its major competitors. Yet, on the other hand, the United States was a leader in national income, productivity, and export growth in the early part of this century. Its relative stature today is less than it was in the 1920s.

The early business schools in the United States, of which Wharton was the first, grew up teaching the practices that made U.S. businesses the largest and most powerful in world history. Joseph Wharton wanted to build an educational institution to train the managers for the expanding corporations that he and his peers led.

The teaching of business at Wharton started slowly. The early focus was on economics, with the founders of the American Economic Association being Wharton faculty. It was due to this legacy that Simon Kuznets and Lawrence Klein joined the faculty much later and did their pioneering work at Wharton, which earned them Nobel Prizes in economics. But the school also developed business classes, especially to teach the new skills of accounting, finance, and insurance, and eventually marketing and management. Up to the 1960s, it ran a time-motion laboratory funded by the widow of Frederick Taylor.

The experiences of other schools were not so different from those of Wharton in terms of the content and structure of teaching. Functional lines evolved in almost all U.S. business schools. Except for an occasional department of real estate, the emphasis of business schools has been to develop the functional and managerial skills of students without regard to specific industrial needs.

This functional emphasis was reflected in the Wharton curriculum up to the current years. Figure 1.1 provides a simple schema of the educational requirements and electives available to the MBA student who matriculated at Wharton during the 1980s. At the end of two years, a student graduated with little classroom exposure to the integration of functional skills that would be part of working life.

We should not underestimate the tremendous advancement in business education over this century. In the late 1950s, the Ford Foundation contracted two professors, Robert Gordon and James Howell, to survey the status of business schools.

Their findings remain startling for anyone educated in a business school in recent years. Up through 1940, only 186 doctorates were given in business, the first Ph.D. being granted only in 1927; only another 978 were given between 1947 and 1958. With one-fifth of all students majoring in business in the 1950s, it is not surprising that only 40 percent of full-time teachers had doctorate degrees; 40 percent of all teachers were part-time. Courses were highly applied; business schools provided frequently no more than a trade training. One 1959 study reported that "an eight-course major at a large . . . university in baking science and management . . . includes courses in Principles of Baking: Bread and Rolls; Principles of Baking: Cakes and Variety Products; Bread and Roll Production—Practical Shop Operation; and finally Cake and Sweet Baked products—Practical Shop operation."[4]

No wonder that the introduction of research findings in operation manage-

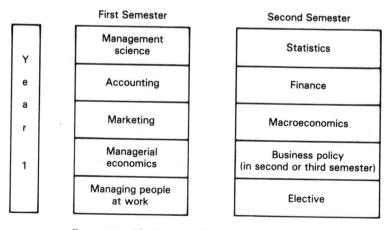

Figure 1.1. The Previous Curriculum Structure.

ment courses that built upon the scientific management heritage of Taylor were seen as representing, and in fact were, major improvements in teaching quality.

The claim that the problem of business schools lies in their emphasis on research strikes us as facetious. In the United States and elsewhere, this view has a considerable history, even with respect to the natural sciences. A distinguished scientist visiting the University of Minnesota in 1908 remarked that "the regents generally regarded research as a private fad of a professor, like collecting etchings or playing the piano, and they rarely interfered with it so long as (the professor) . . . did not ask for money" (Cowley and Williams 1991, 139–140).

The great advancement in the quality of teaching in business schools is linked to the enhancement of and investment in research. Gordon and Howell (1959) openly despaired of the poor quality of research of the 1950s available to the practicing manager. Since this report, research in business schools has moved substantially forward, to the point that fundamental innovations, such as the pricing of securities and options, can be traced to academic publications.[5]

The dilemma facing business schools is that the categories of academic knowledge, as they were determined by the structure of business of the early part of this century, have become increasingly isolated from one another. The new curriculum changes at Wharton, shown in Figure 1.2, and at other business schools, are attempts to maintain functional training but within the context of greater experience in integrated and group problem-solving. New joint departmental committees to coordinate content and to reinforce commonalities across classes have supported these cross-functional efforts.

The current puzzle of research in business schools is that there is no clear idea of what should be the organization of academic efforts that would correspond to these new curricula.[6] Specialization in research has driven the advancement of knowledge since the German university innovations of the 1800s. Must the business school give up this tradition to address the questions of importance to corporations and to its own academic community?

We do not propose the abolition of specialized research, not the least because it is unnecessary. Corporations continue to rely on specialists; cross-functional teams do not eliminate the functions.

The better answer lies in bringing the specialties together. An important side effect of transforming business school curricula is that the process brings into contact faculty from diverse backgrounds. The implications for research are many, but certainly include the promotion of more coordinated, cross-functional projects that are problem-oriented and academically rigorous. The prospects for change in the area of research require the creation of institutional structures within the business school for long-term cross-functional cooperation.

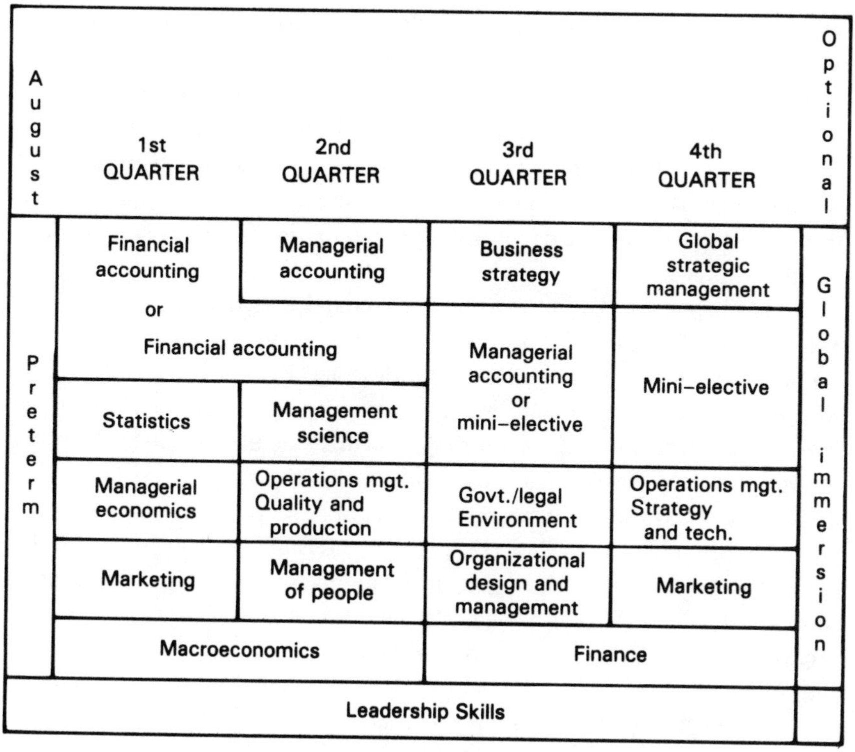

August (vertical)	Preterm (vertical)	1st QUARTER	2nd QUARTER	3rd QUARTER	4th QUARTER	Optional (vertical) / Global immersion (vertical)
		Financial accounting	Managerial accounting	Business strategy	Global strategic management	
		or				
		Financial accounting		Managerial accounting or mini–elective	Mini–elective	
		Statistics	Management science			
		Managerial economics	Operations mgt. Quality and production	Govt./legal Environment	Operations mgt. Strategy and tech.	
		Marketing	Management of people	Organizational design and management	Marketing	
		Macroeconomics		Finance		
		Leadership Skills				

Figure 1.2. The Wharton MBA Curriculum.

The Plan of the Book

The first three chapters in Part I approach the design of the firm from the perspective of its role in a wider network of political institutions and buyers and suppliers. Does the relationship between shareholders, directors, and management need to be reconsidered? Yes, answer Edward Bowman and Michael Useem in their chapter, who cite six widespread practices that upset the balance that should exist between these three parties. Among other anomalies, directors are frequently captives of management, even though they are formally empowered by shareholders. Corporations must change the way power is distributed and information is shared among these three stakeholders if the anomalies of existing practice are to be resolved.

The next two chapters focus more directly on the changing conception of the boundaries of the firm. Globalization, the spread of advanced technology, and the opening of new markets have led to a surge in partnerships and alliances between companies during the past two decades. Elizabeth Bailey and Weijian Shan explain that the form of these alliances depends on the nature of the market and the strengths and weaknesses that firms bring to that market. The authors look at what makes alliances pay off for companies in three types of markets: newly emerging markets such as Eastern Europe, markets where economies of scale provide a critical advantage, and dynamic markets where speed is essential. As the nature of industries change, such as when a government deregulates an industry, a firm must also redesign its boundaries by its alliance strategy.

The chapter by Toshihiro Nishiguchi and Erin Anderson explores the Japanese use of supplier and buyers networks in two industries. They compare the sourcing and buying practices of Japanese and British firms in the United Kingdom. They propose four Japanese organizing principles for network design that can be adopted in other countries: recognize one firm as the leader of the network, employ the win-win principle, involve the supplier at the product design stage, and use multifunctional teams to build products.

The three chapters in Part II look at the internal organizing practices that support speed of product development to the market, variety, and flexibility. Morris Cohen and Deborah Dougherty observe that companies often develop a profitable new product, but they then have trouble repeating their success on the next round—even when they adopt concurrent approaches to product development such as simultaneous engineering or design for manufacturability. They propose a new way for understanding concurrent development. To sustain innovation, concurrence must occur in three dimensions: between functions such as manufacturing and marketing, between a company's overall strategy and the strategy for an individual product, and among the products offered by the company. The authors apply their framework to the results from their field work in an industrial tool company whose efforts to remain innovative met with failure.

The idea that increasing product variety can come at no extra cost to the manufacturer will come as a surprise to many. Manufacturers regard variety as a necessary evil to satisfy the exacting demand of their customers. Companies believe that product variety complicates their operations and drives up costs. But Marshall Fisher, Anjani Jain, and John Paul MacDuffie show that firms in the automotive industry by investing in training, flexible manufacturing processes, and better operations management can increase variety without increasing costs, compromising productivity, or lowering quality. Variety can indeed be free.

Why do the substantial investments made by companies to achieve flexibility so often fail? Chris Ittner and Bruce Kogut show that such efforts do not succeed unless a control system is created that signals the value of flexibility. To make a company more flexible and responsive to the market, CEO's often try a different tactic: they tighten financial controls and create incentives that link managers' compensation to financial performance. Ittner and Kogut find that, contrary to conventional wisdom, these moves can hurt companies' efforts to become responsible and flexible. The authors propose that multiple incentives and measures, resembling those used in research and development (R&D) laboratories, provide better criteria for signaling the importance to managers of flexibility. There should be more emphasis on what measures tell managers to think about, they conclude, than on what they indicate regarding managerial compensation.

The three chapters in Part III analyze the principles of design from the vantage point of form, multinational locations, and the life cycle. Franklin Allen and Peter Sherer begin their analysis by recounting the problems that Salomon Brothers faced when they changed their form from a partnership to a corporation in the 1980s. The main difference between proprietorships, partnerships, and corporations is not how much risk they accept, or the way they divide managerial responsibilities. The critical difference is how freely a company's human and financial resources can move about, or how tightly they are tied to a business. The choice of the organizational form of a corporation is inextricably linked to how it mobilizes its human resources to support its product market strategies.

John Farley and Stephen Kobrin go against the grain. They take a skeptical look at what it means to be a global company and doubt that the design of the organization matters much for the performance of the multinational corporation. What is the glue that holds together global corporations? They believe that being a good global competitor owes more to the mentality of a company's managers than to the company's markets, products, services, or organizational structure.

Who is likely to survive as a high-growth market evolves from creation to maturity to shakeout? How much does timing of entry or strategy matter? In an examination of the magnetic resonance imaging market, George Day and John Kimberly found that being first does not matter very much. The organizational capabilities that support early entry were not the ones needed as the market took off. Shifting people from task to task along the life cycle is a hard trick for many firms to pull off. So with the maturing of the technology, larger firms, especially General Electric, redefined the market to fit their strengths. The organizational strength of dominant firms shaped market demand as much as market demand influenced product strategies.

The final chapter offers our reflections on the trends detected in the contributions to this book. We find that there are two design principles. The first is that the idea of a boundaryless firm may be aptly labeled the question of permeability: how much of what firms used to believe was critical to their success can be placed outside their ownership boundaries? Increasingly, there is a reliance on a principle of external coordination among firms to leverage the strengths of each. This trend of growing permeability is linked to the second principle, namely, the application of modularity in product, organizational, and network design. We discuss how the application of the principle of modular design poses complexes challenges to understanding the size and capabilities of corporations in the coming decades.

These chapters individually present no unified theme. They are problem-oriented analyses of the design of work, governance, and cooperation. As a whole, however, they present the belief that the turn of this century is witnessing a transformation in the principles of design that parallel the vast changes that swept the internal organization of corporations a hundred years ago.

We have a fairly clear record and understanding of the formidable transformation that occurred at the commencement of the twentieth century.[7] From the chaos of firms trying to deal with the growing complexity and size of their operations rose new principles of organization, management, and finance and accounting. In 1900, there were no personnel offices, there was no clear distinction between line and staff in most firms, and there were no accounting rules by which to understand the return on investment, productivity, or business profit.

The corporation has come a long way since that time. The techniques of management are improved. The technologies of finance, manufacturing, marketing, and service have realized stunning gains in productivity. And yet firms are still radically experimenting in new principles of organizing. This book, itself an experiment, is an analysis of these efforts to redesign the firm.

Notes

We would like to acknowledge the research assistance of Vipin Gupta.

1. One of the most important of the many contributions describing this break has certainly been *The Second Industrial Divide* by Michael Piore and Charles Sabel.
2. Comparisons are always difficult. The Fortune sales figures include foreign sales (exports and sales of overseas affiliates). The growth asset size may be an industry "composition" effect; labor-intensive industries may be a smaller percentage of the current 500 than those of previous years.
3. The United States is still usually shown to lead in productivity measures, primarily because Japan and other industrialized countries look so inefficient in their service and distribution sectors. Obviously, one could also argue that the quality of service often depends upon the employment of a well-trained, well-paid work force.

4. Cited by Lyman Porter and Lawrence McKibbin in their recent study which analyzed the quality of business education in the 1980s.
5. See the article by Gerald Faulhaber and William Baumol (1988) who trace financial innovations to basic research in economics and business schools.
6. The Wharton School has undertaken experiments previously along these lines, with the boldest being the Social Science Systems program founded by Russ Ackoff. For a history of this program, see Sass (1982: 327–30).
7. In this regard, the remarkable works of Alfred Chandler remain the preeminent guide to this history.

References

Bowman, Edward. 1995. Strategy history: Through different mirrors. In *Integral strategy*. Ed. Hans Thorelli. Greenwich, Conn.: JAI Press (forthcoming).

Chandler, Alfred. 1977. *The visible hand*. Cambridge, Mass.: Harvard University Press.

Chandler, Alfred. 1990. *Scale and scope. The dynamics of industrial capitalism*. Cambridge, Mass.: Harvard University Press.

Cowley, W. H., and Don Williams. 1991. *International and Historical Roots of American Higher Education*. New York and London: Garland Publishing Inc.

Faulhaber, Gerald, and William Baumol. 1988. Economists as innovators. *Journal of Economic Literature* 26:577–600.

Gordon, Robert A., and James Howell. 1959. *Higher education for business*. New York: Columbia University Press.

INSEE (Institut National de la Statisque et des Études Économiques). 1993. Une Année en demi-Teinte. *Rapport sur les Comptes de la Nation*, Paris.

Kogut, Bruce, and Udo Zander. 1992. The knowledge of the firm, combinative capabilities, and the replication of technology. *Organizational Science* 3:383–97.

Piore, Michael, and Charles Sabel. 1984. *The second industrial divide*. New York: Basic Books.

Porter, Lyman, and Lawrence McKibbin. 1988. *Management education and development: Drift or thrust into the 21st century?* New York: McGraw Hill.

Sass, Steven A. 1982. *The pragmatic imagination. A history of the Wharton School 1881–1981*. Philadelphia: University of Pennsylvania Press.

I

Boundaries, Networks, and Corporate Control

2

The Anomalies of
Corporate Governance

EDWARD H. BOWMAN AND MICHAEL USEEM

Few areas of organizational life are as full of ironies as the governance of publicly traded companies. While the governing board in theory oversees the company on behalf of the owners, in practice, the board is often overseen by management. By law directors are elected by shareholders, but in fact their nomination by management is usually tantamount to election. While executives would emulate a Japanese-style long-term orientation if they could, short-term investor demands foreshorten all strategic horizons. By law managers are empowered to work on behalf of investor interests, yet in fact some investors seemingly prevent them from doing so.

Organizational ironies are curious when isolated. When they become widespread, however, they cease being curiosities and emerge as major challenges to conventional business practice. We have now reached the latter stage in the area of corporate governance. A wholesale rethinking of the theory and practice of governance is in order. Those who wish to redesign the firm need to consider not just the organizational ladder but those who peer over the top rung.

The nature of scientific change can provide a useful analogue here. In his classic treatment of scientific revolutions, Thomas Kuhn focused on those insights in the history of science, like Newtonian physics or Copernican astronomy, that caused major shifts to occur in our basic understanding of nature. He proposed that "normal" science is periodically challenged by an accumulation of abnormal results. The traditional "paradigm" cannot explain the anomalous facts, but its dominance remains long-unchallenged by virtue of the powers of convention. Theoretical reconception, however, eventually wins, bringing both the new anomalies and old facts under the same tent. If scientific revolutions are sparked by accumulating anomalies, so too may be corporate transformations.[1]

The normal governance model for publicly traded firms, enshrined in legal and economic theory, consists of three basic principles:

> Owner sovereignty: Shareholders elect directors to oversee their assets.
>
> Board authority: Directors select managers to increase the owners' assets.
>
> Management compliance: Executives focus on the objectives set by the directors on behalf of the owners.

Six accumulating anomalies in this normal model of corporate governance suggest that a far-reaching redesign in both the theory and practice of corporate governance is overdue. The six anomalous developments are:

1. Boards of directors are formally empowered by shareholders to preside over their assets, but in practice they often exercise little direct control of management.

2. Capital markets are constructed to disseminate information to shareholders as the basis for deciding whether to invest in or disinvest from a firm, though in fact large investors are often unable to readily divest from their largest holdings.

3. Pay for performance and tougher financial oversight are intended to bring managers into better line with shareholder interests, but such efforts run counter to other broadly accepted principles of human resource management.

4. Principal-agent theory anticipates that principals take steps to align their agents, yet we observe that managers—who are supposed to be the agents of shareholders—sometimes take steps to realign their shareholders.

5. In response to shareholder pressures, organizations have reorganized their internal structures, but little reorganization of the governance structure has followed.

6. Institutional investors press poorly performing companies to improve, others to perform steadily, yet investors bring little familiarity with corporate strategy, design, or other foundations of company performance to the table.

The restructuring should, in our view, focus on reconfiguring the flow of information and influence among a company's owners, directors, and managers. Formal hierarchy among the three parties would give way to a horizontal network among them. Each would have more routine contact with, divulge more information to, and exercise more influence on the others. Company strategies and performance would be developed through informed and integrated input from all three parties, replacing defensive jockeying among them.

Of course, many organizations are exceptions to the rule. Contrary to the first development, for instance, the boards of some firms are observed to exercise tight reign over management. The forced departures of several Fortune 500 CEOs in 1992 and 1993 proved what powers directors can sometimes wield. It is too early to say that these anomalies have been resolved by the emergence of a new paradigm for corporate governance, but such developments were surely suggestive.

We elaborate the six anomalies of corporate governance and then turn to their practical resolution through organizational redesign. Our assessment draws on a broad range of academic research and business practice. It also builds on the commentary of fifty-eight large institutional investors interviewed in mid-1992.[2] It is based as well upon the commentary of a number of company executives interviewed for two other studies completed during the period from 1989 to 1993 (Useem 1993).

The Inversion of a Hierarchy

In the normal legal and economic theory of the firm, boards are elected by the shareholders to monitor their investments. Directors are the shareholders' agents, and managers are agents for both as they are selected by directors who are elected by investors. Corporate behavior is, or at least should be, disciplined down this chain of command. "From an agency perspective," theorized one analyst, "boards can be used as monitoring devices for shareholder interests." When directors effectively communicate and inform, "top executives are more likely to engage in behaviors that are consistent with stockholders' interests" (Eisenhardt 1989, 65; Fama and Jensen 1983).

This legally sanctioned model is officially presumed to guide the governance of publicly-traded firms. Lest we lose sight of the model, business associates and companies periodically reaffirm its validity. The *Business Roundtable* (1990) reminds its constituencies that "the board of directors is ultimately accountable to the shareholders for the long-term successful economic performance of the corporation consistent with its underlying public purpose." The ITT Corporation annually refreshes its own shareholders' memory of much the same. Its 1991 annual report stated that the "Board of Directors is responsible for establishing broad corporate policies and for overseeing the overall performance of ITT" (ITT Corporation 1991).

Yet the de facto powers of the board are found to be much at variance with its purported de jure influence. We know this from inside scrutiny of boards ranging from Miles Mace's pioneering study, *Directors: Myth and Reality,* to the extensive update by Jay Lorsch. In *Pawns or Potentates,* Lorsch concluded that directors ought to act more like the "corporate potentates the law intends them to be than the management pawns they have too often been in the past" (Mace 1971; Lorsch 1989, 193).

Boards sometimes intervene when a crisis seems beyond management. Otherwise, the norms are quiescence over challenge, consensus over conflict. Paul Stern, a former chief executive and director of several major corporations, offered an experienced assessment that could stand for many: "For years, boards have lacked cohesion, operated within limited time frames, [and] have had limited knowledge about operations of the business. . . . More importantly, directors have had a rubber-stamp mentality adverse to 'rocking the boat' or 'criticizing the CEO' who all too often they have been beholden to for their position on the board. The old style has been for boards to confirm and conform" (Stern 1993, 13).

These are norms of necessity. Corporate control had gradually slipped from the hands of founding owners and investors to nonowning professional managers. This was the "managerial revolution" identified by Adolph Berle and Gardiner Means in their 1932 landmark study of corporate organization and governance, *The Modern Corporation and Private Property* (Berle and Means [1932] 1967). The founding family and favored financier, observed Alfred Chandler, had relinquished all but residual control over company decisions. "They could say no," observed Chandler, "but unless they themselves were trained managers with long experience in the same industry and even the same company, they had neither the information nor the experience to propose positive alternative courses of action" (Chandler, 1977, 491). Later analysis confirmed that ownership control of the corporation by the 1970s had been replaced with managerial control in a substantial proportion of the nation's largest firms. Boards of directors, crucial links in theory between owners and managers, had often in practice entered the realm of missing links (Herman 1981).

Corporate behavior almost never conforms precisely to what theorists have forecast. Rarely, however, are the two at such complete odds. With myth and reality in overt contradiction, activist shareholders found fertile ground during the late 1980s and early 1990s for investor campaigns to strengthen director powers over managers, and investor influence over both. A newsletter for corporate investor-relations specialists published by their association, the National Investor Relations Institute, so concluded in 1991: "Virtually all of the . . . organizations studying or advancing investor activism agree that the agenda is now focused on making corporate boards truly independent of management" (Mahoney 1993).

A crescendo of investor pressures on the General Motors board during the early 1990s sounds the potential of such independence. In the spring of 1992, the General Motors' independent directors demoted the president and the chief financial officer, removed two executives from the board, and lifted the CEO from his chairmanship of the company's executive committee. Then, just six months later, the outside directors forced the resignation of the CEO and several associates. Extraordinary losses underlay the rebellion. GM's earnings had abruptly turned from black to red at the start of the 1990s. In 1988, it had earned $4.86 billion. By 1990, it had lost $1.99 billion; in 1991, it hemorrhaged $4.45 billion, the largest one-year loss in business history. A management crisis had stimulated the board, and institutional investors pointed the way. The board's show of force in crisis might presage a more forceful exercise of power out of crisis.

The Inefficient Market

Normally, relevant company information travels relatively quickly to interested investors. With good information, shareholders make informed but simple equity decisions: to buy, sell, or hold. Market institutions and securities laws serve to enforce the model. The New York Stock Exchange and U.S. Securities and Exchange Commission set forth a host of rules to facilitate the spread of accurate data across a level playing field.

While this theory characterizes much shareholder behavior, anomalies appear at the high end. For large institutional investors, the three-way choice is often reduced to one: hold. With $10 billion or more under management, large institutions—pension funds, bank trusts, insurance companies, investment firms, and nonprofit endowments—are often unable to divest readily when they do not like what the information tells them about a company. For one thing, the only potential buyers are usually other institutions, who are just as likely to be apprised of the bad news. The disposal of large blocks of stock may thus require substantial time, management costs, and price adjustments, all of which may be viewed as more costly than pressing management for change. For another, even if the dissatisfied seller is able to find a not yet dissatisfied buyer, with investments already spread among most large companies, the seller may be faced with a shortfall of appealing alternatives. And a common practice among many large investors, the "indexed" placement of funds among a pre-set list of companies such as the Standard and Poor's 500, is by definition a hold decision (Lowenstein 1991).

The College Retirement and Equities Fund (CREF), with 1990 investments of approximately $35 billion, described such a limitation facing all funds of its size (1990). CREF "is not in a position to divest itself of a company's stock when it disagrees with the action of that company's management. Furthermore, CREF's obligations to its participants preclude it from making speculative investments. Accordingly, CREF believes that it has a responsibility to use its rights as shareholder to protect shareholder values." The chief investment officer of the California Public Employees' Retirement System (Calpers), presiding over 1992 investments of $68 billion, had reached much the same conclusion: "We realized we don't have the option of voting with our feet. The only course availble is to see [that] companies are effectively run." The same course of action was foreseen by the controller of New York City, who served as investment adviser to the New York City Employees Retirement System, a fund with more than $40 billion invested in 1992. "We are long-term investors. We can't get out of these companies. We want to break up the concentration of power at the top, create more accountability, provide checks and balances" (Grant 1992).

With the hold option often the only real avenue for many large investors, the nature of investor decisions changed, and this in turn altered the kinds of information required for informed decisions. When a company's performance plummeted, investors traditionally exercised the "Wall Street rule" and simply disposed of their holdings. Whether a company was well or poorly governed was largely irrelevant. Investors alternated between what Albert Hirschman had termed the options of "loyalty" or "exit." Investors faced a hypothetical third option of "voice" in which they would express their dissent, but virtually all saw such a course as pointless (Hirschman 1970).

When a company's performance deteriorates in an era of concentrated holdings, however, major investors are faced with a different set of options. Owners could communicate their dissatisfaction to management. They could support shareholder proxy resolutions that would reshape company governance, such as rescission of antitakeover defenses or division of the chairman and chief executive roles. They could back opposing slates of directors or, in a corporate variant on the tradition of moral protest, "just vote no" on management proposed slates. Or they could support hostile takeover initiatives that would install a new board and management. Whatever the options, they expanded their course to include the third choice of "voice" (Black 1990, 1992a, 1992b; Grundfest 1993).

Confirmation of this expansion in investor options was evident in the comments of large institutional investors interviewed in mid-1992. What emerged from our interviews was a picture of a market with only partial resemblance to the traditional version. Consistent with that vision, many investors still reacted to bad news by simply moving their funds from poor performers to good. Others engaged in painstaking research to minimize the risk of investing in companies that could disappoint. Still others, however, sought a sustained dialogue with poor performers that research had failed to screen out and with which they were now stuck. Yet in seeking to understand why the inadequately performing companies had fallen into that category, a number of investors complained of inadequate information. Company financial disclosure was generally regarded as amply forthcoming, though some would have preferred more breakdown of segment and product earnings. But on the governance front, company disclosure was less well regarded. For instance, proxy information on executive compensation, a key parameter of the governance picture, was widely viewed as limited, confusing, and even misleading. Symptomatic of the problem's depth, the SEC instituted new proxy-reporting and shareholder-communication rules in 1992. The reforms focused not on improved financial reporting, as they might have in the past, but on improved governance procedures (Useem et al 1993; Zall 1993).

Like corporate behavior, market behavior never mimics theory in precise detail. But again, the disparity between market theory and market practice is pronounced enough for one to wonder about the traditional paradigm. If large shareholders could not readily sell, the traditional market mechanism for investor discipline of directors and their managers lost much of its meaning. Disgruntled investors groped for new mechanisms of control through the governance process, but quality governance information essential for such oversight was still in short supply (Pound 1992).

Motivating Management

In a normal theory of the organization, individuals are motivated by opportunities for personal gain. Self-interest may not always be good, but it constitutes an indispensable driver. The art of effective organizational design is to harness private motivation to shareholder ends. When management behavior failed to reflect investor expectations, it could be seen, in part, as failures in managerial incentives. Much of the financial restructuring of large companies during the 1980s was directed at correcting those failings.

This theory generated two corrective actions. First, it was argued, senior managers should have more of their compensation at risk; compensation should be more contingent on company performance as defined by shareholders, not managers; and the compensation of more managers should be made contingent. Managers, in short, should be transformed into mini-owners, the only sure way to align their interests with investors' (Jensen and Murphy 1990).

Second, senior managers should have less of the company's resources at their disposal. When executives retain control over a company's uncommitted cash, even well-designed compensation incentives could not prevent misuse of the funds for management gains. The gains were not necessarily narrowly personal. They often came in the form of company expansion, product diversification, and incumbency protection. But all came at the expense of "shareholder value," the growth of company dividends and share price that all investors want in some combination (Jensen 1989).

While this theory well describes much managerial behavior, an anomaly appears here too. We know from extensive research that management incentive systems can be a powerful driver of company performance. Yet we also know from many other studies that managers can be as motivated by the gratification of getting a job done well on their own as by the satisfaction of receiving a good paycheck for doing what they were told to do. There is little reason to believe that top executives are more likely than middle managers or the rank-and-file to require a working environment that stresses control through directives rather than objectives.[3]

We also know from other organizational theory that rigid discipline of free cash disposal can hinder, not foster shareholder ends. The concept of "organizational slack" provides a useful reminder here. Slack is defined as the surplus that remains after all essential costs are covered, and it can serve as a stabilizing resource with which organizations adjust to abrupt environmental changes, as a cushion against adversity, and as a fund for seizing opportunity (Cyert and March 1963).

This affirmative view of discretionary management control stands in contrast to one line of corporate reform that purports to go far toward solving the incentive and slack problems, the leveraged buyout. In this form of governance transformation, all shares of a publicly traded company are repurchased with funds borrowed against its assets. Managerial incentives are radically tightened by making top executives partial owners of the company. Organizational slack is radically contracted by the imposition of fixed schedules for debt retirement (Crawfold 1987; Fox and Marcus 1992, 68–70). But this is precisely what is wrong with leveraged buyouts. When flexibility is called for, as is often the case with organizational leadership, this rigid incentive and resource discipline of agents is likely to backfire against the principals that imposed it.

A study of eighty-three major leveraged buyouts completed between 1985 and 1989 offers confirming evidence: it was a period in which cash flows became especially hostage to debt payments, and twenty-three of the buyouts had defaulted by mid-1991. If economic downturns make fixed payment schedules impossible to meet, bankruptcy is the limited option of the shackled executive, suspended dividends the option of the flexible manager (Kaplan and Stein 1991).

If we lived in a world of narrowly prescribed job descriptions and financial incentives, such solutions to agency problems might well work. But much individual behavior is also motivated and constrained by social networks, power relations, implicit understandings, and management ideologies. Traditional governance practices have underestimated their behavioral powers.[4]

When Managers Replace Shareholders

In principal-agent theory, principals seek complete control over their agents' work. This is inherent in the act of hiring agents to execute a task that the principals have neither the time nor wherewithal to do themselves. Securing complete control, however, is another matter. Agents find numerous ways to bias their reporting and interject their own agendas. Yet such hindrances are viewed as temporary, momentary imperfections, which in due course should be resolved by the parties. After all, owners of the firm have unlimited authority to insist on full compliance among those whom they have temporarily granted power to run their company. If compliance is not forthcoming, in theory, the shareholders also have unlimited power to discipline or replace their agents.

While the theoretical logic here is straightforward, the empirical reality is not. Companies are in fact observed to do just the opposite of what principal-agent theory might expect: they sometimes replace their owners. According to a study of 761 publicly traded companies responding to a 1989 survey, a significant number had taken such actions. One in six had sought more institutional investors, two in five had gone after more individual shareholders, and more than one in three had recruited more employee and director shareholding. Moreover, the actions were driven by efforts to secure better protection of managements against shareholders who were challenging their prerogatives. Companies thus sought greater employee shareholding and lesser institutional shareholding when they were threatened by hostile takeovers and short-term investor pressure. Instead of submitting to owners' discipline or threats, managers sought to rid themselves of those imposing the discipline or making the threats (Useem and Gager 1993).

The extent to which employee and other "safe" ownership can be enhanced through concerted intervention is illustrated by McDonald's Corporation during the years 1986–1992. The company expressed fears about excessive volatility in stock price that it believed can come with high institutional ownership. "The risk of high institutional ownership is the risk of the herd mentality," warned McDonald's vice president for financial communications and investor relations. "I don't know how [investor relations] people can sleep at night with extremely high institutional ownership." The company encouraged employee, supplier, and franchisee shareholding through a variety of programs, wrapped, as is typical of such initiatives, in the ideology of general benefit. "[W]e believe," the company asserted, that employee "share ownership encourages performance that serves the long-range interests of shareholders." Between 1986 and 1992, the fraction of inside ownership nearly doubled (Figure 2.1) McDonald's Corporation 1992, 1).

This result suggests that principal-agent adjustments can sometimes be reversed. Though agents by definition are working for principals, their efforts to discipline their agents can lead the agents to replace them. Rather than shareholders throwing out underperforming managements, managements jettison overly controlling shareholders. The application of traditional marketing techniques does much of the work: little attention is directed at unwanted stockholders, while the firm's investment virtues are extolled among more desirable groups. Whether through outside brokers or inside incentives, the company's image as an investment opportunity is burnished among both individuals and employees.

Management actions to reconstitute its ownership base are not surprising given the powers that management commands. And if company executives believe that the risks and rewards sought by current investors do not well match the firm's new strategic directions, changing that clientele would seem entirely appropriate. The anomaly here is evident, however, in the redefinition of the meaning of ownership. Traditionally, owners occupied hallowed ground: a company's ultimate source of legitimacy and authority could only be its ultimate

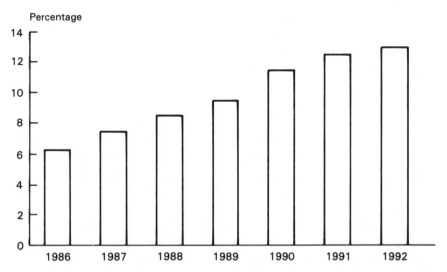

Figure 2.1. Ownership of McDonald's Corporation Shares by Employees, Franchisees and Suppliers, 1986–92. (*Source:* McDonald's Corp. 1992.)

source of capital. If, despite management arguments about the value of a new strategic directions, investors are still unwilling to accept a new direction, by the normal model we would anticipate managerial retreat. Yet we see that actual behavior often departs from this conception; managers moved to change owners they found objectionable.

Looking Down, Not Up The Hierarchy

Organizational change is often directed from above, sometimes it emerges from below, and occasionally it is a powerful product of both.[5] While the 1980s and early 1990s witnessed all the above, several dominant elements emerged in redesigns fostered by the executive suite: (1) authority to succeed and fail was moved lower in the organization, giving managers and operating units greater operating autonomy; (2) headquarters staff were scaled back and workrolls were pared; (3) top managers invested more time in managing and developing their successors; and (4) managerial decisions and promotions were more explicitly judged on the basis of anticipated value to stockholders.

If a new set of practices was pushed down the firm's hierarchy, few new practices were pushed up. Empowerment, decentralization, and flexibility became the new "best practices" below the chief executive, but they found little application above. The absence of change was not for want of fresh ideas. A host of proposals were circulated for redesigning virtually all major aspects of the governing board, ranging from its election and information to compensation and composition. On the last issue, for instance, leading proposals, most coming from outside management, included an increase in the ratio of outsiders to insiders, expansion in the number of outsiders fully independent of management, election of directors more responsive to shareholder interests, and separation of the position of board chairman from that of the chief executive. Related changes included limiting the nominations and other key committees to outside directors, and equipping boards with better means, such as independent staffs, and shareholder advisory committees, for exercising oversight.[6]

Drawing on a chapter from contemporary debates over national electoral reform, one analyst even found merit in setting terms for directors. A ten-year tenure limit, for instance, would force turnover in 1991 of five of General Motors' directors and six of Sears, Roebuck, ensuring at least new personnel if not a pronounced change in generic composition. The rationale: "By pruning some deadwood—and even active, constructive board members whose creative thinking days may have passed—term limits on directors could push companies to do better" (Barnard 1991a, 1991b).

However, though investors and companies often stood on the common ground of the need for change, they proposed different paths to achieve it. Shareholders, for instance, more often preferred electoral reform, managers compensation reform. One negotiated effort in 1991 found a single voice; a select group of company and investment managers issued a "new compact for owners and directors," urging that shareholders regularly evaluate the performance of directors and that directors regularly evaluate the performance of managers. But this common effort was unique. On most major matters, the landscape was marked by conflict, not compromise (Working Group on Corporate Governance 1991.)[7]

Restructuring has occurred within the ranks of many corporations. It has made little headway, however, at the top; the conflicting postures of investors, directors, and managers accounted for much of the inaction. Whatever the causes, corporate change was relatively rare at the apex of the organizational chart, though notable below that level.

Corporate Strategy and Plebiscite Management

A company's strategy can be a critical driver of its success or failure. Effective strategies shape an organization's design, investments, and products, and, ultimately, its performance (Chandler 1962; Porter 1985, 1987).

When institutional investors press poorly performing companies to improve soon and well-performing companies never to stumble, they seldom tell them how to do so. It is an attempt at influence by objectives, not directives. Yet there are notable exceptions. Several public pension funds sought a voice in General Motors' decision on a CEO succession in 1990 (their offer was accepted); several private money managers asked Chrysler Corporation to consider a specific executive for a CEO succession in 1992 (their advice was rejected); and various investors pressed USX in the early 1990s to divide its steel and oil business (their urging led to the creation of separate classes of stock linked to the two businesses).

An occasional investor advisory on a company's strategy raises few concerns for corporate governance. After all, many companies are already well familiar with unsolicited suggestions from a host of would-be interveners, particularly in the wake of publicized disasters and scandals. When occasional comment slips into frequent intervention, however, concerns do arise. Paramount among these is the extent to which investment managers are familiar enough with market conditions, company history, and strategic options to render effective advice. Many managers do not think they are; the chief executive of a large telecommunications services company offered a public assessment that would be privately expressed by many: "There is a move by pension funds to assert that they can assist management. But I have never seen a list of great triumphs of those who manage money who go out to manage a company. There is nothing to tell me that these state pension groups in New York, California and New Jersey know anything about how to run a company" (Useem 1993, 155–56).

The new-found powers of concentrated holdings may lead institutional investors, acting alone or collectively, increasingly to press for improved performance. But if their interest goes beyond the objectives to consider the means, companies could be faced with a kind of owners' vetting of its business plans. Routine management decisions would be transformed into the nonroutine. Plebiscite politics is inherently unwieldy, and plebiscite management would be much the same.

Redefining Power Relations

In identifying the six anomalies in normal governance, we have sought to describe where the model no longer fits observed behavior. We now turn to resolution of the anomalies. And in so doing, we move from the largely descriptive to the more prescriptive. While recognizing that there are alternative paths for overcoming each anomaly, we have also sought to find a path that would help to resolve them all. It would be premature to offer a highly specific road map, but we do propose general criteria for redesigning the firm at the top.

A normal conception of the firm posits an unambiguous hierarchy of control. Shareholders preside, directors guide, and managers execute. The vision of one observer is symptomatic of the world view. "Shareholders come first, other capital contributors thereafter, and other constituencies in the order that they contribute to the long-term profitability of the business. Public companies are not in business to reward creditors, inspire devotion of their employees, win the favor of the communities in which they operate, or have the best plants or products. These are all means to an end—making shareholders richer" (Seeley 1991, 36).

Resolution of the six anomalies described here, however, point to a different vision. The formal hierarchy running from shareholders down through directors to managers would be replaced by a horizontal network among them. Organized networks facilitate two-way flows of information and influence, and their establishment here would help achieve what takeover threats, proxy battles, and other blunt forms of "communication" between owners and companies have so often failed to achieve in the past.[8]

Investors, directors, and managers are still at the table. But formal principal-agent relations would give way to negotiated treaties among them. The hierarchy of organizational control would diminish as investors, directors, and managers all exercise claims on the firm. Primacy could be claimed by none. The hierarchy of market control would also flatten. Neither institutions nor companies could assert sovereignty over the other.

This revised model of governance provides room for other company constituencies to enter the negotiated order. While it is true that companies are not in business to inspire employee devotion or win community favor, in reality these other stakeholders already make it difficult for companies and investors to ignore them. Though they have no formal or legal claim on the corporation akin to that of stockholders, if they can mobilize the might to enter the negotiated order, they can do so. And they already do so, the traditional conception of the firm notwithstanding, though the impact is often episodic. The revised governance model would open the way for more regular engagement of these other company constituencies, which should make their impact less uneven and more constructive.

Consider just the effects of collective bargaining on investor holdings. In a study of two-tier wage agreements negotiated during the early 1980s, Thomas and Kleiner (1992) found that these innovative provisions, in which new hires were compensated at a lower rate than existing employees for essentially the same work, led to above-average returns of 2-to-4 percent during a ten-to-twelve-week period following their announcement. Conversely, failure to reach agreement and an ensuing strike can have a negative impact on investor value. In an analysis of strike data for the years 1962-1982, Becker and Olson (1986) report below-average returns of about 4 percent, mostly coming in the wake of the strike rather than in anticipation of it. Other management actions affecting large numbers of employees have no consistent effects on the level of stock prices but do affect price swings, according to a study by Abowd, Milkovich and Hannon (1990) of nearly 650 such announcements by 256 companies in 1980 and 1987. Focusing on changes in compensation, staffing, plant closings, and related events significant enough to warrant *The Wall Street Journal* coverage, they found abnormally high price swings in the immediate aftermath of plant shutdowns and permanent staff reductions, but neither positive nor negative net effects. To exclude labor and other stakeholders from the governance picture, then, is theoretically tidy but empirically foolhardy.

The revised governance model also implies that the preferred directions for the redesign of a specific company's governance system are contingent upon the existing balance—or imbalance—of power among investors, directors, and managers. If a firm's ownership becomes concentrated among a small set of major investors, management's relative autonomy to act may be overly constrained. Conversely, if a company's ownership becomes dispersed among a large set of small holders, its relative autonomy to act may be too unconstrained. Similarly, if a company board is dominated by insiders, it may be prudent to bring on more outsiders if the directors are to have independent standing among the primary strands of the governance network. Conversely, if outsiders dominate to the exclusion of insiders, it may be desirable to reverse this bias. The notions of checks and balances among the three branches of government offer a useful analogy here.

The normal definition of directorship duties includes review and approval of major company decisions, selection and oversight of top management, compliance with the law, and changes in ownership. Directors also play important roles in shaping the company's strategic directions, supporting the chief executive, and, in periods of crisis or long-term decline, more directly intervening and even challenging or replacing top management. Much of the board's action is transacted outside the boardroom itself, since its meetings are generally formal affairs in which policy differences are only indirectly aired. Committees undertake more of the board's real business, ranging from annual compensation for the chief executive to the nomination of new directors. Because of governance norms that discourage director challenge of the CEO, dissidents usually express their concerns informally through private communication. One active board member and former CEO characterized the informal channels this way: "Much of the contact between a CEO and an outside director is outside the board room [during] meals before and after board meetings, special 'off-campus' planning sessions and personal visits and telephone calls about company business. . . . It is a process which is normally subtle, non-directive and well-mannered (Richman 1993, 8).

With a more equitable balance of power among directors, investors, and managers, the process of board decision making and director wielding of influence may be little different from the normal model. The content, however, can be expected to be substantially revised, placing the distinctive concerns of investors and other stakeholders more clearly at the table than in the past.

Redefining Information Systems

The flow of company information reaching large shareholders markedly improved during the 1980s. This is evident from annual surveys of institutional investors between 1981 and 1991. The investors reported continued expansion in the amount and quality of information supplied by companies, the willingness of firms to meet with investors, and the frequency with which companies initiated contact with the institutions. This can be seen in the averages for 1987-1991 reported in Figure 2.2.

Yet the information flow is primarily in the area of financial indicators. There is little doubt that this remains critical to investors. Financial informa-

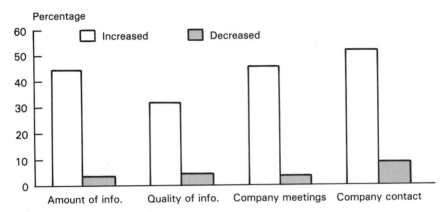

Figure 2.2.   Investor Evaluation of Company Imformation and Contact, 1987–91 Averages. (*Source:* Greenwich Associates, 1992 and earlier years).

tion is the foundation of expectations, and forecasts are the foundation of investment decisions. One study confirmed the contemporary importance of such expectations. Comparing actual performance of a set of 408 large, publicly traded companies during the early 1980s period with what analysts had expected of their performance, it found that when a company came on hard times, analyst expectations were a better predictor of a chief executive's downfall than was actual company performance. But if relatively high quality characterized financial reporting, relatively low quality characterized governance reporting (Puffer and Weintrop 1991).

In nearly all directorship elections, the board nominates a number of candidates precisely equal to the number of board openings. Nominee information presented to shareholders is almost always limited to the candidates' employment record, other corporate directorships, and company shares. Information about the nominees' views or records on matters of special interest to shareholders virtually never appears.

The 1987 proxy statement by Lockheed Corporation illustrates the information formally provided to shareholders. It contained the conventional biographies of the thirteen nominees standing for re-election to the board's thirteen openings. The data comprised the minimum mandated by the Securities and Exchange Commission: the director's age, principle business experience, first year on the board, and shares held in the firm (Table 2.1 displays the data for five of the nominees). It was from this profile that shareholders were to decide if the nominees would faithfully govern in their interests. All thirteen of the board-nominated nominees were elected to the Lockheed board.

On those rare occasions when the one-nominee/one-opening convention is not followed, the information flow usefully illustrates what could be more

TABLE 2.1.   Descriptions of Five Director Nominees for the Board of Lockheed Corporation, Company Proxy Statement, 1987

Name	Age	Director Since	No. of Shares	Principle Business Experiences
Roy A. Anderson	66	1971	66,401	Former Lockheed chief executive; director of 6 other companies
Michael Berberian	53	1973	300	Secretary-Treasurer, Berberian Brothers
Jack L. Bowers	66	1986	0	CEO of Lockheed subsidiary; director of 1 other company
Joseph P. Downer	64	1976	300	Retired Vice Chair., Atlantic Richfield Co.; director of 1 other company
Houston I. Flournoy	57	1976	300	Professor, University of S. California; director of 3 other companies

Source: Proxy Statement of Lockheed Corporation, March 31, 1987 (descriptions of principle business experience are abbreviated).

generally available to investors. A 1990 campaign by NL Industries to take over Lockheed included the formal constituting of an alternative slate of director nominees. The board-nominated and alternative slates offered voters distinct alternatives, and the two sides delivered substantial information to the voters on how the slates differed. Investors learned, for instance, that the incumbent Lockheed directors standing for reelection had recently rejected a measure to adopt confidential shareholding voting, a provision valued by many institutional investors. By contrast, investors also learned that each of the directors proposed by NL Industries had endorsed the introduction of secret balloting. The two rosters also differed on the poison pill and other governance issues of tangible interest to shareholders. In sharp contrast to conventional practice, the nominees' campaign platforms, not just their biographies, were carried directly to the voters. One newspaper advertisement by NL Industries, partially reproduced in Figure 2.3 showed the differences.

Lockheed countered with its own media campaign to reach its investors, asserting that its "Board will continue to make the hard choices we believe will enhance shareholder value." It urged its shareholders "to reelect your board, which is committed to maximizing values for All shareholders" (Lockheed Corporation, 1990). No such information or claims about the official director nominees had been made available to Lockheed shareholders in 1987, let alone an alternative slate. Such choices and information about them were available to shareholders on only exceptional occasion. By convention—and by contrast—

Lockheed and Shareholder Rights

NL Industries and the Lockheed Board take contrasting positions on several shareholder rights issues.

Here is where the two sides stand

	NL Nominees		Incumbents	
	For	Against	For	Against
Adopt Confidential Voting	X			X
Opt Out of Anti-Takeover Law	X			X
Eliminate Poison Pill	X			X
Prohibit Greenmail	X		X	
Forbid Golden Parachutes	X			X

When you decide whom to support in the election of Lockheed's Board of Directors, we urge you to ask yourself where you stand.

Figure 2.3.   NL Industries Newspaper Advertisement for Nominees to the Board of Directors of Lockheed Corporation, 1990. (*Source:* NL Industries, 1990.)

stockholders were without choice or information in virtually all other board elections. Enhanced choice and information do not necessarily bring management defeat. Lockheed's 1990 nominees still received some 62 percent of the shareholder vote.

Improved management disclosure of information on a range of governance practices and policies would significantly improve the capacity of investors to make informed decisions. Moreover, our revised, tripartite governance model would also direct attention to improved disclosure of governance information by the two other parties. Shareholders presently disclose very little. We know from our 1992 interview study of large investors that most have written policies concerning their voting on shareholder and management proxy resolutions (an example of one appears in Table 2.2). Yet few make these policies publicly available, nor do many announce their proxy decisions on governance resolutions. Discrete company inquiries to the investors can often produce such information on a case-by-case basis, but even then company executives may be hard pressed to discern the outlines of a policy. Public announcements of such policies by Calpers and CREF remain the exception, not the rule (Useem et al 1993).

Directors disclose even less. Rarely, if ever, do they talk with the shareholder community about their company. When our interviewed investors were asked if they had personal contact with directors of any of the companies in which they held major stakes, the answer was a resounding no. Indeed, direc-

TABLE 2.2.   Policies for Voting Company Proxies by a Large Fund Manager, 1992

General Policy: Proxies must be voted in the best interests of the shareholders.

Routine Issues: We will vote with management. Routine issues include election of directors, approval of stock option plans, and ratification of auditors.

Social and Political Issues: Unless instructed by a client, we will usually vote with management. Included here are restrictions on business activities in certain countries and limitations on controversial products.

Governance Issues: We will usually vote against proposals that limit shareholder sovereignty. Such proposals include elimination of cumulative voting and approval of poison pills.

Non-Routine Business Issues: We will vote on a case-by-case basis. These matters include restructurings, acquisitions, and divestitures.

Source: Fund Manager Documents, 1991.

torship decorum requires directors to deflect any efforts by investors to contact them personally, usually with the simple suggestion that the owners speak with management directly. Since boards formally represent shareholders to the company, this informal practice of avoiding all contact with shareholders is an ironic variant on the concept of representation.

The Forces for Reform

If investors become restless over management performance, directors should be the first to know. When the interests of shareholders receive short shrift, directors should be the first to complain. The rising tide of shareholder power and activism during the late 1980s and early 1990s in theory, therefore, should have first been felt in the boardroom. Yet in fact directors were usually the last to hear, and then, typically, they heard from the firm's management, not its shareholders.

The predominance of reactive rather than preemptive board behavior derives from the power relations that had long prevailed among the companies' three major stakeholders. Though the official pyramid placed shareholders on top, directors in the middle, and managers below, the actual picture was upside down. Board control of management was honored more in the breach than in practice.

Perhaps no single indicator better captured this decoupling of accountability than the electoral process itself. Investors almost never enjoyed a choice of candidates. So impervious were companies to electorate preference that shareholders seldom bothered to suggest a choice, even though they are legally entitled to do so, and annual company reports invite nomination. A 1989 study by the Conference Board confirms a nearly complete absence of shareholder initiative in this arena. Only 17 of 589 large firms surveyed reported that institutional investors had suggested or requested that they, the investors, play a role in selecting directors. And only a single company said that it had acceded to a demand from a major shareholder to add another outsider to its board. Without accountability, amnesia was next. Some twenty-six chief executives were asked in 1985 to identify their chief concerns. Only a single CEO mentioned shareholder value (Bacon 1990, 16; Bowman 1986).

Whatever the evident anomalies of the present governance system, any redesign is likely to face daunting barriers. During the early 1990s, however, divergent forces converged on the need for change. Some institutional investors clamored for reform. In our own 1992 study of large investors, two-fifths asserted that creating an independent board was the critical ingredient for an effective governance system (Useem et al 1993). Organized groups such as the United Shareholders Association and Council of Institutional Investors added their collective voice. The Securities and Exchange Commission received a host of governance-related proposals, and in 1992 it implemented major changes in both corporate reporting (better data on executive compensation was required) and owner challenges (investors were freer to organize opposition to incumbent management).

Many directors and managers themselves backed reform. A 1991 survey of 653 company directors reported that 70 percent believed that directors should be required to own stock; 53 percent backed development of a process to facilitate shareholder nominations of directors; and 20 percent even supported giving shareholders a chance to vote on management tenure (National Association of Corporate Directors 1992).

Some companies, moreover, initiated reform. The proportion of outside directors, according to one annual survey of large companies, edged modestly upward during the 1980s, standing at some 75 percent by 1993. More companies created nominations and compensation committees consisting solely of independent directors. And some also separated the roles of chairman and chief executive, enhancing the board's capacity to oversee management. When the board of General Motors forced its chairman and chief executive into early retirement in 1992, it divided his titles, giving the former to the outside director who had led the revolt against inside management. Though only a fifth to a quarter of large companies had separated the two posts by the early 1990s, the GM action drew widespread attention. So too did related actions by other companies, including Digital Equipment Corporation's forced retirement of its founder and chief executive in 1992, and Sears, Roebuck's removal of its chief executive from the chairmanship of the board nominations committee (Korn/ Ferry International 1993; Bacon 1990; Lublin 1992).

Alternative Models

While the momentum for change is evident, alternative models are less evident, unlike internal organizational innovations ranging from quality management to information systems. The Japanese and German systems are much discussed, but little more than the rudiments could be readily transplanted.[9] This is because their governance schemes are integral parts of complex business systems and cannot be readily extracted from them. Certain elements are certainly suggestive of what the United States might consider: the central role of banks and large long-term investors in Japanese and German companies imply that we should surely consider the known advantages of what is sometimes known as "relationship investing."

Perhaps because the changes required to resolve the anomalies required such wholesale revision of the governance system, and possibly the entire business system, widely admired best practices were slow to emerge in the United States. Underlying any revised governance model, however, should be a relative power symmetry among the three major parties. Central to this agenda is an enhancement of the power of the board. A host of steps is likely to contribute. These include increased outsider membership, reduced board size, stronger board committees, term limitations for directors, separation of the positions of chairman and CEO, annual performance reviews of both top managers and directors, and openly contested elections for the board. Some of these are likely to make more of a difference than the others, and certain are likely to be more acceptable than others. But some combination will be essential if the board is to achieve a greater presence.

Altered power relations in turn require altered information relations. A governance hierarchy normally implies that those at the top extract information from those below, with little reciprocation in return. A governance system of negotiated treaties, by contrast, implies widespread information sharing. If investors are to be effective partners in governance, they need an understanding of how the company operates. If directors are to exercise their oversight on behalf of investors, they require an informed view of what investors want and what management can give. And if managers are to manage their place in the tripartite arrangement, they deserve improved data on how the institutions operate. Table 2.3 identifies what would be more freely disclosed if information is to follow and support the improved power balance among the contending parties.

TABLE 2.3. Disclosed Information in a Redesigned Governance System

Managers	Directors	Investors
Compensation schemes	Nomination criteria	Performance measures
Strategic directions	Director policy views	Governance policies
Business organization	Board organization	Portfolio practices

Under a revised governance model, managers, owners, and directors would have access to far better information about one another. A company's managers and directors would know, for instance, the investment strategies and proxy policies of its major shareholders. Directors, not just managers, would meet periodically with the large owners, listening and sometimes heeding the owners' concerns, but also informing and occasionally educating owners on long-range company concerns. Board nominees would not stand for election on uncontested ballots as hand-picked successors of incumbent managers or directors, but rather as representatives of the several constituencies they are formally charged to represent. Company executives, board directors, and investment managers would form enduring relations, frequently informing and consulting one another, fully mindful of the others' interests and constraints.

The changes, however, are likely to come in modest measure. While wholesale redesign might be preferred for theoretical reasons, actual efforts are likely to focus on specific steps of limited scope: a board's decision to add an independent director to the board, an investor's decision to serve on a board, a chief executive's decision to relinquish chairmanship of the board. Given the resisting powers of the contending parties and the risks accompanying untested alternatives, incrementalism is prone to prevail. While Thomas Kuhn's anomalies of normal science may be the genesis of scientific revolution, our anomalies of normal governance are more apt to see an evolution.

Emerging Issues

Even with an evolving resolution of these governance issues, however, a new set of governance issues hovers on the horizon. The basic elements of contemporary governance practices were established in an era when centralized control of the company was gospel. Despite the appearance of the multidivisional form and other innovations for devolving authority, headquarters had retained tight control. The emergence of strategic business units and the more general decentralization of central management functions, however, is now altering the way companies do business (Galbraith and Merrill 1991; Taylor 1991; Golden 1992).

Top managements exercise less stringent decision-making oversight, while applying more stringent performance criteria. They place less stress on controlling inputs and more on ensuring outcomes. As a result, the firm's internal control systems are being revamped. Executives acquire stronger oversight through the more indirect but also more powerful mechanisms of managerial and divisional accountability.

A corresponding set of changes may be required in governance at the top. For instance, when a company operates a highly autonomous set of strategic business units, a board may want to consider establishing miniboards to oversee each. Kohlberg Kravis Roberts does this, in effect, for the some twenty companies it owns, and this may be a practice that could be duplicated inside firms seeking to approximate a KKR-type holding company. Governance reforms on top of those already in the offing could well be in store. Learning from experience in governance design may be just as important as in organizational design.

Perhaps the most general challenge for governance and redesign of the firm is least addressed in these debates. Lindblom reminds us that politics become important when markets fail (Lindblom 1977). And markets frequently do fail to solve widely felt social problems. Whether environmental quality, demographic diversity, or employee training, companies may value change but find few advantages in doing so. While toxic dumps abandoned by bankrupt firms pose hazards to all, the costs of clean-up will be borne by none of those responsible. The political arena generates solutions, but without company cooperation, many solutions are sure to be stillborn. In its most general form, then, corporate governance is concerned not just with achieving shareholder value but also with realizing societal goals.

Notes

The authors would like to thank the Institutional Investor Project of the Center for Law and Economic Studies of Columbia University, Price Waterhouse, and the Reginald Jones Center for Management Policy, Strategy, and Organization of University of Pennsylvania for support; Bruce Kogut, Anthony M. Santomero, Raymond Bromark of Price Waterhouse, and other participants in the conference on designing the firm for helpful comments; and Jennifer Myatt and Craig Irvine for research assistance.

1. Thomas Kuhn (1962). This is a predicate of much analysis of the impetus for change, whether in Kurt Lewin's (1952) and Edgar Schein's (1987) metaphor of organizational "unfreezing," or David Nadler and Michael Tushman's (1988) concept of organizational "congruency."
2. Useem, Bowman, Irvine and Myatt (1993). The institutional investors were drawn from among the forty largest public and private pension funds, forty largest investment funds, and the twenty largest foundations.

3. The impact of senior management incentives on company performance is examined in a volume edited by Ehrenberg (1990); the impact of work and organizational design on managerial motivation is explored in Lawler (1992); and impact of information on managerial work is examined in Zuboff (1988).

4. The importance of management networks, power, contracts, and ideologies is developed in Granovetter (1985), Etzioni (1988), Fligstein (1990), Pfeffer (1991), Powell and DiMaggio (1991), and Shleifer and Summers (1988).

5. Examples of organizational innovations that emerge from below and are embraced from above are chronicled in Beer, Eisenstat, and Spector (1990).

6. A sampling of both calls for reform and resistance to them can be found in Porter (1992), Monks and Minow (1991), and Business Roundtable (1990); and assessments of relevant research are available in Walsh and Seward (1990) and Hoskisson and Turk (1990).

7. Working Group on Corporate Governance (1991).

8. The structure and power of networks as mediators of economic exchange and organizational influence are developed by Granovetter (1985) and Powell (1990).

9. Analysis of the Japanese and German governance systems can be found in Gerlach and Lincoln (1992), Roe (1993), Kester (1991), Porter (1992), and Franks and Mayer (1992). Constraints in the transfer of organizational models across national boundaries are developed in Westney (1987) and Cole (1989).

References

Abowd, John M., George T. Milkovich, and John M. Hannon. 1990. The effects of human resource management decisions on shareholder value. *Industrial and Labor Relations Review* 43:203S–216S.

Bacon, Jeremy. 1990. Membership and organization of corporate boards. New York: Conference Board.

Barnard, Jayne. 1991a. Reducing tenure in the boardroom. *New York Times*, December 22, p. F11.

Barnard, Jayne. 1991b. Institutional investors and the new corporate governance. *North Carolina Law Review* 69:1135–87.

Becker, Brian E., and Craig A. Olson. 1986. The impact of strikes on shareholder equity. *Industrial and Labor Relations Review* 39:425–38.

Beer, Michael, Russell A. Eisenstat, and Bert Spector. 1990. *The critical path to corporate renewal*. Boston: Harvard Business School Press.

Berle, Adolph, Jr., and Gardiner C. Means. 1967. *The modern corporation and private property*. New York: Harcourt, Brace and World (reprint edition).

Black, Bernard S. 1990. The legal and historical contingency of shareholder passivity. *Michigan Law Review* 89:520–608.

Black, Bernard S. 1992a. Agents watching agents: The promise of institutional investor voice. *UCLA Law Review* 39:812–93.

Black, Bernard S. 1992b. The value of institutional investor monitoring: The empirical evidence. *UCLA Law Review* 39:896–939.

Bowman, Edward H. 1986. Concerns of the CEO. *Human Resource Management* 25: 267–85.

Chandler, Alfred A., Jr. 1962. *Strategy and structure.* Cambridge, Mass.: MIT Press.

Chandler, Alfred D., Jr. 1977. *The visible hand: The managerial revolution in American business.* Cambridge, Mass.: Harvard University Press.

Cole, Robert E. 1989. *Strategies for learning: Small-group activities in American, Japanese, and Swedish industry.* Berkeley, Calif.: University of California Press.

College Retirement Equities Fund (CREF). 1990. Letter of November 8, 1990 to U.S. Securities and Exchange Commission. New York: College Retirement Equities Fund.

Crawford, Edward K. 1987. *What management should know about leveraged buyouts.* New York: John Wiley.

Cyert, Richard M., and James G. March. 1963. *A behavioral theory of the firm.* Englewood Cliffs, N.J.: Prentice-Hall.

Ehrenberg, Ronald G. 1990. Introduction: Do compensation policies matter? *Industrial and Labor Relations Review* 43: 3S–12S.

Eisenhardt, Kathleen M. 1989. Agency theory: An assessment and review. *Academy of Management Review* 14:57–74.

Etzioni, Amitai. 1988. *The moral dimension.* New York: Free Press.

Fama, Eugene, and Michael Jensen. 1983. Separation of ownership and control. *Journal of Law and Economics* 26:301–25.

Fligstein, Neil. 1990. *The transformation of corporate control.* Cambridge, Mass.: Harvard University Press.

Fox, Isaac, and Alfred Marcus. 1992. The causes and consequences of leveraged management buyouts. *Academy of Management Review* 17:62–85.

Franks, Julian, and Colin Mayer. 1992. Corporate control: A synthesis of the international evidence. Conference on Corporate Control, University of California, Davis, May 15–17.

Galbraith, Craig S., and Gregory B. Merrill. 1991. The effect of compensation program and structure on SBU competitive strategy: A study of technology-intensive firms. *Strategic Management Journal* 12:353–70.

Gerlach, Michael L., and James R. Lincoln. 1992. The organization of business networks in the U.S. and Japan. In *Networks and organization theory*, edited by Robert Eccles and Nitin Nohria. Boston: Harvard Business School Press.

Golden, Brian R. 1992. SBU strategy and performance: The moderating effects of the corporate-SBU relationship. *Strategic Management Journal* 13:145–58.

Granovetter, Mark. 1985. Economic action and social structure: The problem of embeddedness. *American Journal of Sociology* 91:481–510.

Grant, Linda. 1992. GM shuffle may be watershed in reining in CEOs. *Los Angeles Times*, April 13, D1–2.

Greenwich Associates. 1991. End of the tunnel? [Institutional Equity Services, Report to Participants]. Greenwich, Conn.: Greenwich Associates.

Grundfest, Joseph A. 1993. Just vote no: A minimalist strategy for dealing with Barbarians inside the gates. *Stanford Law Review* 45:857–937.

Herman, Edward S. 1981. *Corporate control, corporate power*. New York: Cambridge University Press.

Hirschman, Albert D. 1970. *Responses to decline in forms, organizations and states*. Cambridge: Harvard University Press.

Hoskisson, Robert E., and Thomas A. Turk. 1990. Corporate restructuring: Governance and control limits of the internal capital market. *Academy of Management Review* 15:459–77.

ITT Corporation. 1991. Notice of annual meeting and proxy statement. New York: ITT Corporation.

Jensen, Michael C. 1989. Eclipse of the public corporation. *Harvard Business Review* 89(5):61–74.

Jensen, Michael C., and Kevin J. Murphy. 1990. CEO incentives—It's not how much you pay, but how. *Harvard Business Review* (May-June): 138–53.

Kaplan, Steven N., and Jeremy C. Stein. 1991. The evolution of buyout pricing and financial structure in the 1980s. Unpublished paper, University of Chicago.

Kester, W. Carl. 1991. Governance, contracting, and investment time horizons. Cambridge, Mass.: Harvard Business School, unpublished manuscript.

Korn/Ferry International. 1993. Board of directors: Twentieth annual study, 1993. New York: Korn/Ferry International.

Kuhn, Thomas. 1962. *The structure of scientific revolutions*. Chicago: University of Chicago Press.

Lawler, Edward E., III. 1992. *The ultimate advantage: Creating the high-involvement organization*. San Francisco: Jossey-Bass.

Lewin, Kurt. 1952. Group decision and social change. In *Readings in social psychology*, G. E. Swanson, T. N. Newcomb, and E. L. Hartley. New York: Holt.

Lindblom, Charles. 1977. *Politics and markets: The world's political economic system*. New York: Basic Books.

Lockheed Corporation. 1990. Advertisement. *New York Times*, March 27, p. D11.

Lorsch, Jay W. 1989. *Pawns or potentates: The reality of america's corporate boards*. Boston: Harvard Business School Press.

Lowenstein, Louis. 1991. *Sense and nonsense in corporate finance*. Reading, Mass.: Addison-Wesley.

Lublin, Joann S. 1992. Other concerns are likely to follow GM in splitting posts of chairman and CEO. *The Wall Street Journal*, November 4, p. B10–11.

Mace, Myles. 1971. *Directors: myth and reality*. Boston: Division of Research, Harvard Business School.

Mahoney, William F. 1993. *The active shareholder*. New York: Wiley.

McDonald's Corporation. 1992 Annual Report 1991. Oak Brook, Ill.:McDonald's Corporation.

Monks, Robert A. G., and Nell Minow. 1991. *Power and accountability*. New York: Harper Business.

Nadler, David A., and Michael L. Tushman. 1988. *Strategic organization design*. Glenview, Ill.: Scott, Foresman.

National Association of Corporate Directors. 1992. 1992 Corporate Governace Survey. Washington, D.C.: NL Industries. 1990. Advertisement. *New York Times*, March 27, p. D7.

Pfeffer, Jeffrey. 1991. *Managing with power*. Cambridge, Mass.: Harvard Business School Press.

Porter, Michael. 1985. *Competitive advantage*. New York: Free Press.

Porter, Michael. 1987. From competitive advantage to corporate strategy. *Harvard Business Review* 65:43–59.

Porter, Michael. 1992. Capital choices: Changing the way America invests in industry. Washington, D.C.: Council on Competitiveness.

Powell, Walter W. 1990. Neither market Nor hierarchy: Network forms of organization. In *Research in organizational behavior*, edited by Barry M. Staw and L. L. Cummings. Greenwich, Conn.: JAI Press.

Powell, Walter W., and P. J. DiMaggio, ed. 1991. *The new institutionalism in organizational analysis*. Chicago: University of Chicago Press.

Puffer, Sheila M., and Joesph B. Weintrop. 1991. Corporate performance and CEO turnover: The role of performance expectations. *Administrative Science Quarterly* 36:1–19.

Richman, John M. 1993. Corporate governance: The U.S. experience. Paper presented at a conference on Creating a Corporate Governance for the Global 21st Century Enterprise, the Wharton School, University of Pennsylvania, January 7–8.

Roe, Mark. 1993. Some differences in corporate structure in Germany, Japan, and the United States. *Yale Law Journal* 102: 1927–2003.

Schein, Edgar H. 1987. *Process consultation*, vol. 2. Reading Mass.: Addison-Wesley.

Seely, Michael. 1991. A vision of value-based governance. *Directors and Boards* 15:35–6.

Shleifer, Andrei, and Lawrence H. Summers. 1988. Breach of trust in hostile takeovers. In *Corporate takeovers: causes and consequences*, edited by Alan J. Auerbach. Chicago: University of Chicago Press.

Stern, Paul G. 1993. Corporate governance: beyond the hype. Paper presented at a conference on Creating a Corporate Governance for the Global 21st Century Enterprise, the Wharton School, University of Pennsylvania, January 7-8.

Thomas, Steven L., and Morris M. Kleiner. 1992. The effect of two-tier collective bargaining on shareholder equity. *Industrial and Labor Relations Review* 45:339–51.

Useem, Michael. 1993. *Executive defense: Shareholder power and corporate reorganization*. Cambridge, Mass.: Harvard University Press.

Useem, Michael, and Constance Gager. 1993. Employee shareholders or institutional investors? When managerial agents replace their shareholder principals. Unpublished paper, University of Pennsylvania.

Useem, Michael. Edward N. Bowman, Craig Irvine, and Jennifer Myatt. 1993. U.S. investors look at corporate governance in the 1990s. *European Management Journal* 11:175–89.

Walsh, James P., and James K. Seward. 1990. On the efficiency of internal and external corporate control mechanisms. *Academy of Management Review* 15:421–58.

Westney, D. Eleanor. 1987. *Imitation and innovation: The transfer of western organizational patterns to Meiji Japan.* Cambridge, Mass.: Harvard University Press.

Working Group on Corporate Governance. 1991. A new compact for owners and directors. *Harvard Business Review* 69:142–43.

Zall, Charles C. 1993. *1993 annual report and proxy rules of the Securities and Exchange Commission.* Philadelphia: Packard Press.

Zuboff, Shoshana. 1988. *In the age of the smart machine: The future of work and power.* New York: Basic Books.

3

Sustainable Competitive Advantage Through Alliance

ELIZABETH E. BAILEY AND WEIJIAN SHAN

The business press is full of stories about corporate alliances: KLM and Northwest Airlines, Xerox and Fuji, Caterpillar and Mitsubishi, Amgen and Kirin Brewery, IBM, Siemens and Toshiba. Information about alliances is not limited just to the news stories. Recently, a clever advertisement in *The Wall Street Journal* asked "What have Bill Gates, John Sculley, Scott McNealy, John Young and Larry Ellison agreed to cooperate on?" The answer: to establish an alliance between Oracle and four other computer companies.

In recent years, the number of alliances has grown at an explosive pace. But what is the incentive for these arrangements? Who cooperates with whom? And what form do these cooperative ventures take? In this chapter we will focus on three of the major forces driving this trend—the increasingly global nature of competition, the accelerated pace of technological change, and the opening of new markets such as Eastern Europe—and how firms, and governments, are creating networks of alliances that yield sustainable competitive advantage.

Changes in the External Environment

The most fundamental trends since World War II are the increasingly global nature of competition and technological innovation. All major markets have seen a sharp increase in international competition. Firms have seen their foreign rivals make inroads into what had been their domestic markets. So they, in turn, found it necessary for their financial success to be present in foreign markets. As customers became more global, so too did successful suppliers to those businesses, whether an airline that flies all over the world or a hotel chain with properties on every continent. The result has been that in business after business the number of competitors capable of world-class competition has grown. These competitors have made competition more demanding and less forgiving. Their backgrounds are Asian and European, not just American.

Partnerships have formed to enable firms to find sustainable competitive advantage in this global marketplace. The idea is to win together by creating economic value through alliance. Manufacturers are giving their strategic suppliers more say in designing parts and systems through concurrent engineering. Manufacturers and suppliers are becoming partners in production and are selling and servicing each other's production. A product can have a recognizable U.S. brand name, yet it may have been assembled overseas, using components produced in many countries. Companies have begun forming direct research links, especially at precompetitive stages, such as new battery technology for electric cars. Multinational firms have become adept at using alliances to overcome trade and investment barriers imposed by their governments.

A more recent phenomenon is the opening up of new frontiers, such as China, the former Soviet Union, and Eastern Europe. These underdeveloped markets offer challenging opportunities to multinational firms, as well as to the countries themselves. These new markets are likely to be politically, culturally, institutionally, and economically different from those markets with which multinational companies are familiar. Learning to do business effectively and efficiently in these new markets requires costly investment and takes considerable time. Therefore, alliances with insiders can be efficient entry vehicles to the benefit of both parties. Often, the inside partner is a governmental entity. The nature of the partnership involves access to the market in return for up-front investment and expertise.

There continues to be an infusion of new technologies. These technologies are becoming increasingly complex. An automobile used to be an assembly of metal and mechanical parts; it now contains advanced electronics, computers, and even special ceramics. As such, it has become increasingly difficult for one single company to possess all the technologies needed for the final product. Frequently, parts containing new technologies must be custom-made because they cannot be found in the open market. The convergence of technologies requires alliances between firms possessing different types of technologies. This sharing of cost, risk, and complexity provides a motivation for alliances among large multinational firms. For example, among other advantages, the European Airbus consortium pools the technological capabilities of the partners to create the technology-intensive commercial aircraft.

The life cycles of technologies are becoming curtailed. One needs only to observe the accelerated introduction of models of personal computers based upon ever-newer generations of microprocessors and built with new materials. The trend is ever-faster, smaller, and energy-efficient machines. The first PC was introduced only about a decade ago. Today, PCs based upon Intel 8086 and 80286 microprocessors are hopelessly out of date and virtually worthless. The same is true in many industries of high technology. Even during the lifetime of a technology, the ensuing competition in search of new sources of profits quickly erodes the monopoly of the innovator. There is a real danger that a new product could become obsolete even before it is introduced, or become a near commodity soon after (just think of facsimile machines and cellular phones).

The trend is ever-faster, smaller, and energy-efficient machines. The first PC

Therefore, there is every incentive for an innovating firm to expedite the R&D process and to formulate an alliance for a more rapid commercialization of a new technology. Firms are constrained by the limited resources and capabilities under their ownership. The capabilities that complement their own and may allow them to capture maximum value from their investment in technology might reside within the boundaries of other organizations, and vice versa. Therefore, as technological change accelerates and as technological life cycles become ever shorter, domestic and international alliances are becoming ever-more necessary if firms are to enjoy sustainable advantage.

The Sustainability Framework

Several recent concepts from the academic literature—in particular, the concept of sustainable competitive advantage, but also the notion of core competence and the concept of economies of scope—provide a framework and a set of prototypes to draw upon in analyzing the rationale for corporate alliances.

According to the sustainability framework, firms are positioned along a spectrum based on the rate of product imitability (Williams 1992). Imitability is very slow in monopolistic environments where companies are shielded from competition (slow-cycle or sheltered markets). Product imitability is moderate in oligopolistic environments (standard-cycle markets). Imitability is rapid in dynamic, entrepreneurial, "Schumpeterian" environments (fast-cycle markets).

Companies in each cycle find competitive advantage in ways that are different from companies in other cycles. Successful firms in sheltered environments achieve advantage through a local monopoly or exclusive rights to a territory. Economies of scale provide advantage to successful firms in oligopolistic environments. In entrepreneurial environments, the laurels go to firms that can sustain a high rate of innovation and change.

These sources of competitive advantage are summarized in the middle panel in Table 3.1. The external trends of globalization and innovation (the left

TABLE 3.1.   Enhancing Economic Benefit through Alliance

External Trends	Source of Sustainable Competitive Advantage	Incentives for Alliance
Opening new markets	Sheltered market	Public–Private: Access for resources
Globalization	Scale and scope of operations	Transnational: Sharing cost, risk, and complexity
Innovation	Dynamic environment	Developer–Innovator: Speed of adoption

panel) provide new sources of economic benefit, which can be captured through alliances, such as those depicted in the right panel. The sustainability framework embraces the notion of competitive fit. The objective of its analysis is to achieve, through appropriate strategies, a tight competitive fit between the firm's idiosyncratic skills and its environment. One of the strategies available to management is that of alliance. If a firm's capabilities do not match well with the capabilities it needs in a changing environment, an alliance may well offer it the best path to achieve its goals. Alliances may aid it in establishing operations in foreign countries, in rapid achievement of some benefits of vertical or horizontal interaction, in gaining a resource infusion not otherwise available to it, or in gaining a first-mover advantage.

The sustainability framework is closely allied to the notion of core capability. The idea of core competence focuses on the capability set a firm wishes to create (Prahalad and Hamel 1990; Stalk, Evans, and Shulman 1992). The sustainability analysis identifies specific capabilities that contribute to each source of economic advantage. For example, a scale-based advantage is associated with a control orientation that is driven by cost and quality. Capabilities linked more with market timing and intelligence, with speed of entry and exit, are likely to be associated with dynamic advantage. Capabilities based on guildlike, long-term relationships or country-specific advantage are linked to command of sheltered markets, through local monopoly or territorial advantage.

There is a link between the sustainability framework and contestability theory, due to the effect of expansion of a firm's scope of operations has on enhancing scale (Baumol, Panzar, and Willig 1982). The concept of economies of scope distinguishes between profit enhancement resulting from a geographically wider scope of operations versus that arising from a larger scale of operations.[1] The important feature is that enhancing the scope of operations magnifies overall scale for any given level of individual scale. An alliance that involves a trade of access for resources may have the double benefit of enhancing scale and of operating in a sheltered market.

Our approach encompasses a firm's current competitors. But, in addition, we include those potential competitors who are positioning themselves to enter an industry at a future date. Thus, when a firm undertakes an alliance for sustainable competitive advantage, its plan is to create long-term value that other current and potential competitors will be unable to duplicate rapidly. Often, firms will forge alliances that strengthen the advantage from their current place in the competitive cycle, as well as enhance advantages across the competitive cycle.

Motivations for Alliance by Firms with Sheltered Markets

Sustainable competitive advantages associated with slow-cycle, sheltered markets arise from establishing a geographic monopoly or a unique set of product attributes. A product design that is just right may dominate its market for decades. Research-and-development expenditures have led to a not-easily-imitated product, such as a complex software system, an airplane design, or a drug protected under the patent laws. The key aspect of these advantages is that the firm has been able to achieve an idiosyncratic one-of-a-kind capability, that is likely to erode slowly over time.

Since shielded advantages are often geographic, it is not hard to see that the opening of markets in Eastern Europe and Russia offers a strong motivation for alliance. Figure 3.1 depicts the advantages and disadvantages over time, from

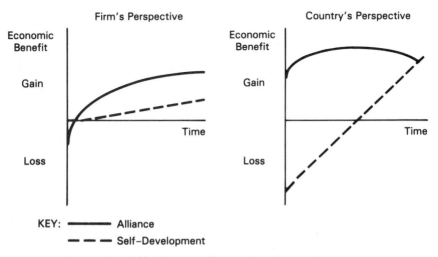

Figure 3.1.   Public–Private Alliances for Plant Modernization.

the perspective of each of the players, of an alliance involving plant modernization in Eastern Europe. A firm is severely constrained from entering these
markets on its own because the country may not permit access. By forming a
public/private alliance, a firm can increase the scope of its operations; it will
incur initial costs, but at the reward of long-term economic benefits in this
shielded market. From the country's point of view, where the state had been the
monopoly producer in the past, its capital base has weakened. So it seeks an
alliance in which a partner offers an initial investment of capital, as well as key
operating capabilities and skills. The country can expect to achieve a significant
gain financially in the early years of the alliance with this infusion of foreign
capital and know-how. Because of overall capital constraints, the alternative
path of self-development is an inferior alternative for the country, as it would
take a long time to build this capability internally. The country is in a position to
seek competitive bids, set the terms of the alliance, and thus ensure an immediate flow of benefits to itself.

A specific example might be the recent agreements various countries in
Eastern Europe have made with multinational tobacco companies. Each country currently has a monopoly franchise of tobacco in its region. Multinational
tobacco companies, from such countries as the United States and France have
bid for these rights. These companies will provide needed capital and expertise
in plant modernization and marketing in return for the right to manufacture
and sell their own brand names in the new territory, along with local brands
they will help produce. By enhancing their scope of operations, they increase
their scale-based advantages and obtain sustainable advantages from the new
sheltered market. Eventually, they may either increase or sell off their equity in
these foreign alliances as skills and knowledge are transferred and as the entities become sufficiently successful to be candidates for privatization.

A second example of a teritorial alliance involves energy conservation in
Russia and Eastern Europe. These countries face a significant backlog of maintenance and repair in their public infrastructure. A consortium of firms has
allied to offer a long-term performance contract that guarantees operating savings (mostly in energy) over a number of years. Capital is provided up-front to
modernize all aspects of the energy system. A complex set of contractual alliances with producers of energy systems components and suppliers of the energy
itself is created so that savings from energy usage can be used to pay back the
initial infrastructure investment.

Such performance contracts are also being undertaken in an effort to open
new markets within the United States. The public incentive may be purely a
trade of access for resources, rather than an alliance based on a transfer of
knowledge. Alliances between Honeywell and local school boards are illustra-
tive. Honeywell offers to modernize the school plant and improve the learning

environment at no financial outlay to the district. The school board can direct all its investment dollars to its educational mission and pay back Honeywell through the transfer of some amount of the energy savings. From Honeywell's perspective, the alliance opens up a vertical market opportunity. The company is working with the public sector to enact legislation that permits such performance contracting (only fourteen states now permit this). And it has to develop a complex selling capability tailored to each customer. This capability is local, but in can be re-used in each locality, whether it is a school system in the United States or a local government building management agency in Moscow.

Alliances motivated by rents from shielded markets may be based on technology instead of territory. There are a number of high-technology firms, such as Oracle, that have developed software products over time and offer specialized customer-specific services. Oracle has allied itself with SUN, Apple, Microsoft, and Hewlett-Packard so that software applications could be developed more rapidly than otherwise for the new cooperative-server database of Oracle. The incentive for Oracle to ally with these hardware and software companies is to have its innovation become a standard in the marketplace, thereby co-opting continued development of competing systems and giving itself a larger long-term shielded market. The incentive for the other members of the alliance is to get early access to Oracle's new database system and share in the rents its new capabilities offer to users. [2]

Motivation for Alliance by Firms with Scale-Based Advantages

A different set of economic advantages arise from the building of capabilities of a traditionally oligopolistic nature. (The classic text on the oligopoly environment is Porter's 1980 *Competitive Strategy*.) These capabilities entail coordination of large teams of workers and large-scale standardized production and distribution processes to serve mass markets, both national and global. These organizations are scale-orchestrated because profit leadership requires tight resource control at high volume. Companies within these industries, such as those producing automobiles and appliances, fast food, and credit card services, face a higher degree of resource-imitation pressure than companies in slow-cycle, shielded markets. Rather than a one-of-a-kind advantage, competitive advantages in oligopolistic environments arise from repeated transactions, from orchestrating complex processes.

The nature of alliances is somewhat different for industries whose advantage comes from scale of operations. Here, alliances tend to form where players have complementary capabilities, and where the joining of these complementary capabilities is forced by the increasing globalization of markets. A second important motivation for transnational alliances is that even major national markets may be too small to support efficient business operations. Manufacturing economies of scale have been an important factor in several major industries (automobiles, construction equipment, and semiconductors). A third driver is the ever-increasing cost of development of new commercial technologies, in industries such as microelectronics, jet aircraft, and telecommunicatons. Each player gains sufficiently from the alliance in the early years relative to the expense it might otherwise incur that it offsets some loss of economic benefit in later years compared to the profits it would have enjoyed under self-development (Kogut 1988; Kobrin 1993; Shan and Hamilton 1991).

The aviation industry provides an excellent example of scale-based alliances. Deregulation has created impetus for a more global, scale-based industry (Bailey and Williams 1988). American, United, and Delta, the big three U.S. carriers, have purchased the former international routes of PanAm and TWA. They have thus become powerhouses in Europe, as well as the United States (see Table 3.2). Smaller U.S. carriers, such as Northwest, USAir, and Continental, are seeking alliances with foreign airlines to provide a similar global capability. For example, KLM significantly strengthened Northwest financially through an infusion of equity. Then, it proposed a legal framework under which the two carriers could operate as if they were a single firm. The agreement involves joint advertising, combination of sales forces and schedule planning, coordination of pricing and commission programs, and the like. Similar alliances between USAir and British Airways, and Continental, SAS and Air Canada have recently been concluded. The incentives for alliance are the

TABLE 3.2. Joining the Ranks of Global Megacarriers

	1991 Revenue Passenger Miles (Billions)
American	82.33
United	82.29
British Airways/ USAir*	73.66
Northwest/KLM*	71.04
Air Canada/SAS/ Continental*	68.71
Delta	67.34

* Proposed alliances.

Note: Ranking excludes Aeroflot.

creation of full-operation synergies to enable the combined entities to be global players of comparable scale to American and United.

It should be noted that governments can be a kind of hidden partner in an oligopolistic alliance. In the airline case, the Netherlands recently signed an open-skies trade agreement with the United States, thereby lessening opposition to its proposed alliance. In contrast, the opposition to the USAir and British Airways alliance is based in part on current restrictions on access to Great Britain. It is significant that the senior partner in these scale-based alliances are European carriers. Under European Economic Community rules, purchase by a U.S. airline would mean that the European airline would lose its status as a community carrier and thus its access to the internal European market. Clearly we have here a situation in which asymmetries in government policies are important elements in determining the degree and form of alliances.

A number of alliances between oligopolistic firms have taken place in the automobile industry. An interesting alliance is that between Ford and Mazda. Holding equity stakes in each other, Ford has long had a cooperative relationship with Mazda in which each complements the territorial strength of the other. Each of the companies traded their territorial advantage for access to global markets in which they were weak: Ford agreed to have Mazda sell Ford-made Mazda cars in Europe and Mazda agreed to have Ford sell Mazda-made Ford cars in Japan.[3] Thus, the alliance has its roots in trading territorial or scope advantage; however, as we have shown, such a trade also serves to satisfy each firm's desire to enhance its scale of operations.

Other examples concern access to the Japanese market. The Japanese market is difficult for a foreign firm to penetrate because of its peculiar distribution system, institutional relationships, and government policies. Xerox, however, successfully penetrated the Japanese copier market through an alliance with Fuji, even as the Xerox home market was being relentlessly invaded by a dozen or so Japanese competitors. Many U.S. multinational companies achieved their successes in Japan through similar strategies. These include the joint ventures between Merck and Banyu, between Eli Lilly and Shionogi, and between Caterpillar and Mitsubishi, to name just a few. While such alliances are motivated primarily by the need for a global scope of operations, each partnership promotes economic benefits from larger scale and from the gain of access to a shielded territorial market.

Mushrooming costs of developing and producing advanced computer chips has led to a joining of three global competitors (IBM, Siemens, and Toshiba) in one alliance and two other global competitors (Advanced Micro Devises and Fujitsu) in another to develop a new type of memory chip. The motivations are complex and clearly include both cost and risk elements, as well as scale and antitrust considerations. If each of the firms in such an alliance makes complementary improvements to the technology, the advance in the technology will go much faster. All firms have incentives to join the consortium since no major player wants to be behind the technology frontier and thereby risk losing a major market.

Table 3.3 summarizes some of the alliances formed in this industry in recent years and indicates the type of purpose or capabilities offered by the alliance. The alliances currently tend to involve joint development; in the past, a looser form of alliance involving licensing agreements was considered sufficient. Alliances in these areas will cause some interesting rethinking on the national origin and control of technology. If such alliances are successful, the new technology that is developed will be a world technology, not an American or Japanese or European technology. There could arise the opportunity for a global shielding of a major technology break-through, under which governments might not have the ability to intervene as they have traditionally done in the past.

Motivations for Alliance for Firms in Dynamic Environments

The third generic category of economic benefit applies to Schumpeterian rents, where the capabilities are those generated in dynamic, entrepreneurial environments. Considerable competitive advantage can be obtained in a short amount of time, but the expectation is that the product or process innovation will rapidly diffuse. Therefore, it is critical to commercialize and adopt the new idea quickly, before the window for economic benefit disappears. Often factories built to manufacture such products are designed for compressed lives of only two or three years. Product life cycle, prior to imitation, will often be even shorter.

Therefore, there are strong incentives for alliance in industries whose operating environment has a fast competitive cycle. Here, it may be that one new product can only flourish if there exists a set of complementary products that simultaneously comes to the market place (PCs and software, VCRs and programs). In such cases, there must be networks among innovators (De-Bresson and Amesse 1991). Ideas tend to spring up in many small companies. These firms find it attractive to ally themselves with larger firms that have expertise in product development. The smaller companies may be unable to obtain financing in the capital markets and therefore look to the deeper pockets of the larger firms. The time pattern of benefits and costs to each of the partners over the life of the product entails a cost to the multinational firm in the early years and produces a benefit in later years; the innovator firm tends to benefit in the early years, while it sacrifices profits in later years. In general, the shorter

TABLE 3.3.   International Alliances for New Memory Chips

Date	Companies	Purpose	Status
July 1992	Advanced Micro Devices Fujitsu	Joint development, manufacturing, marketing	New
	I.B.M., Toshiba, Siemens	Joint development	New
	I.B.M., Toshiba	Technology sharing	New
June 1992	Micron Semiconductor, NEC	Mutual supply, marketing	New
February 1992	Sharp, Intel	Technology sharing, mutual supply	Active
November 1991	Texas Instruments, Hitachi	Joint development	Active
July 1991	I.B.M., Siemens	Joint development	Active
July 1990	I.B.M., Motorola	License agreement	Abandoned in 1990
February 1990	Advanced Micro Devices, Sony	Technology sharing	Active
1986	Motorola, Toshiba	License agreement	Active

the life of the product and the higher the initial development cost, the more likely that alliance will be attractive to the entrepreneurial firm.

The example of EMI, the British company, provides an illustration of what can happen if an innovator tries to go it alone rather than form an alliance. EMI was responsible for introducing one of the century's great medical innovations: the CAT scanner. Its chief scientist received a Nobel Prize in Medicine for the innovation. Yet, EMI failed to profit from its revolutionary innovation because it lacked downstream commercial capabilities, especially in the United States, the major market for its machines. EMI did not expect that the potential of their revolutionary machine would attract twelve imitators and competitors in less than two years, including giant companies in medical equipment such as General Electric, which developed a superior product. EMI finally commissioned its new manufacturing facility in the United States just in time to see the saturated market plunge. Soon after, the company was bought out by the French company, Thorn, which liquidated the money-losing CAT scanner division. An early alliance with a firm with downstream capabilities in the United States and with technical expertise might have allowed both EMI and its partner to profit handsomely from the CAT scanner revolution.

The pharmaceutical industry is probably the most R&D-intensive of all industries, with R&D expenditure around 16 percent of sales in the United

States. By some estimates, it costs approximately $250 million to bring a drug through R&D, the governmental approval process, and to the market. Moreover, the introduction takes ten years on average. Typically, when a drug finally arrives in the market, it has just a few years of patent life (shielded advantages) left. As many companies are competing with each other to generate drugs with similar indications (for example, anti-ulcer drugs), first-mover advantages in the marketplace are important, but may erode rapidly.

Both Amgen and Genetics Institute (GI) were engaged in R&D for an anticancer drug, erythropoietin (EPO). Both are start ups with limited financial resources and downstream capabilities, and neither possesses any capabilities in overseas markets. Amgen established two strategic alliances, one with the established pharmaceutical house, Johnson & Johnson, and another with the Japanese Kirin Brewery, in an effort to become the first mover in both the U.S. and the Japanese market. GI, on the other hand, formed strategic alliances with the Japanese Chugai Pharmaceutical and the German Goehringer Mannheim. In the end, Amgen won the patent battle against GI in the United States, but GI became the first company to bring its version of EPO into the Japanese market through Chugai. Either might have lost the race completely without strategic alliances with established firms. Thus, this industry provides an example of firms with dynamic innovative capabilities, who ally with firms having scale-based marketing and distribution capabilities, in order to capture quickly a few remaining years of monopolistic rents.

The challenge to many firms, particularly new biotechnology companies, is to be able to commercialize a new product as soon as possible and in as many markets as possible to recoup the investment in R&D. Biotechnology companies might possess superior capabilities for discovering new biotechnology drugs, but they lack downstream capabilities, such as the experience to navigate through regulatory approval processes, or experience in distribution, manufacturing, and marketing, and particularly so in foreign markets. On the other hand, both domestic and foreign-established firms have downstream capabilities but struggle to feed them with new products. It is not surprising, therefore, as Figure 3.2 shows, that almost all biotechnology firms maintain multiple alliances with domestic and foreign firms with complementary capabilities. By forming alliances, partners can benefit from both the R&D that start-up firms offer, and downstream capabilities offered by multinational giants. These advantages will confer shielded and scale-based advantages if they are given patent protection; otherwise, if speed is critical, the economic benefits will come from attaining dynamic advantage.

Another illustration of an international consortium based on the hope of dynamic advantage includes AT&T (the U.S. telecommunications group), Matsushita of Japan (the world's leading consumer electronics company), Masubeni

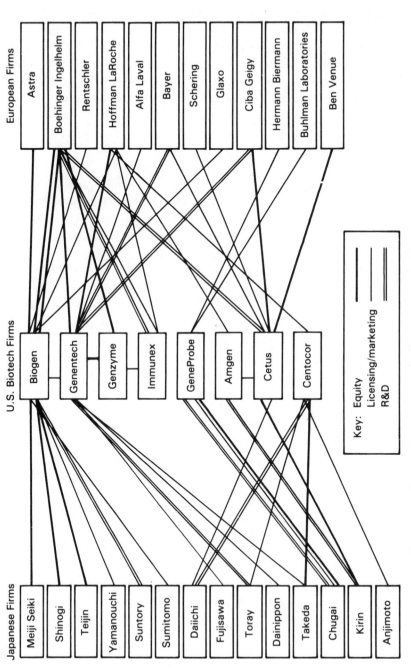

Figure 3.2. Patterns in International Alliance Partners. Biotech firms have multiple parallel alliances with their partners. (*Source:* Bioscan 1990.)

(the large Japanese trading house), and EO (a California computer designer). They are joining together in an effort to win the race to launch the world's first "personal communicator"—a combined pocket telephone and personal computer. The device will combine voice telephone, electronic mail, facsimile, and a personal word processor that accepts handwritten input. This is a clear example of a growing number of cross-industry and global alliances being formed as advances in technology start to erode the boundaries between the computer, consumer electronics, and telecommunications industries.

Conclusion

Alliances based on isolating mechanisms or firm capabilities can provide sustainable economic advantages. Alliances help in filling deficiencies in each partner's capability set and enable the building of new capabilities. Our approach has identified a number of generic situations in which gains from cooperation are possible. It provides a framework and a set of prototypes that make it clear how alliances enhance the competitiveness of private firms and how they can aid in strategically enhancing the international competitiveness of a country. We have broadly classified incentives for alliance for firms whose capability sets reside mainly in shielded, scale-based, or dynamic advantage. The economic synergy generated by the alliance comes about because each agent has a capability or resource for the other's needs, and there is some aspect of potential benefit from alliance that dictates that this intermediate system of governance offers a higher degree of sustainable competitive advantage than would going to the market or going it alone.

For markets whose benefits are embedded in sheltered or shielded market advantage, the nature of the trade tends to be an infusion of resources and organizational knowledge in return for access to territory. For markets with scale-based advantage, alliances take the form of a sharing of cost, risk, and capability. In markets with dynamic advantage, alliances offer innovative firms the resources and skills to move more quickly to development. For an alliance to have long-term stability, it seems as if the skill base of both partners must remain somewhat different. If the skills become sufficiently close, through learning, then the need for the alliance dissolves. During the period in which the alliance persists, the benefits issuing from the alliance derive from the strengths of the partners. Thus, alliances often involve the generation of benefits from more than one of the three types: territorial, dynamic, and scale advantages.

Many of the prototypes we describe involve the public sector, as well as the private sector. Often, restrictive governmental policies or lack of public resources shape the infusion of new economic benefits through alliance. As we design public and firm policies for the 1990s a new, more expansionary vision should be taken. Instead of a go-it-alone, we-they mentality, the clarion call is for cooperation that leads to a positive-sum outcome with benefits that can be enjoyed by both the public and private sectors. Both sectors must recognize that firms provide forward momentum for countries. The benefits from alliances must be of sufficient magnitude to ensure that firms can move profitably into an increasingly complex future.

Notes

The authors are grateful to Barry Rand of Xerox Corporation, Jeffrey Williams, Herb Addison, Allan Alter and participants in the Wharton Conference on "R(Designing) the Firm" for thoughtful comments on an earlier draft of our paper.

1. Economies of scale over more than one product/nation are a weighted sum of the individual scale economies associated with each product/nation multiplied by a factor involving economies of scope. Enhanced scope of operations can confer scale where none existed before and always serves to magnify scale. It should be noted that contestability theory defines sustainability in an equilibrium context that differs from the competitive cycle context we are focusing on in this paper.
2. A cautionary note might be sounded here. Getting together to create a standard, such as a computer operating system, is not always effective at providing sustainable competitive advantage. IBM created such a standard, but then many competitors entered with this same standard. Apple has a different system yet remains a viable competitor.
3. A further alliance in which Mazda and Ford would build cars together in Europe was recently scrapped. By helping Mazda become a local producer, Ford risked building cars that would compete with its own models in the slumping European Community market.

References

Bailey, Elizabeth E., and Jeffrey R. Williams. 1988. Sources of economic rent in the deregulated airline industry. *Journal of Law and Economics* 31:173–202.

Baumol, William J., John C. Panzar, and Robert D. Willig. 1982. *Contestable markets and the theory of industry structure.* New York: Harcourt, Brace and Jovanovich.

DeBresson, Chriss, and Fernand Amesse. 1991. Network of innovators. *Research Policy* 20:363–79.

Kogut, Bruce. 1988. Joint ventures: Theoretical and empirical perspectives. *Strategic Management Journal* 9:319-32.

Kobrin, Stephen J. 1993. Transnational integration, national markets and nation states. In *The state of international business inquiry*. Quorum Books.

Porter, Michael E. 1980. *Competitive strategy*. New York: Free Press.

Prahalad, C. K., and Gary Hamel. 1990. The core competence of the corporation. *Harvard Business Review* XX:79–91.

Shan, Weijian, and William Hamilton. 1991. Country-specific advantage and international cooperation. *Strategic Management Journal* 12:419–32.

Stalk, George, Philip Evans, and Laurence E. Shulman. 1992. Competing on capabilities: The new rules of corporate strategy. *Harvard Business Review* XX:57–69.

Williams, Jeffrey R. 1992. How sustainable is your competitive advantage. *California Management Review* 34:29–51.

4

Supplier and Buyer Networks

TOSHIHIRO NISHIGUCHI

AND ERIN ANDERSON

Many discussions of "Japanese business practices" center around the complex and (by Western standards) unusual manner in which Japanese manufacturers are thought to deal with their suppliers. Many anecdotal accounts of Japanese practice paint a picture of a tightly woven web characterized by elevated levels of service, innovation, and efficiency. These impressive results of Japanese buyer-supplier transactions are usually achieved with little of the well-publicized rancor that often characterizes the ever-changing lineup of players in many conventional supplier-buyer transactions. It is tempting to conclude that Japanese buyer-supplier relationships operate as smoothly as though everyone involved worked for the same company. However, that conclusion is tempered by the observation that such results are not often achieved even when it really *is* all one company.

Obviously, not all Japanese supplier-buyer relationships are as successful as the growing mythology of Japanese management prowess would have it. Yet so many Japanese buyer-supplier relationships achieve such impressive results that the thoughtful manager must ask how they do it. How do Japanese manufacturers acting as buyers of components from outside suppliers manage to have it both ways? That is, how can they purchase from an outside specialist supplier, with all the advantages that entails, *and* enjoy the closeness, reliability, and continuity that are the objective of manufacturers who supply all their needs in house? And, just as important, can we redesign a Western firm to achieve comparable results?

We argue that current explanations of the success of Japanese supplier-buyer networks are incomplete. Some accounts point to specific techniques and suggest that if some (or all) of these are implemented, non-Japanese firms will also enjoy the success of Japanese networks. Other accounts are more pessimistic about the transferability of these networks, arguing that their workings are hopelessly embedded in Japanese culture and cannot be used by non-Japanese firms. We argue that a fundamental basis for the success of Japanese supplier-buyer networks is that the players are using four principles *that anyone can utilize*. We detail these four "portable principles" and explain why Japanese managers are comfortable with them—and why they are not as foreign to Western managers as they may seem.

The issue of cross-cultural transferability of a management system is both old and new. Recent debates on the transferability of the Japanese management system to a foreign environment have rekindled this traditional problem. Briefly, what is currently understood as Japanese methods of managing employees involve treating employees with fairness, rewarding them well, investing in them, and assuring stability of employment in exchange for high levels of performance. Yet, Japanese employment practices are less egalitarian than they may seem: it is clear who is the boss, and the legitimate authority of the boss is seldom questioned. These practices characterize many of Japan's largest firms, though they may or may not represent the approach of smaller firms.

This description of how Japanese managers, at least in large firms, treat their employees has an analogue in how Japanese supplier and buyer *organizations,* at least the larger ones, treat each other. We argue that supplier-buyer networks in Japan bear a strong resemblance to employment systems. Our arguments are based on hundreds of interviews with Japanese firms and their competitors, both suppliers and buyers, conducted over a number of years by Toshihiro Nishiguchi, as well as on the growing body of research on Japanese management practices.

The Bedrock of Japanese Buyer-Supplier Networks: Four Principles

We note that Japanese networks of buyers and suppliers exhibit four properties:

1. Both parties practice win-win behavior consistently;
2. Suppliers and buyers share vulnerability;
3. The more powerful party involves and rewards its counterpart;
4. The system has a recognized leader.

Below we will argue that these four properties constitute principles for re-designing the firm's buyer-supplier relationships so as to reap the benefits noted in chapter three of this book. We suggest that these organizing principles help explain successful buyer-supplier collaboration. We argue that, while these principles may be more compatible with the Japanese management paradigm, they *can* be transferred outside the Japanese context to form a new outsourcing paradigm for Western firms.

Before delving further into the principles, let us briefly review how Japanese sourcing networks developed. Compared with common practices in the United States and the United Kingdom, contemporary supplier relations in Japan are characterized by investments specific to certain contracts and/or customers. This is a historical (*not* cultural) product of the strategies of large Japanese manufacturers from the 1960s onward. Faced with increasing manufacturing complexity and product proliferation in the rapidly growing, competitive domestic market, these firms gradually converted many of their suppliers, previously used chiefly for instrumental reasons and for simple processing tasks (such as machining and treating the surface of metals), into contract assemblers and systems components manufacturers, performing much more complex tasks.

In this process, firms transferred technology to suppliers. Customers taught multiple skills to their suppliers in the interest of maintaining product quality. Asset-specific features of contract assembly and systems components manufacture contributed to stabilizing contractual relations. In turn, stability provided further opportunities for suppliers to grow. Over time, the proportion of development and design input from suppliers increased (for example, black box design, in which customers provide basic ideas and specifications while suppliers work on details), and suppliers even began to provide self-developed technologies to their customers.

For principal manufacturers, the new arrangements secured ongoing sources of production for part of their own products (frequently of a small-lot, specialized, and mature kind) without investing heavily themselves. In this way, they were able to allocate newly freed resources to state-of-the-art technologies and to the development of new products, including the product variety discussed in chapter six of this book. Outsourcing a variety of production and development activities to external organizations shortened overall lead times and product cycles, while enabling many Japanese manufacturers to maintain the full product-line strategy they pursued in the wake of a high-growth economy. Principal manufacturers benefited from the new arrangements by being able to adjust to shifting demand and thereby got ahead of the competition; suppliers enjoyed relatively stable contractual relations together with enhanced responsibilities and increased commitment from their customers.

Along with the development of contract assembly and systems components manufacture, a well-defined clustered structure for manufacturing control—"clustered control"—came into being. For instance, parts procurement for particular systems components, or for contract-assembly products, could be concentrated on select first-tier suppliers. Such a first-tier supplier acted on behalf of the principal manufacturer, but the control function resided with the supplier, who managed that function for other suppliers in the lower tiers in the pyramid. Thus, first-and lower-tier suppliers formed a series of clusters for controlling manufacturing and purchasing functions. Again, this new organization relieved the principal manufacturer from the increasingly complex control functions that accompanied product proliferation and rapid technological progress; at the same time, first-tier suppliers enjoyed prospects for stable growth and enhanced responsibilities.

In short, systems developed in which suppliers took on unusual levels of responsibility for customized products they supplied to a set of buyers. The ability to delegate such responsibility, in spite of the customized nature of the products, in turn, freed up manufacturers to turn to the other demands of their principal business. Essentially, suppliers exchanged volume, stability, and growth for a measure of dependence, as they concentrated more and more on meeting the specialty needs of a single manufacturer.

This is the system that has attracted considerable attention for the results it achieves. What enables this system to work are the four portable principles.

The first principle of Japanese management of supplier-buyer relationships is that both sides practice win-win behavior. By this we mean that both suppliers and buyers seek to find ways to create benefits for both sides. Typically, they do so by trying to enlarge the pool of benefits that is being divided. (In contrast, many Western buyer-supplier networks are strained because one party tries to win at the other party's expense by taking a bigger piece of a fixed pie of benefits.) For example, in Japanese buyer-supplier networks, powerful buyers institutionalize certain mechanisms (for example, joint value analysis meetings and cost reduction conferences) to work with suppliers to achieve cost savings jointly. When the savings are achieved, the supplier cuts its price to the buyer—usually by 50 percent but not to the full extent of the savings—in exchange for the de facto guarantee of long-term commitments. Thus, even with a lower price, the supplier achieves a return on its improvements in efficiency, thereby protecting its profits and at the same time stabilizing the contractual arrangement. In contrast, powerful Western buyers often impose unilateral price reductions upon their suppliers, leaving the suppliers to figure out how profits can be protected while giving them little or no prospect of continued trading.

An important feature of win-win behavior is that parties pass up short-term gains that come at the partner's expense: this would constitute win-lose behavior, which is unacceptable. Because the relationship is valued for its long-term potential, windfalls are not reaped at the other party's expense.

This is all well and good, but on what basis can the weaker party trust the stronger party not to violate the win-win ethic? The answer lies in the second portable principle: that both parties have some weakness in the relationship because they share strategic vulnerability. Japanese buyer-supplier networks rest on a bedrock of mutual need, deliberately created and enhanced by the players themselves, who make sure that each side would suffer significant losses, long- and short-term, were it to walk away from the relationship.

Strategic vulnerability is created in a myriad of ways. One of the most common is to limit the number of trading partners to a handful. As noted above, suppliers are willing to concentrate on just a few buyers. The buyers reciprocate; they rely on only a handful of suppliers, often going as far as single sourcing an item. This is a marked contrast to the common Western practice of keeping a stable of suppliers available, routinely splitting business among them.

Another way that supplier-buyer networks share vulnerability is to make investments in each other. These investments can be in the form of equity, but they are more often in the form of dedicated facilities, equipment, practices, and personnel. By "dedicated" we mean tailored to the relationship. A supplier, for example, could adapt its factory, its processes, and even its location to the needs of a particular buyer. That buyer, in turn, could invest in developing an intimate working knowledge of the supplier's personnel and procedures. Personal bonds, specialized knowledge, tailored equipment, convenient siting— these are examples of experience-based assets that grow slowly and represent a substantial investment in the other party. When such assets are in place, the advantages they create make it difficult to walk away from the relationship. When the supplier is in trouble, there are incentives for the buyer to help. Depending on the degree of trouble, it is not unusual that a "rescue" team comprising engineers and other specialists is dispatched from the buyer's company to the supplier and stays there until the problem is solved. Contrast this with the common practice of trying to keep suppliers as interchangeable as possible so that they may be played off against each other.

If shared vulnerability pins parties to their place in the network and if both parties practice win-win behavior (motivated by their shared vulnerability), relationships should be cordial. But will they be productive? An insurance policy against complacency in these relationships is the third portable principle: involve and reward your counterpart. A good illustration is the automotive industry, in which outside suppliers fill a much higher proportion of parts needs than they do in the United States. (The United States may be an extreme: outsourcing is much more common in many European markets.) Buyers (for example, Nissan and Toyota) frequently are more powerful than their suppliers. The buyers involve their suppliers heavily in problem solving and decision making. To do so, they share confidential information (for example, proprietary designs and plans) early. Suppliers are expected to use their information and access in order to be innovative and responsive to the buyers' needs. Performance on these dimensions is rewarded in terms of awarding or renewing a contract with an increased volume.

A further insurance policy against complacency in stable relationships is the fourth portable principle: one of the parties in the network should play the role of leader and be recognized as such by the other players. The leader in Japanese buyer-supplier relationships possesses a legitimate authority *in the eyes of the other players,* in that the leader's suggestions and initiatives are respected and followed. The leader role is essential because without it the parties in the network have difficulty achieving closure on projects and settling disagreements. The leader breaks deadlocks and circumvents inertia. As deadlocks and inertia occur readily in systems from which neither party can exit readily, the leader's role is critical. Notably, the type of leadership exercised in these systems is not a simple exercise of oligopoly power, an exercise that threatens the followers' autonomy and create power struggles. Rather, the leader in question makes sure that various constituencies within the networks do not operate at cross-purposes, which would lead to their disintegration.

Who will be the leader? Who will be tacitly granted legitimate authority? Leaders in Japanese buyer-supplier networks are organizations that are proven performers. Their good performance leads their partners to attribute expertise to the leaders and to defer in case of deadlock. But when performance slides, the leader's role is in jeopardy; if the faltering leader's role were to be maintained, oligopoly power, if any, would to have to be exercised to compensate for the decline in the leader's legitimate authority. Clearly, this is not functional, and it should be stressed that not all Japanese networks are functional; only networks headed by the better performing firms are effective.

These four portable principles (practice win-win behavior, share vulnerability, involve and reward your counterpart, acknowledge a system leader) are interlocking. Each principle is necessary—and not one by itself is sufficient. Sharing vulnerability insures against exploitation (the degradation of win-win behavior). The system leader makes the mutually vulnerable partners take initiative and risk, thereby renewing and extending their relationships and blocking the threat of stagnation. Against the assumption of stability without exploitation, win-win behavior encourages cooperation. And with that cooperation as a norm of the relationship, involvement and reward bring out the performance that has attracted attention to Japanese buyer-supplier networks and that encourages a level of outsourcing that is unusual by traditional Western standards.

(An appendix to this chapter offers an empirical demonstration of the Japanese supplier's willingness to invest in a handful of prime customers, thereby practicing the second principle of tolerating strategic vulnerability.)

The Issue of Transferability

How difficult is it to transplant Japanese patterns? How portable are these portable principles?

Many "Japanese" practices can be and have been successfully transplanted, with or without the presence of Japanese managers to implement them. Even employment practices, which are widely thought to be so inherently Japanese that they cannot work elsewhere, can be transplanted. If employment practices are portable, so are outsourcing practices because they share a similar philosophy.

A Brief Debate History

During the period when the influence, if any, of Japanese management practice was limited mainly to cheap manufactured exports, culturalist explanations of transferability prospered. Organizational theorists and industrial sociology suggested the inseparability or "embeddedness" of organizations within their societal environments; the implication was that Japanese organizations were so deeply rooted in Japan's own distinctive culture and the characteristics of employment relationships, including the acquiescence of Japan's "docile" and "feudal" workers, that the factors that made these organizations successful were not transferable.

However, a wave of Japanese "transplants" in various parts of the world has produced overwhelming counterevidence that the Japanese management system, especially its production organization, *is* interculturally transferable *with a few practical constraints*. A striking case is New United Motor Manufacturing Inc. (NUMMI). It should be recalled that Toyota took forty years to develop and perfect the Toyota Production System (TPS) to the current level with Japanese workers and suppliers. In contrast, NUMMI, a Toyota-GM joint venture in California, was almost an instant success with a unionized work force among the most militant in the United States and many local suppliers. Over the last forty years in Japan, Toyota's productivity and product quality increased from a negligible level to among the world's highest. By the time the NUMMI project was put into operation, the efficacy of TPS had been tested out in Japan. Almost instantaneously, NUMMI proved itself to be among the most efficient and highest quality assembly plants in North America (Krafcik 1986).

The issue does not now appear to be whether the Japanese management style is transferable: it is. The question is how to do it. In particular, can the diffusion of a new system be successfully made *without* the direct involvement of Japanese management? Existing evidence of successful transfers, be they "transplants" or technical consulting, invariably appears to be associated with direct involvement of the Japanese. However, a systematic study of transfers is needed to establish definitively whether a Japanese presence is truly essential or merely helpful.

Is It Enough to Copy Pieces?

Recent evidence demonstrates that it is not so difficult for Western producers to import and implement institutional artifacts of the Japanese system. Many manufacturing firms in the United States and Europe have introduced a whole shopping list of the "Japanese techniques": teams, quality circles, *Kaizen* (continuous improvement) activities, fewer job classifications, suggestion systems, buttons for workers to stop the assembly line, multimachine operations, U-shaped lines, suppliers' early involvement in design, self-certified suppliers, "black-box" design of components, simultaneous engineering, project managers, cost targeting, profit sharing, joint product design, and just-in-time supply of manufacturing.

It has proven to be difficult, however, to implement and maintain the new system in its totality. Our field interviews in the United States and Europe with product purchasers and suppliers alike have consistently suggested difficulties in gaining expected results. Copying selected pieces of the system does not appear to approximate the system well. Our interviewees often have implied that the new system's transfer without direct involvement of Japanese producers could be categorically difficult.

Can Japanese practices be exported without being implemented by Japanese personnel? Many Japanese managers are more comfortable with our portable principles than are many Western managers. Yet, these principles are not as foreign to Westerners as they may seem. On this basis, we suggest that our four portable principles, which are a condensation of much that underlies Japanese practices in outsourcing, can be usefully employed outside the Japanese indigenous context by a broad range of firms.

We focus on two themes: fairness and the basis of legitimate authority. Japanese and Western cultures approach these issues differently, accounting in large part for why Japanese suppliers and buyers are often more comfortable with such principles as win-win behavior, sharing vulnerability, involving and rewarding participants, and recognizing a leader. However, we argue that Japanese viewpoints about fairness and authority are compatible with Western values.

The Meaning and Importance of Fairness

Let us contrast the Japanese idea of fairness in outsourcing (win-win behavior) with its traditional Western counterpart, which, as noted later, is changing rapidly and has been obsolete for years in a number of Western firms.

When trading behavior is assumed to be dictated by market forces in the tradition of neoclassical economic theory, the application of the concept of fairness, if any, is simple. Give fair opportunities to competing agents in the market place, let them bid, and give contracts to those who bid the lowest. The traditional bidding pattern of U.S. automotive producers, for example, has been that and often still is.

While Detroit was perfecting the concept of fairness through market competition Japanese producers were working on their own version of a "fair" trading system based on radically different principles. Along with the development of contract assembly and systems components outsourcing, which made it dysfunctional to rely on market prices, the cost-targeting method was developed. Increasingly, complex cost structures were decomposed into parts and cost-sensitive elements were identified item by item. For this purpose, buyers and suppliers shared cost data, an unusual step for Western supplier-buyer pairings. Rather than negotiating price downstream, buyers and suppliers alike began step by step to look at the possibility of reducing costs at the source by means of joint problem solving based on the objective value analysis (VA) method. Moreover, suppliers became involved in design to further reduce costs, using joint value engineering (VE) techniques. An important point is that these VA and VE techniques were applied to the supplier chain, not restricted to within the corporation. As a result, continuous cost reduction was systematized during the course of a product cycle, and fifty-fifty "profit sharing" rules, which embody win-win behavior, were established.

The cost-targeting and profit-sharing rules work as follows. The cost targeting of product development is based on the market-price-minus, rather than cost-plus, principle. The sale price of a new car model is first determined: for example, X dollars, with Y profits and Z costs. The cost of each part is then evaluated. Through this process, the cost for a console box in a car, for example, is targeted to be C dollars. Within this cost, the required specifications for the part, such as performance, quality, durability, feel, and appearance, must be met. By jointly evaluating various possibliities—in view of functionalities for the consumer—in design, materials, surface treatment, mechanisms, manufacturing methods, and the like, the aggregate of individual part costs must be reduced step by step so as not to exceed the target while keeping the required specifications constant.

VE techniques are particularly useful in this process. Suppliers' proposals are encouraged because of their intimate professional knowledge of the part concerned. After the commercial launching of a new product, design modifications to reduce costs further are continuously pursued. VA techniques are especially helpful at this stage.

Concomitant with the cost targeting of new product development was the emergence of "profit-sharing rules" between purchaser and supplier during the 1960s in Japan. If, for example, as shown in Figure 4.1, the price for an instrument cluster in the dashboard was agreed to be 120 points for the first car model year, during which time 110 points, a target price for the second year, was in fact achieved by their "joint" efforts, then, the purchaser paid the supplier 115 points, thus sharing the incremental profit evenly. If, however, further cost reduction was achieved during that period, say, down to 108 points, then, the balance went to the supplier. In other words, the buyers did not ask for a cheaper price than the second-year target price. In the second year, the assembler paid either 109 or 110 points net, and further cost reduction was continuously pursued by encouraging additional supplier proposals.

This Japanese rule setting was a significant departure from the traditional practice, in which supplier incentives for improvement were frequently dis-

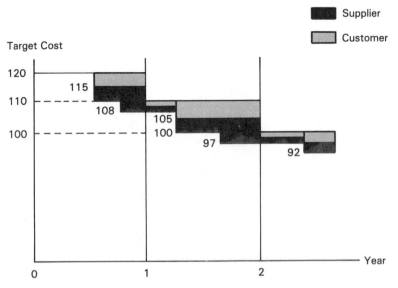

Figure 4.1.   Profit Sharing. (*Source:* TN/EA 1993.)

couraged by the purchaser's attempts to try to monopolize the benefits of its suppliers' new ideas. In contrast, the Japanese approach kindled supplier entrepreneurship and lead to a virtuous circle of buyer-supplier competition and cooperation in Japanese manufacturing industries, led by autos and electronics (Nishiguchi 1993).

Referring to the profit-sharing norm, a manager of a European multinational brake supplier remarked (our interview 1991): "The Japanese customers are tough negotiators. But at the same time they are the most fair."

Similarly, a sales director of a Japanese multinational wire harness supplier located in the United States commented in a 1988 interview: "We do business with almost all the major auto assemblers in the world. On an operational level, our Japanese customers are perhaps the most demanding. But unlike Western customers who tend to sever business relationships lightheartedly, we can be one-hundred-percent sure that as long as we show them the result of our continuous improvement, the Japanese customers never say, 'Hey, we no longer need you next year. Good-Bye.'"

The Importance of Legitimate Authority

However much emphasis is placed on harmony, partnership, and collaboration between buyer and supplier, it is ultimately the buyer-leader who exercises authority in Japanese buyer-supplier relationships. Orders are always given by the buyer to the supplier. Final decisions are invariably made by the purchaser.

What is of concern in practice, especially in a situation in which radically new systems are transplanted, is how this authority is legitimated. On what basis is the buyer's "authority" justified by those who exercise it, and on what basis is that authority accepted by those who obey it? We reiterate that this authority is not statutory: it is tacitly awarded to the buyer by its suppliers, and as such is a form of legitimate authority that depends on the acceptance of the follower (supplier). Should there be no fair rules or procedures equally *shared* between trading partners, or no rationality in the behavior of those who command authority in the eyes of those who receive it, the whole project could potentially collapse. The predictable result would be that new practices sooner or later would revert to the domain of old mechanisms which were sustained by other means of support (for example, the raw exercise of oligopolistic power).

Innovative management by leader-buyers in interorganizational relations is likely to be accepted only if suppliers perceive it as reasonable and effective. Undermined expectations and loss of trust and respect, due to ineffective management, cannot easily be recovered. A deterioration of trading and industrial relations will follow.

As in the case of NUMMI, many Japanese transplants, which brought in Japanese employment and supplier management practices to the United States and the United Kingdom, appear to be serving to reconcile previously antagonistic supplier relations (Dunning 1986; Florida and Kenney 1991). This experience suggests that close supplier relations a la the Japanese model are not antithetical to Wesern business practices.

Can Westerners Adopt "Japanese" Practices?

A Western firm's outsourcing practices can be redesigned along Japanese lines. Recent evidence in the United States and Europe indicates that insofar as institutional arrangements are concerned, Western, and, in particular, North American, producers are already fairly advanced in their efforts to establish new outsourcing organizations (for example, long-term contracts, suppliers' early involvement, resident engineers). However, distrust and timidity, a result of long-standing adversarial relations, are still problems, say managers of buyers and suppliers alike. A director of a U.S. brake systems supplier commented:

> On official occasions, our customers trumpet the benefits of concurrent engineering and supplier involvement. But in reality harsh relationships still exist. For example, one of our customers did not inform us of a design change in the suspension system of a car model. A juddering problem occurred in steering. But the same brake unit is used in another car model of this customer, and there's absolutely no problem. You see, increased responsibility has often been used for covering up inefficiencies in our customer's own organization.

A manager of an independent electronic components supplier in the Midwest remarked:

> Unlike the court system in this country, suppliers are guilty until they are found to be innocent. Even the most harmonious supplier relations in the United States are very adversarial compared to Japan.

In a similar vein, a director in charge of quality at a French producer commented:

> We have installed all the new programs, from early involvement to supplier suggestions to profit sharing. But our suppliers never respond. They are afraid they may be preyed upon in a new way. More seriously, they don't know how to suggest a new idea, not even how to create a new idea.

These comments indicate that there appears to be substantial "social distance" between purchaser and supplier in the West to be overcome.

Nonetheless, progress is being made at a rapid pace. "Japanese" principles and practices are being used and improved upon more and more frequently by Western firms. The widespread reduction in the number of suppliers, the adoption of just-in-time supply, increasing interest in concepts such as fairness, commitment, partnership, alliance, gain sharing, and trust are all indicators of a growing willingness to experiment with alternative approaches (Anderson and Weitz 1992). Indeed, a wave of interest in close relationships has led to a sharp increase in their importance and usage in North America and Europe (Dwyer, Schur, and Oh 1987; Frazier, Spekman, and O'Neal 1988), as well as closer examination of the mutual vulnerability that these relationships entail (Heide and John 1990) and the performance improvements they offer (Noordeweir, John, and Nevin 1990). Concurrently, the business press has rediscovered anecdotal evidence that many Western firms practiced at least some of the four portable principles well before they came to be viewed as "Japanese management." Hence, these principles are indeed portable, though in many settings they will be viewed as novel. A decade from now, these practices will no longer be seen as unusual—or even particularly Japanese.

Appendix: Concentration and Investments in Contract Assembly

In this appendix, we describe supplier-buyer networks in Japan, contrasting them with the United Kingdom, to illustrate some of the prototypical differences between Japanese and Western outsourcing practices. We take as an example the contracting out of assembly work. We focus on original interview data collected in the electronic components industry to show the relatively greater willingness of Japanese suppliers to practice the second principle: tolerate strategic vulnerability.

One of the most striking contrasts between Japan and the West in industrial sourcing organization is the prevalence of contract assembly and subassembly work in Japan, as opposed to a relative lack thereof in the United States and Europe. In general, a Japanese firm is much more likely to outsource components that Western firms insist on producing in-house. The high level of vertical integration that Western practice entails is a major feature of the design of Western firms. We argue that the portable principles explain, at least in part, how Japanese supplier-buyer networks are able to produce such a substantial range of components.

Dividing industrial sourcing (excluding purchase of raw materials and services) into three broad categories—assembly or subassembly, components manufacture, and discrete treatment (for example, plating, painting, machining, and the like)—we found that assembly or even subassembly is relatively rare and often almost nonexistent in the United States and Europe. These differences are not only the results of different producer strategies (Nishiguchi 1993) but also have significant repercussions on supplier-buyer networks.

Contract assembly or subassembly consists of a combination of *contract-specific* technologies and *customer-specific* know-how. For example, a combination of special machines, tooling, and processes, often not readily applicable to other contracts, is required. Besides, *end-product* manufacturing for a specific customer requires the same level of idiosyncratic organizational input (for example, settling the division of labor, cycle times, the degree of mixloading, staff training) as the customer's in-house production. Furthermore, the longer the trading relationship, the more likely a supplier is to develop customer-specific expertise through continual operations. For example, the supplier might readily understand hidden codes and omissions in the customer's drawings based on its own judgments derived from previous experiences without further consultation. In both visible and invisible aspects then, contract assembly or subassembly tends to be more asset specific than discrete treatment or standard components manufacture.

When this type of idiosyncratic asset sourcing describes the main feature of transactions between traders, frequent switches of partners can be costly. Extensive arm's-length relationships may be shunned. In the interest of preserving vested interests in the long run, apparent short-term losses may even be accommodated between the parties. Thus, what to outsource defines how to outsource; the four principles come into play to protect the relationship.

A Demonstration of Strategic Vulnerability

Anecdotal evidence abounds to the effect that Japanese suppliers are willing to make themselves relatively dependent upon their buyers, while Western suppliers typically are less willing to do so, preferring to preserve a greater degree of independence. There is cross-sectional evidence of this tendency in a prototypical industry, electronic components. Electronic components are the pieces and subassemblies that go into a wide range of both consumer and industrial manufactued goods. It is a broad, varied, and generally competitive industry that differs from automotive manufacture (the sector from which many of our examples are drawn). In electronic components, we see a wide range of practices, some of which are characteristically Japanese. Japanese electronic component suppliers, compared to their counterparts in the United Kingdom, are a great deal more willing to concentrate their sales in a handful of buyers, as well as to make investments that are specific (customized) to those buyers.

CONCENTRATION OF SALES

Conventional wisdom indicates that concentrating sales in one or a few customers renders a supplier dangerously dependent on a buyer. We contrast Japanese and United Kingdom supplier behavior in terms of their propensity to diversify. We base this on original interview data collected in the mid-1980s from a cross section of seventy-four Japanese and fifteen United Kingdom suppliers of a broad range of electronic components of varying levels of technological sophistication (Nishiguchi 1989). Each supplier provided the proportion of its sales coming from its first, second, and third largest customers (buyers), as well as the number of buyers that the supplier considered to be regular customers (who, on average, placed an order more frequently than every four months). The details of our analysis are presented in the background note that follows this appendix. Below, we sketch the major differences between U.K. and Japanese suppliers.

Our sample of Japanese and United Kingdom suppliers differ dramatically in terms of their propensity to diversify their sales (see Table 4.1 for details). On average, United Kingdom suppliers followed the prudent practice of diversification, allowing their top customer to account for 31 percent of their sales, in apparent observance of the "one-third rule" (letting no more than a third of sales come from one source). In contrast, the relatively reckless Japanese suppliers averaged a striking 81 percent of their sales coming from a single customer. This differential is so great that, in spite of the smaller United Kingdom

TABLE 4.1.   Statistical Significance Testing of
Differences: Japanese vs. U.K. Suppliers

	Mean	T Statistic for Mean Difference
Proportion of Sales Accounted for by Regular Customer 1		
Japanese	80.817	6.223*
English	30.60	
Proportion of Sales Accounted for by Top Three Customers		
Japanese	94.404	6.121†
English	58.800	
Number of Regular Customers		
Japanese	9.623	2.13†
English	30.692	

*Significant at $\alpha = .01$ level.

†Significant at $\alpha = .025$ level.

The assumption of equal variance in the two populations is satisfied in the test of mean differences.

sample size, it is unlikely that the British and Japanese suppliers are drawn from a population in which the propensity to diversify is the same.

The picture changes little if one examines the top three buyers combined. The United Kingdom suppliers, on average, allow 59 percent of sales to come from three buyers, in apparent observance of a two-thirds rule. In contrast, the Japanese figure (which cannot rise much higher than the 81 percent going to the biggest buyer) climbs to 94 percent, again a statistically significant difference.

It seems likely, then, that the United Kingdom suppliers would keep a larger stable of regular customers, and this they indeed do: on average, thirty-one buyers are "regulars" for United Kingdom suppliers, while only ten buyers are regulars for Japanese electronic component suppliers.

Of course, this comparison makes no allowance for differences among the eighty-nine suppliers. We will deal with the issue of different types of outsourcing activity and their relationship with concentration of sales later. Table 4.2 shows the results of an analysis that duplicates that shown in Table 4.1 but controls for some important differences in the profile of the supplier firms. In this analysis, we examine the logarithm of the "odds ratio," which is the ratio of the supplier's proportion of its sales to its top customer to the proportion to all its other customers combined. For example, the average Japanese supplier has an

TABLE 4.2.   Concentration of Supplier Sales in Customers (Logodds)

	Concentration in Top Customer Coefficient (Standard Error)	Concentration in Top 3 Customers Coefficient (Standard Error)
Intercept	1.062 (.887)	2.767* (.736)
U.K./Japan dummy	2.288† (.866)	1.618† (.719)
No. Employees	−0.007* (.003)	−0.003 (.002)
No. Regular customers	−0.078† (.003)	−0.091* (.028)
	$R^2 = .51$	$R^2 = .56$
	$F_{(3,43)} = 14.87^*$	$F_{(3,42)} = 17.56^*$

* Significant at .01 level.
† Significant at .05 level.

odds ratio of about 4.3 (that is, 81 percent to the top customer vs. 19 percent to all other customers), while the average United Kingdom supplier has an odds ratio of about .5 (31 percent/69 percent). (Using the logarithm of the odds ratio dampens the possible distorting effect of extremely high levels of concentration.) We model the log of the odds ratio (using ordinary least squares regression) as a function of several supplier characteristics.

Our analysis indicates that the more regular customers any supplier has, the lower its concentration of sales in the top customer. This also proves to be the case when one examines the top three customers combined. In addition, the larger the supplier (as measured by its number of employees), the lower its concentration in its top customer (though this effect disappears for the top three customers combined). This suggests that larger firms, be they Japanese or British, tend to allow a lower proportion of their sales to go to their single largest customer.

Yet, even after controlling for differences in size and in the number of regular customers, electronic component suppliers are more likely to concentrate sales in one or several customers if they are Japanese than if they are British. The conclusion suggested here is that nationality indeed appears to be related to concentration.

MAKING INVESTMENTS SPECIFIC TO THE BUYER

To what extent will a supplier make investments that are "specific" (that is, customized or idiosyncratic) to a buyer? Such investments allow the supplier to better meet the buyer's needs, yet also deepen the supplier's dependence on the buyer, due to the likely difficulty of redeploying assets specialized to a single buyer. The analysis in the background note of the relative willingness of Japanese and U.K. suppliers to make such idiosyncratic investments indicates that Japanese suppliers are considerably more likely than are their United Kingdom counterparts to be operating in activities that demand they tailor their operations to their customer base and to concentrate business in a handful of customers to a substantial degree, a degree that is not encouraged or frequently observed in many Western economies. In general, the larger the proportion of asset-specific sourcing, the more concentration of transactional partners in the interest of preserving vested interests in the long run. On the one hand, this factor indeed makes traders vulnerable to each other. But, on the other hand, it forces them to cement their relational contracting because frequent switches of partners based on extensive arm's-length relationships are costly for both the buyer and the supplier and inconsistent with the intent of new outsourcing networks.

Background Note: Asset Specificity

The degree to which a supplier invests in assets tailored to a single customer is somewhat difficult to assess precisely. Scholars who study this phenomenon typically use proxy variables designed to capture the nature of the work performed, on the theory that some types of work inherently involve more tailoring to customers than others.

In the case of electronic components suppliers, the type of work they do for their own customers is reflected in the type of work they themselves subcontract to their own suppliers. Firms that do more work of the nature of complete assemblies, for example, will subcontract to more makers of complete or subsystems assemblers, all else constant, while firms that make more discrete components will also subcontract out to more makers of discrete components or treatments.

We use a proxy variable for the idiosyncracy of the assets in the relationship ("asset specificity"), which is constructed as follows. Five categories of industrial sourcing activity (excluding raw materials and services) were identified and assigned a score *a priori* to reflect, in an approximate fashion, the degree to which the category of work was likely to entail making investments (human and physical) peculiar to the customer. The category likely to involve the most asset specificity is complete assembly of a finished product: this category was assigned a score of five. Subsystems assembly, somewhat less likely to entail idiosyncratic investments, was scored four, while single components were scored three, discrete treatments were scored two, and miscellaneous activities received the lowest score, one (Nishigushi 1989, ch. 5). For each supplier, the number of subcontractors it uses in each category of work was supplied by managers interviewed by the principal investigator. The number of subcontractors used in each category was multiplied by the category score to derive an index of the amount and type of subcontracting the supplier does. To the extent this index reflects the nature of the supplier's business, it serves as a proxy for the supplier's level of investment idiosyncratic to members of its customer base.

Table 4.3 shows the results of an ordinary least squares regression on the score of asset specificity. These results indicate that Japanese suppliers are considerably more likely than are their United Kingdom counterparts to be operating in activities that demand they tailor their operations to their customer base. This is true regardless of the number of regular customers and regardless of the size of the supplier. The insignificance of indicators of size is important here because it suggests that our results reflect more than the sheer amount of subcontracting activity occurring.

TABLE 4.3.   Specificity of Assets

	Coefficient (Standard Error)
Intercept	7.722 (30.902)
U.K./Japan dummy	34.131* (17.977)
No. employees	−0.057 (0.054)
Proportion of sales in top three customers	−0.158† (.311)
No. regular customers	0.751 (.751)

* Significant at .05 level.
† Significant at .01 level.

Notes

Presented at the conference on "Designing the Firm," October 9, 1992, at the Wharton School. The authors gratefully acknowledge the benefits from the conference participants' comments on our presentation, including John Burke of Unisys Corporation, as well as the suggestions of Bruce Kogut. The authors also thank the Reginald H. Jones Center Management Policy, Strategy, and Organization for financial support and Rosemary Morrison and Sharmila Chatterjee for capable research assistance.

References

Anderson, Erin, and Barton Weitz. 1992. The use of pledges to create and sustain commitment in distribution channels. Journal of Marketing Research 29:18–34.

Dunning, John. 1986. Japanese participation in British industry. London: Croom Helm.

Dwyer, Robert F., Paul H. Schur, and Sejo Oh. 1987. Developing buyer-seller relationships. Journal of Marketing 5:11–28.

Florida, R., and Martin Kenney. 1991. Transplanted organizations: The transfer of Japanese industrial organization to the U.S. American Sociological Review 56:1–18.

Frazier, Gary L., Robert E. Spekman, and Charles R. O'Neal. 1988. Just-in-time exchange relationships in industrial markets. Journal of Marketing 52:52–67.

Heide, Jan B., and George John. 1990. Alliances in industrial purchasing: The determinants of joint action in buyer-supplier relationships. Journal of Marketing Research 27:24–36.

Nishiguchi, Toshihiro. 1989. Strategic dualism: An alternative in industrial societies. D. Phil dissertation, University of Oxford, U.K.

————. 1993. *Strategic industrial sourcing: The Japanese advantage.* New York: Oxford University Press (forthcoming).

Noordeweir, Thomas G., George John, and John R. Nevin. 1990. Performance outcomes of purchasing arrangements in industrial buyer-vendor relationships. *Journal of Marketing* 54:80–93.

II

Speed, Variety, and Flexibility

5

Product Innovation in Mature Firms

DEBORAH DOUGHERTY

AND MORRIS A. COHEN

Launching an innovative product is one thing, sustaining innovation is another. All too often, firms successfully produce one or two innovative products, then fail to replicate their success (for example, IBM's PC or GM's Saturn project). This is especially true for firms that have been operating in stable markets for some time. Old habits and routines can thwart attempts to become innovative, even when management sets up interdisciplinary teams, encourages coordination and information-sharing across functional lines, and embraces other tenets of concurrent engineering.

How can older organizations transform themselves so they can sustain innovation? Bringing together all the functions involved in developing a new product is important, but insufficient. Firms must also align new products with their current product offerings and their overall corporate strategy. Sustained innovation requires concurrent management, not just concurrent engineering.

The framework introduced here defines at least three critical requirements for becoming innovative. The framework is based on the concept of concurrence, or simultaneity, whereby different functions, projects, and organizational units coordinate their innovation activities. This framework goes beyond concurrent engineering, which focuses on coordination across business functions, to include two other dimensions—concurrence within the portfolio of new and existing products and concurrence with respect to different institutional levels of managemnet.

We apply this framework to the case of Machco Machinery, a century-old firm which attempted and failed to become more innovative. By looking at what people at this firm did and did not change, and what happened as a result, we can understand the challenges of becoming more innovative and begin to ferret out what managers can do to transform the firm.

Background of MACHCO

MACHCO is a multibillion dollar machinery and equipment concern that was started more than a century ago with the invention of a steam-driven drill for mining. By 1988, the company had grown to four major business segments with a total of ten groups, with fifty-five plants around the world, and sold everything from huge engines to tiny bolts. Our research concerned the efforts of one of the ten business groups to improve its product development capabilities. This is the Production Equipment Group, which sells a variety of small electrically powered machines (engines, pumps, drills, gauges) used in industrial manufacturing, assembly, and repair processes.[1] For the most part, these were mature, almost ancient markets.

Like other oldline firms, MACHCO's Production Equipment Group had over the years developed a reputation for being "the Cadillac" of assembly equipment in several of its segments. They made profits for years, according to one manager, and, not surprisingly, had settled into a "fat and happy" stasis. The Group's main plant was located in Springton, a small rural town in the Midwest, while the division headquarters (comprised mainly of marketing and sales) was about four hours away by car. MACHCO's factory dominated the small town, since most of its residents worked at the plant. Jobs ran in families, and many shop floor people had fathers and grandfathers who also worked for MACHCO.

Befitting a firm older than Taylorism, Springton historically operated on the principle of segmenting work into the smallest steps that could be measured and controlling work flows and processes tightly. The plant, as well as the firm as a whole, had been organized functionally for years, and this segmentation was carried through to product development, where each group had its own separate task to perform. An engineer explained that marketing always handled all the "external" work on product specifications, while his group did all the internal work. A manufacturing person said: "It used to be, marketing would come in here and tell us what to do. They would throw the specs over the wall. They never talked to the engineers, so both groups hated each other. And manufacturing hated new products, period. They distrusted the whole process and it hurt the numbers."

Relationships between engineering and manufacturing were worse than those between marketing and engineering. Traditionally, according to one manager, manufacturing would wait until a product was completely designed with all drawings final. Then the drawings would go to industrial engineering, who would work out the process, and then on to the shop. They handled the interdependencies by taking plenty of time to work issues out. Not surprisingly, each department also blamed the other for taking too much time. For example, a technical person explained: "Normally, manufacturing would take six to nine months to process parts, so they didn't need all the pieces to fit together all at the same time. In our usual process we would just throw a design over to them and let them take as much time as they wanted." Contrast this explanation with one from a manufacturing person: "It's hard to get engineering to move on things. We work over here on schedule and we are evaluated on keeping to the schedule, but the engineers have a blank check on time."

Not only did the people in different departments harbor a degree of contempt for each other, they saw the same things very differently, and did not really appreciate one another's concerns.[2]

The strong separation between the departments did not hamper their work much, since the products themselves were not integrated with each other or with resources. Managing product lines was the functional province of marketing and sales personnel, most of whom were located at group headquarters. Product strategies were not used at the plant to guide decisions. This astrategic approach worked well for a long time, according to one, because changes were rarely made: "Production machinery made god-awful gobs of money, and there was no pressure on innovation as we know it now. We had an 80 percent market share." They developed few new products, although the product line had evolved incrementally over the years. As of 1988, the plant produced hundreds of different kinds or models of small production machinery, an array that had evolved from and was continually upgraded in response to specific customers, through the addition of "specials" or "buy-outs" to fill in lines.

Resources were allocated in a standardized, generic fashion as well, reinforcing the standardized products. Not a great deal of investment was made in product engineering, and MACHCO had closed its technology center in the late 1970s. Their core product "architecture" was a class of extremely rugged electric motors, used to power many of their machines. MACHCO people invented this motor years ago, and since then had been tweaking it to make different sizes and speeds. As one put it: "We built a company that knows everything about industrial grade electric motors."

The manufacturing technology was also mature, based on the forging and machining of metal parts. Everyone referred to what they did as "making chips" and "cutting bar stock." One engineer who had recently joined said: "This was an excellent machine shop. They would machine something or work on it so they can machine it, even if other technologies are better. They'd keep backing up and beating themselves trying to do what they knew best. It was inbred in people." Manufacturing resources were managed departmentally rather than by different product lines, and controlled by a system of standard costs which emphasized gross volume over flexibility. Manufacturing managers understood that their jobs were to "keep up productivity levels and not show a negative variance." Everyone in manufacturing, from the machine operators to the managers, was judged on volumes shipped, use of equipment, and adherence to standards. An engineer explained: "Once stuff hit the shop floor it was all automatic. They were not set up to make any adjustments." Needless to say, their emphasis was also short term, as this manufacturing manager explained: "We did not look forward. We worried about costs, and we looked at things from month to month. If we had a bad month, we would hope to make it up the next. The corporation looked at things quarter to quarter."

The only strategic guides used in the day-to-day decision-making at the plant were abstracted rules of thumb concerning costs and volume production. This segmented, incremental approach to resource allocations worked well enough for years, but it had an inherently conservative bias. As far as Springton was concerned, keeping costs low was the objective, not spending money was the strategy, and meeting weeky schedules and cost targets were the key performance criteria.

In addition to the compartmentalized approach to work and the departmental approach to resource allocation and development, Springton had a particular, often unspoken, social system. Nor surprisingly, the plant and the firm more generally comprised a world with a unique culture and institutionalized practices that people followed without thinking.[3] Three aspects of this culture are important to the story of becoming more innovative.

One important aspect was how people decided what work to do. To sort among the many possible choices—work on this enhancement, fix that performance problem, respond to this customer's requests—they relied on an informal network of incremental, day-to-day deal-making and negotiating, with long time employees who knew the system playing key roles. One explained that getting work done ". . . depends on the informal system. It comes down to this person having or developing a working relationship with others who have the technologies he needs to access, and his ability to keep a door open to his supervisor so he doesn't have to go through the chain of command every time he needs something."

A product line manager explained how he would follow the network system rather than official procedure as well: "The guys are so busy here. You have to constantly push for your stuff, face to face, even to get something small done. . . . I go over to engineering all the time to work out quality problems or other problems. I should go to manufacturing, but I go ask the project engineer. We have lots of people who have been here for twenty-five years who know a lot of stuff, so its' easiest to go to them." He also explained that since engineering chose the problems they would work on via political nudging and firefighting, he routinely asked engineering for much more than he really needed to manage his line well, just to make sure he was always on people's agendas. This process was incremental and reinforced the scattered sense of product strategy. It was also very much an insider's game, and people who had been at the plant for only a few years felt like outsiders.

A second important aspect of the social system was its hierarchical nature, based on top-down control. Senior management, ensconced at Group headquarters, "called the shots" regarding production and product lines, and Springton executed. There was no real communication or interaction between the strategic and the operating worlds, so that informal networking emphasized day-to-day, piecemeal execution of tasks and trouble shooting. The connection between senior managers and the plant had become a thin thread of control around cost and "invoices." Nearly everyone at Springton, regardless of function, pointed out that they had been driven by costs. One said: "We look for cost reductions on products without thinking of the final effect on the product." The emphasis on cost control had been so strong for so long that people would not risk $5,000 worth of scrap to experiment with a new design or process. Senior managers were making money while Springton was making production machines, and their very limited interaction was comfortable to both sides as long as these two goals did not conflict.

Third, because of the constricted, top-down, authoritarian relationship, people at the plant felt that they could not discuss matters with management, and routinely hid any problems from them: "If there is a problem, they will more than likely cover it up—you know, in quality, delivery. . . . People are scared to let divisional know about problems because of the backlash. Also, it [hiding problems] comes from the bottom up—people say: 'Hey, I live next door to you . . .'"

Another attributed this hiding to a fear of punishment: "Everyone in manufacturing is thinking they will be brought out to the woodshed if they screw up." He said that failure also was not acceptable: "We don't like to admit that people make mistakes . . ." And an old timer explained that they hide mistakes because they cannot really trust senior managers to react fairly: "We don't hide problems, but we will gloss over them. Upper management says: 'We are all one big happy family, so if you have a problem tell us.' But one time that we did, the whole top of our head comes off and blue smoke fills the room. . . . You can't turn it on and off, because the next time you will not tell them about problems. Besides, you got your manager sitting there and you don't want to get him in trouble."

As of 1988, MACHCO's production equipment business was based on segmentation: segmentation of departments from each other, of resources from products, and of operations from strategy. They routinely made few tradeoffs, except around "cost" in the abstract. The plant was good at machining and volume production of clearly designed parts. The engineers were good at adjusting and tinkering with established products. The sales people were good at calling on established accounts. The rift between the operating and strategic levels had become large. Changes had indeed occurred during the 1980s. The group had invested in a number of programs to modernize manufacturing, such as improved worker-management relations, which emphasized development of the labor force, quality circles, shifts toward just-in-time inventory processing, and a capital improvement plan. They had also developed cellular manufacturing and implemented a state of the art CAD system. On the engineering side, they actively recruited more college-educated engineers to broaden their skill base. People who had joined the firm during that period said that MACHCO's Springton plant was more advanced than many in other established industries such as automobiles and engines.

But these changes did not improve their product innovation abilities, since it took them an average of four years to get a new product out. Despite the time, most of the new products were me-too designs that did little to increase their market share. MACHCO had not introduced any truly innovative products in some time, and even their "bread and butter" products were being superseded by low-cost foreign competition and innovative domestic competition.

The Fix/Phase I

In late 1987, division management decided that their deficiencies in product innovation were no longer tolerable, since they were facing increased competition in all their markets. An "innovation champion," Jim Fox, a business manager at group headquarters, was charged with the task of devising and implementing a new product development process. Fox researched product innovation, and came up with a process outlined in Figure 5.1. The project characteristics listed in Table 5.1 reflect some of the key characteristics that are embedded in the flowchart: (1) interdisciplinary teams with team ownership of the product's development; (2) full customer and supplier interaction throughout; (3) careful product conceptualization and project-objective setting with respect to product performance and development cycle time; and (4) adequate phase reviews so that connections between the project and the rest of the organization were organized around joint problem solving and effective resource allocation. These characteristics are part of proficient product innovation that studies of innovation have uncovered,[4] so Fox had done his homework well.

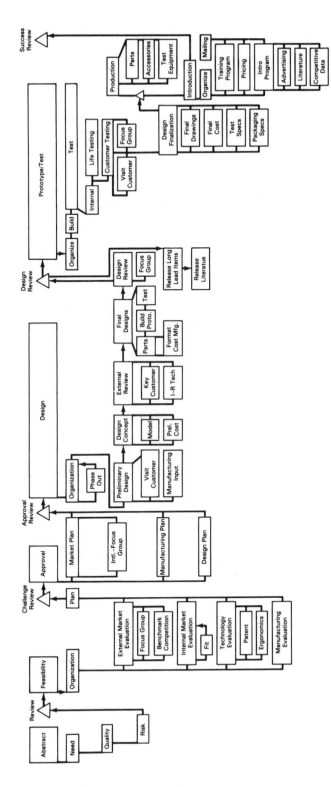

Figure 5.1. Machco Division's New Product Development Process.

93

TABLE 5.1. MACHCO's Four New Products Compared

Project Characteristics	Venus Grinding Machine
Functional concurrence	
All departments throughout	Yes, but manufacturing not fully involved
Team-owned product concept	Team created
Team in charge of details	Yes
Joint customer visits	Yes
Portfolio concurrence	
Project scope fit 1 year frame	No, 3 models, change to 1 in development
Product strategy clear	Yes, emphasis on clearly superior product
Technical feasibility assessment	Yes, but shell problem occurred
Manufacturing feasibility assessment	No, not thorough
Institutional concurrence	
Good support from departments	Yes, except manufacturing role process not clarified
Access to resources	Yes, funds as necessary
Effective phase reviews	No
Joint problem solving with top management	Strategic input, hands-off management
Project outcomes	
Team satisfaction	High
Time to market target	Met for first model, others delayed
Product and project costs	Overage
Customer acceptance	Very High
Overall project success	High

Mars Engine Starter	Jupiter Drill	Saturn Drill
No, IE late, manufacturing not involved	No, began as engineering team, others only partly involved	No, began as engineering team, others only partly involved
Team created	No, different ideas in different departments	No, concept changed by management not team
Yes	No, intervention from others	No, intervention from others
No	No	No
Yes, came up with 1 model	No, 5 models, too large	No, multiple models
Yes, enter as newcomer	No, too vague, too big	No, strategy changed, objectives conflict
Yes, decided to use existing product	Partly, but need new tech platform	Yes
No, all parts outsourced.	No, major problems late in development	No, some problems late in development
No, team on its own, marginal status	No, roles not clear, manufacturing not ready	No, marketing and manufacturing not connected
No, low priority, limited access	Yes, funds as necessary	Partly, funds limited
No	No	No
Team avoided management	Management intervened in details	Management intervened in details
Medium	Low	Low
Late	Very Late	Very Late
Very Close	Close	Overage
High	Very High	Very High
High	Low	Low

MACHCO's process was also deliberately tailored to resolve what group managers saw as their major problems. For example, by centering on inter-disciplinary teams, they attacked the historical "over the wall" (sequential) development process. The flow chart also carefully laid out what to do and how, which gave people a path to follow as they went about this very new kind of activity. Management included a very ambitious one-year time frame as well, in part to break through what headquarters saw as Springton's tendency to avoid risk and stick to their usual methods and to respond to emerging competitive pressures. However, the new process did not lay out the roles for senior management or others at Springton, except for participation in review meetings.

A new finishing machine, to be called Venus, was selected as the first new product, because MACHCO's existing machine suffered from a low-market share, a poor performance image, and the effects of a series of unsuccessful attempts to win market share through product redesign. They recognized that if the company did not do something with this product, they would soon be out of that business all together. Management felt that if they could go back to the drawing board and come out with a product that was demonstrably better than the competition's, they could realize growth at the expense of the competition. In addition, this machine was relatively simple, and as one team member put it: "We figured if we couldn't innovate here we couldn't do it anywhere."

In late January 1988, a memo was sent to the function heads in Springton outlining general objectives for the project, which included developing a whole line of machines, doubling market share within three years, and using modular design and design for assembly procedures. A tight schedule of market research, commercial and technical feasibility studies, and extensive customer visits was laid out. By March, a person from each department had been appointed to the team. The marketing person commuted to Springton, but engineering and manufacturing people were co-located and assigned full time.

Working in a multidisciplinary team required a new approach to taking responsibility and understanding one's role, as one recalled: "It was very differ-ent from our usual approach. The whole team was responsible to go find out what the market wanted and what the customer needed, and then move the product into design and manufacturing. We never did that before. We had no infrastructure on how it should work."

Despite the uncertainties, the team went right to work evaluating the market and customer needs by visiting customers (including users, buyers, and facility managers) and distributors together. The direct exposure to customers gave them many insights and ideas, and helped to define the product strategy further. By May the team had developed a business plan, which included meeting specific measurable features (for example, durability, repairability, safety). An important insight from all the customer visits was that the machine should be ergonomically sound: safe, easy to use, and comfortable. As shown in Table 5.1, the product scope was large, consisting of three different models and many accessories. The team also concluded that a significant performance improvement was needed if they were to meet the general business objectives of the project. An incremental improvement would lead to a quick response by their major competitor, who, as market leader, could lower price and/or quickly match incremental product enhancements.

In the next three months, the team brought the product concept alive, working with a design house to develop various mockups. By July, the team came to realize that the new finishing machine would have to be radically different from current designs in order to deliver all the customer attributes they developed in the planning phase. The machine's shape needed to fit into the operator's hand, which meant that the body had to be made from plastic, not metal. To fit the motor and other parts inside this radical housing, they would have to redesign the machine and add an internal shell made of bored composite to hold all the parts. The group made the decision to take the radical approach, even though working with plastics and bored composite was completely new to the plant.

Over the next six months, the team worked on all the new parts, including the new shell. Throughout the process, senior management maintained a hands-off stance. They did not get involved with day-to-day problem solving, but did make the necessary resources available by holding the MACHCO's normal rules of avoiding costs in abeyance. They also made it clear that the one-year cycle time target could not be compromised.

By January of 1989, however, they ran into trouble manufacturing the internal shell. The part called for production methods that they had no experience with, and one person observed that they did not build the connections with manufacturing very well:

> The flaw in our organization turned up when we moved into manufacturing. The magnitude and scope of the change was too much for the people involved. They had to wear hats they never wore before. A whole lot of decisions had to be worked out all at once because as the product moved into the plant, there are a lot of loose ends in production control, planning, shipping. . . . The coordination effort was the hard part. Normally . . . we would just throw it over to them and let them take as much time as they wanted. Here, everything was to be done at the same time. All of our GANTT charts were all laid out on top of one another. We weren't prepared to handle that.

The team decided to source the troublesome part externally for the time being, hoping to solve the problem when they could, but that doubled the part's already high cost. Their inability to produce the internal shell also had forced the team to reduce the original product scope significantly from three different models to one.

By February, they put prototypes with customers and learned that their newly designed machine was a hit. By June, the machine was formally introduced to the market, only two months later than the date they set the year before. Initial sales ran 20 percent above previous levels even though there was only one model, and they lacked the benefit of advertising or structured promotion. The compressed development time and word of mouth alone generated significant interest in the marketplace. Several big problems remained, particularly that the shell was still being produced externally at twice the planned cost, which significantly increased the cost of the machine (to the point where its profit margin was eliminated). The continued inability to work out this manufacturing problem made the whole team feel burned out. Management declared a victory, however, because the new innovation process had indeed produced a demonstrably superior and commercially viable new product in one-third the usual time. In addition, manufacturing ultimately (after a year) mastered the composite boring process and were able to bring its fabrication in house.

The Fix/Phase II

During the next year production equipment group managers decided to launch three more new efforts with the same development process and the same one-year time frame. Unfortunately, all three were over time and budget, as the status summary in Table 5.1 indicates.

The Mars Engine Starter (a special motor to turn over industrial diesel engines) started in September 1990. As shown in Table 5.1, this effort also had many more of the innovation characteristics in Fox's flow chart than the other two projects. The Mars project relied on a multidisciplinary team, but the day-to-day work was carried out in engineering, and there was no participation from industrial engineering or manufacturing initially. The team had little customer input because they felt that they already knew about this market. The product conceptualization was done well. One member explained that the team spent a lot of time up front on the concept development: "We really beat it out." Relationships between the project and the rest of the plant and senior management were handled primarily by avoidance. The Mars team also did not let development problems "go upstairs" to group management. The project was also disconnected from resources in manufacturing, in that all the new parts necessary to produce their elegant design had to be made outside.

The Jupiter Drill project was begun in late 1989 with a one-year development plan, but it was almost three years before two of the five models were "signed off," or approved for sale. Jupiter also has cost problems that have not yet been resolved. The Jupiter drill is a $1,500 to $15,000 piece of equipment, depending upon design, used for boring and screwdriving in mass production processes, especially for automotive assembly.

As Table 5.1 indicates, the Jupiter project did not embody many of the characteristics of an effective innovation. There was no interdisciplinary team in the beginning, and only occasional true teamwork later on. Jupiter's product conceptualization was weak, its scope large. Some said that the project goals and objectives were so broad that each day they would "make one step forward and three back." The product required significant advances in technology for Springton, such as new motor designs and clutches and use of computers, and the basic machine had over 130 parts, vs. 30 for the finishing machine. People at group headquarters disagree, however, and argue that the product was not a major technological advance.

The project ran into significant delays in manufacturing, partly because of a lack of coordination and partly because the product required new know-how. They were using standard micrometers to test the new parts, but these did not measure the various dimensions adequately. The parts fit the drawings, but, since they were made from composites, they had different properties than metal. Management authorized new testing equipment, and by July the plant had produced parts that both performed and fit together. The project's relationships with senior managers were also strained.

The Saturn Drill project began in early 1990; it was less technically complicated, but still a challenge. This drill would sell for several hundred rather than thousand dollars and was designed for professional repair shops. The development team was managed from engineering again. Neither marketing nor IE was assigned full time or co-located, and the team as a whole made no visits with customers. The product's conceptualization (as summarized in Table 5.1) only partially embodied the necessary attributes, and the goals were changed by management significantly after about eight months. In December of 1990, management decided to be the only producer of this kind of drill in the United States, and to erect such significant entry barriers—patents and high capital costs—that foreign competitors could not copy the product. The team was given one year to accomplish the new objective. Again, the vertical relationships became quite strained. Management felt that the people at Springton were not working creatively or thoughtfully, so they increasingly intervened to solve problems in the project itself (that is, by requiring the team to submit a weekly schedule).

By July of 1992 it looked like all three new products would finally be going into production. MACHCO people had learned about managing innovation, team work, how to solve problems creatively, and, from the school of hard knocks, where they had remaining weaknesses. By January of 1993, MACHCO (finally) had several very good new products. But everyone was extremely frustrated. Senior managers felt that the delays were at least partly avoidable, while operating people felt that they were being asked to do the impossible. All four innovation projects ran into problems with manufacturing. None of the products were "simultaneously designed" for function and manufacturing. All four competed with each other for resources (the rest of the Venus models were being developed at the same time as the Mars, Jupiter, and Saturn). So, while the official product development process contained a number of the characteristics of effective innovation, often these characteristics were not put into practice.

Let us step back from these particulars for a moment to analyze what happened by drawing on the many studies of innovation and its relationship to organizations. One important insight is that MACHCO's problems are within the range of "normal," because many organizations have difficulty breaking down functional barriers, keeping teams going, getting resources, and so forth.[5]

Another insight is that the implementation of new technologies is more successful when accommodations are made in administrative policy and organizational structure at the same time. Ignoring organizational change happens often, however, one writer estimates that 50 percent to 75 percent of U.S. firms have experienced failure in implementing manufacturing technologies, because they have overlooked necessary organizational changes.[6]

A third important insight is that organizations constitute systems of know-how and culture that are "interlocking, complex, and tenaciously held."[7] The configurational nature of organizations suggests that change will be difficult, and not simply because employees themselves resist change. Innovations introduce dynamics that can get truly gummed up in the interlocked set of organizational beliefs and practices, because unforeseen mismatches betwen an innovation and the organization's existing procedures inevitably crop up. For example, new equipment may need debugging, but is often put into full operation right away, or a new process may negatively affect measures used to judge the success of certain people or operations, or pressures for continued productivity creates maelstroms of conflict when the activities of innovation hinder volume production.[8]

Therefore, to become an innovative organization is to also manage complex, challenging organizational changes. Piecemeal tweaks or incremental shifts, such as putting in a few teams or decentralizing some decisions, is not enough. Managers need to grab the configuration and shift it all at once. This did not happen at MACHCO. In fact, for the three new products that followed the initial effort, we can see that MACHCO's established ways of working, summarized in the beginning, still dominated.

One model of change management suggest some dynamics that we can develop for MACHCO.[9] According to this model, people cannot even begin to change until they see that the current system no longer works and that another system is available. This step is called "unfreezing," which occurs when the worth of the current configuration is disconfirmed; at the same time, people are motivated to change and provided with a sense of "psychological safety" to do so. Change can be a confusing and frightening process, and people are reluctant to change without this kind of help. Change occurs by "cognitive restructuring," or learning, which provides people with both a new perspective and the specific skills to see and feel differently. Finally, the new configuration is "refrozen" by integrating it into a new set of relationships.

A study of a poorly performing automotive plant illustrates this change process. The plant was attempting to change from an autocratic to a quality-oriented, decentralized management style, but for two years not much happened because changes were made in a piecemeal fashion that merely conflicted with the existing culture. They made no effort to provide people with insights into what the new system would look like, nor the psychological safety to begin to change. The people experienced the pressures to change as a "squeeze through the eye of a needle, where the safety of an effective production culture was being left behind but the new culture remained only a poorly understood theory."[10] Change finally took place when people developed metaphors through which they could envision their new roles and the new system. The metaphors enabled them to see through the eye of the needle, to transform their understanding and understand how to get from "here" to "there."

Toward a Model of Organizational Transformation

The people at MACHCO were definitely feeling as though they were being squeezed through the eye of a needle. The old way of working that did not enable innovation had been disconfirmed, and all but a few people recognized that they needed to change. But try as they might, they could not carry out the innovation activities listed in Table 5.1 very well. We think that they did not because they were mired in their old segmented system, and the new innovation process did not help them break out of that old system entirely.

We propose that MACHCO needs to change three dimensions of organizational practice all *at once* in order to become innovative. We use the term *concurrent management* to describe the overall idea: "concurrent" because the three changes occur together, and each change requires a high degree of coordination within its specific domain; and "management," to emphasize that firm-wide change is needed. The three dimensions that managers need to change at the same time, in order to unfreeze and change the three kinds of segmentation that trapped MACHCO are: the horizontal dimension to integrate the various sets of functional expertise (*functional concurrence*); the new to old dimension to connect the new product with the existing patterns of products and resources (*portfolio concurrence*); and the top to bottom dimension to align strategic with operational orientations (*institutional concurrence*). These three concurrences "make sense" individually at MACHCO, and so can be useful metaphors for change. The project characteristics associated with each dimension are listed in Table 5.1.

Functional Concurrence

The need to integrate the functions around new product development, is widely recognized, and team development has been widely discussed,[11] so we will not belabor this point here. However, MACHCO did not fully achieve functional concurrence in any effort. They did achieve the close, trusting team relationships on the Venus and Mars projects, which shows that, despite their highly functionally segmented work before the innovation, they could indeed create teams. But in no project did they achieve simultaneous engineering, wherein the design and manufacturing are worked out together, up-front. And in two cases marketing was disassociated enough from the projects that the initial designs were rejected. It is obviously hard to create complete functional concurrence, in which people jointly conceptualize the product and jointly bring it alive. To do so, people need roles that encompass the entire project rather than only a step in it, a rich understanding of one another, considerable trust, and the ability to make decisions for their particular function based on the whole.

Comments from Jupiter participants highlight the fact that MACHCO's historical lack of appreciation and trust between manufacturing and engineering was carried forward into this project. An engineer attributed most of the problems in manufacturing to the industrial engineering department: "We had involved industrial engineering, and they were familiar with the parts, but they did not pay attention to how critical the new parts were in the design so they didn't focus up front. They assumed standard processes would be acceptable." Yet an industrial engineering (IE) person explained that engineers did not give them good specifications:

> There were so many stumbling blocks, it wears on you. In December we wanted it so bad, but it seemed like we took three steps backward every time we solved a problem. We spent Christmas and New Year's in here

building tools and testing them. We gave it all we got, and we found out uh oh, it's not here. The engineers were somewhat tight on design, and they didn't know if they needed those parts that tight. It was a downer. We would ask the engineers: "What do you have to have," and they would say: "We don't know." They wanted the parts in this condition to validate them, but they were not sure of the design. We didn't know what to give them.

In the Saturn project, a manufacturing engineer explained a major rift between marketing and design: "Marketing along with their consultants wanted a mechanism in front of the tool because it would be easy to operate and innovative. The engineers said that would increase costs because it would make the handle longer. Marketing wanted someone to come up with a mechanism that would work on the front, and engineering already had a solution that they preferred. They felt it was a waste of their time to work on the valve when they had other problems to solve." His words reflect a lack of appreciation and trust and hint that each group was digging in, not opening up.

Many more examples could be listed. The point is that, even though effective teamwork could and did happen, it often did not. We suggest that the lack of concurrence in the other two dimensions, in fact, made functional concurrence almost impossible, especially the more rigorous concurrence required by simultaneous manufacturing; to do that requires that people fundamentally alter the way they normally work. Putting people on teams and even building team relationships will not help those people decide between innovation vs. routine products, learn how to participate in designing effectively, allocate resources among competing businesses, or align innovation with strategic issues. The failure to unfreeze these other two dimensions led to a situation where the functional work, we think, kept refreezing and so day-to-day work returned to its normal, functionally disconnected mode.

Portfolio Concurrence

A new product is not developed in a vacuum. Many new products in established firms fit into an existing line as an enhancement, addition, or replacement. Even entirely new categories of products need to connect to the existing portfolio because they may be sold to existing users, use an existing distribution channel, or build on an existing technology. Sometimes demand for products may be correlated, so the introduction of a new product can affect the sales of existing products. In addition, product development is resource intensive, but key labor and capital resources are limited and must be allocated over multiple projects. Moreover, learning can be accumulated over time from the various design efforts. Early versions of a product may "fail" by market or financial standards, but the insights that the developers gained into technology and market issues can contribute to the success of subsequent generations. These interdependencies should be handled systematically, or the inherent ambiguities of product innovation will lead to arbitrary or politically motivated choices—that is, chaos. Chapter seven in this volume summarizes the challenges in developing more systematic decision criteria, and also illustrates what happens when firms fail to do so.[12]

At MACHCO, while each of the products had a strategy, there was no evident connection among the four new products, nor among them overall and the set of current products. The formal process (Figure 5.1) contained the decisions to be made at a project level, but did not provide the decision criteria to be used to make choices and tradeoffs across product lines. Moreover, tradeoffs within a project—time to market and product performance—were not considered explicitly in setting the project's strategic objectives (see Cohen, Eliashberg 1993 for a normative model framework which analyzes such tradeoffs explicitly). MACHCO's existing control "system" was based entirely on rigid and very general cost control, and this system was not changed. The new products competed with each other and with the mature products for scarce tooling, industrial engineering time, and production capacity. For example, even though they had outsourced all their complex parts, the Saturn team planned to have several of its simpler parts made at Springton. But manufacturing decided that the pilot runs of these parts would also be done outside because of resource constraints that the team, at least, felt could seriously hurt the product. As this person notes, they could not work out any alternatives: "The team felt it was important to make these pilot lot parts here, so the plant could get an understanding of the process. But because of the schedule the manufacturing manager said we should put all the parts out. The tool room is so backed up they couldn't handle the load. . . . We suggested that we farm out the tooling for the parts but make them in here, but they didn't want to do that. Having someone else's tools in here is too radical for them."

A manufacturing manager vividly described the more general chaotic conflicts that a lack of portfolio concurrence caused, as the new products conflicted with all the other work people had to do:

> I don't see a universal strategy for new products. Everything is on a micro basis. Is anyone managing the new products overall as a sucker of resources from Springton and the division? No. They micromanage each project with no foresight on what it will do to the others. Plus we are implementing an MRPII program, becoming ISO9000 certified, and we've got 400,000 square feet of shop floor in the back here producing mature products, and that doesn't happen by itself. . . . There is a need to stand back and look at what we have on our plate and determine what we really want to get

done, . . . rather than try to do a hundred things on an inferior level. Things get too segmented on a day to day basis. You have too many hats to wear. Every five minutes you put a new hat on and take the old one off. They only time we can work on something for more than five minutes is when management is coming to town to look at our costs, and we need to come up with another program to reduce people . . .

People at MACHCO had no framework to focus and orient their choices over resource allocation and prioritization. Such a framework is essential in innovation management, because problems and choices come up all the time and cannot be planned for at the project level only. Without any decision frame, MACHCO innovators could not renegotiate targets when problems cropped up, work out conflicts, or solve common problems in a systematic fashion. The existing resources, including time, were fixed, which hurt the innovations in three important ways.

One negative effect was that the fixed time schedule made people feel that the projects were doomed to fail—not a healthy premise. An engineer said: "You need a good handle on the scope of the project and on the technical risk before you set the time period. Otherwise, experienced people who know better will not buy in; they would have no enthusiasm because they know it will fail."

The sense that success was impossible made people "back off" from aggressive pursuit of goals, as this manufacturing person said: "On the development end, if I am given an unrealistic goal, well, I don't stop working, but I take liberties in the back of my mind because I know we will not meet the target date."

Second, the lack of portfolio concurrence—understanding and making tradeoffs among or links between the many issues involved—led to "micromanagement." Upper managers attributed the myriad problems the innovators had to failure on the innovators' part to stick to a schedule or make good decisions, not to the lack of a framework to make choices. Management, therefore, reached down into particular problem areas where they did not have expertise and created even more problems, as this person explained: "They make decisions that they should not be involved in. They are not in here day to day seeing all the problems. So they come in here and say: 'What is the hold up?' We explain the situation and all the ideas we have had, and they say: 'Well, why don't you do this and this.' They don't know that the engineers have already said they don't like that idea or that manufacturing has these kinds of problems."

Third, the inability to make their own choices, as well as the micromanagement robbed the teams of a sense of ownership, which affected their ability to be teams: "Now everyone has their heads in, and the team is not able to make its own decisions. We trade off an enormous amount to get the product out on time, but then every technical decision is reviewed and criticized by people who aren't on the team, and we still get no relief on the time."

We do not suggest that the technical choices he referred to were necessarily correct, or that management's concerns were not well motivated. However, all choices would always be suspect without a system to compare the choices against, and innovators would often make unstrategic choices if they did not know what the strategy was. It should not be surprising that in this very confusing and complicated situation people stayed with what they knew how to do and were rewarded to do. It should also not be surprising that without a more general framework to connect the particular projects to the rest and to set explicit project performance targets people worked with their heads down rather than up and, in so doing, fell into every innovation trap in the book.

It is interesting to note that many firms have adopted reduced time to market or project breakeven times as their standard for product development. The one-year goal for the first phase of the Venus project is a case in point. Motivated by their success at meeting this target (albeit with a product whose main component was being outscourced at a severe cost penalty), MACHCO attempted to use this standard on all subsequent projects. As we have noted, only some of these targets were met. The cause of this failure can be traced in part to a lack of portfolio concurrence. The time/performance tradeoff was not evaluated for each project. Resource allocations across projects also did not necessarily reflect the strategic priorities of each project relative to the company's portfolio of new and existing products.

Institutional Concurrence

One reason that no general objectives or strategic rules of thumb were developed to guide the innovation process is that MACHCO had no way to arrive at them. Even if they have a rational decision-making framework to allocate resources and make project tradeoffs, innovators also face many ambiguities and so must make qualitative judgments and choices, renegotiate deadlines, or reconceive product packages and strategies. Decisions require a framework against which the choices are thought about and played out. Just as a continual dialogue between lateral functions is necessary to design and produce a product, a continual vertical dialogue between managerial levels is necessary to create and recreate a project's connection with the firm's strategy.

Institutional concurrence refers to the vertical alignment of the firm as an institution with innovation and assures that what people down at the plant are doing and thinking about innovation accords with what people up at headquarters are doing and thinking. Institutional concurrence provides the social context that enables the creation and ongoing maintenance of vertical interaction and communication. Such communication is essential if both operating- and strategic-level people are to work together under fundamentally ambiguous conditions. For example, both sides need to appreciate and respond to the shifts in market or technology needs that often occur during a project (for example, the need to go "radical" with Venus, to alter the goals with Saturn), even though the decision points are not precise, and be able to judge how the project is doing, even though the milestones may be blurry. Chapter two in this volume describes how different organizational paradigms regarding "governance" fail to acknowledge the realities of how decisions are made and people are motivated, and thus may not produce effective governance. In the same fashion, divergent paradigms or beliefs about "strategy" and "operations" can disrupt the necessary communications, and thus disrupt innovation.[12]

In all three subsequent innovation projects, MACHCO's established vertical connection of one-way, top-down control and authority did not unfreeze. Indeed, people at Springton from senior managers, hid any exceptions and surprises they encountered in their innovation efforts, even though such inevitable hitches are the primary means to learn. The following comments indicate that people at Springton recognized the need to change the institutional relationships before other change could happen, but, in their usual fashion, they were waiting for senior managers to take the lead:

> There haven't been any real changes. The teams are good, but from a decision-making standpoint we operate as before. We let upper management get too involved in the details, and they do not let the teams do their work. It's a cultural problem at MACHCO, not just at Springton.

> We need a new philosophy. It is not enough to just set up teams and say OK, now this is how we will do business. This requires a whole change in point of view, all the way down to the shop floor supervision. This is just like our attempts to use quality circles. They were never a part of the business strategy, and never a real part of our profitability or cost improvement, and so we never really implemented them.

The major indicator of a lack of institutional concurrence was the failure on everyone's part even to recognize that MACHCO and Springton were institutionalized, configured *systems*, with many tightly interconnected practices and procedures. A simple, seemingly obvious, example came up time and again in people's stories. The need to create new parts and produce prototype quantities violated the usual performance measures based on standard costs (which, in turn, were premised on volume and optimization of labor). One reason for the extended delay of the Jupiter project was that Jupiter's new parts were treated like usual parts and standardized in the usual fashion. One manager explained the problems that usual procedures created on the shop floor: "I was asked to get parts for the Jupiter through. They had already made decisions as to the time it takes to run them and the cost. For example, we would tell the operator to make ten of these an hour. But it turned out that the rates were wrong. We have a pay incentive system. The operator knows for sure that he can run the machine with this other part at a certain rate, but we tell him to run the machine for the new part at ten an hour and he can't. So he comes back and says: 'Hey the rate is wrong, can you fix it?' And we say: "No, that's it.' What's wrong with this picture?"

Parts for the Saturn drill were also delayed in manufacturing because they got caught up in the system, not simply because the team failed. This IE manager explained:

> We were set to run one of the seven new parts on April first. The plan was to run a pilot lot of 100 to 150 pieces through the cells and make sure everything was right. You need to check the gauging, adjust the tooling, and so forth. Well, those parts are still not in stock [three months later]. First the tooling wasn't ready, and then the department foreman ran a production lot through right behind the pilot lot. He was supposed to run the pilot lot all the way through first, but he did a 4,000 lot right behind it to minimize setup time. He is graded on how quickly he uses the tools. So now I am managing a 4,000 part production, not just a pilot lot, but I have no authority over that. Fred [Division Manager] gave explicit orders that he wants all the pilot parts in stock as soon as possible, but the foreman is the scheduler of that department, and he has people above him who told him to run the production lot.

Fred, the manager, reacted to this problem by requiring the IE person to submit a weekly schedule, rather than acknowledging that the existing social system, including manufacturing's performance criteria, had to change. Fred obviously thought that the problem was a lack of proper attention to detail. It is not that the people are stupid and overlook what we see as an obvious conflict. Rather, senior managers did not recognize the configured (and not necessarily rational) nature of Springton plant's existing social system.

The major reason for the lack of appreciation, indeed of awareness, was senior managers' detachment from operations, and vice versa. A person at Springton explained the separation of thinking from doing: "The thinking is the easy part. You can envision how the changes in manufacturing can happen, just like you can envision teaching, your kid to play baseball. But actually doing it, implementing change, is always harder than you thought. Managerially, people envision this happening at a faster and faster pace than it actually can."

Because of the very abstracted and limited view of each other, upper management saw no conflict in asking Springton people to change radically how they work but also keep volumes up and costs down. Springton saw nothing but conflict and felt that they must have more resources to carry out what they saw as a significantly increased work load. Neither side could believe the other, which meant that there was no basis for trust and, thus, none for unfreezing and changing the system. Consider the lack of understanding between levels this comment suggests: "We are trying to take a quantum leap beyond the competition, and you have a tendency to fall when you do that, which becomes very stressful for everyone, right down to the shop floor people who are working very hard for you. From the corporate structure, people start raising hands and saying why does this have to happen? But they are not in here every day. . . . It is difficult to quantify to a corporate VP, who certainly has other things on his mind, so that he can understand why we can't make this machine do what we want."

Each side of the strategic divide continued to look at the other through the knothole of standard cost and other abstracted performance indicators, which did nothing to provide a common understanding of what they were about, as this manager explained:

At our annual meeting, corporate management talks about cost management, profit, and market share. We don't relate to that. We talk units and how many units. I remember when a corporate VP came here. He was very honest about the fact that when he looked at tools he has no idea what they are. But he knows our contribution to the corporation's bottom line down to the last five digits. . . . We try to share more information within the factory with people about market share, but it's difficult, and I don't understand it really. There is also a comfort level. If I meet with you weekly, I can understand your questions and learn to respond. But if it's once a year or once a lifetime, I don't understand you . . .

This engineer was more scathing in his views of senior management, but the lack of appreciation between the operating and strategic levels is quite clear: "Management is driven by dollars, and some are reverting to Theory X management. They think if they beat us up hard enough, we'll see the errors of our ways. . . . Upper management is bored and confused by lines on a drawing. They want a return on investment."

Without the resource allocation system of portfolio concurrence or the strategic guidance system of institutional concurrence, particular decisions end up creating more disruption. For example, we asked one manager if they were getting better at anticipating the kinds of problems that plagued the Jupiter and Saturn projects, and he said: "Yes, now there is a certain amount of anticipation. But we still try to reduce the leadtime. That is the area we go after. Say we say that the time frame for a part will be two weeks. Management says can you get that to seven days or even five days, and we say yeah, we can. But ten days means we will be doing all the modifications to make the a part work, but when you move it down to five days, all the working time for modification is gone."

We can see how such constant pressure on the details eliminates the room to maneuver, experiment, and learn. We can also imagine that it precludes attention to the whole project or to the portfolio of projects. Nobody can really feel in charge or can take charge. No one can quite see through the eye of the needle.

What Now?

MACHCO managers have brought themselves to the brink of transformation to an innovative organization through their efforts in the last three years. We suggest that more deliberate management of all three concurrencies at once would help them go reach that goal. They began innovation by emphasizing functional concurrence, which is necessary, but we think not sufficient. The lack of teamwork occurred not only because people did not know how to work together, but because the total system of management reinforced the segmentation. We suggested two additional dimensions of organizational change that would correct the total system. To perform effectively, the teams need to take joint responsibility for the product's ultimate development and make discontinuous leaps in method and approach. To work in this new way, the current system of resource allocation and decision making must be freed up. To give the teams the ability to make their own decisions, management must back off, move out of the day-to-day work, and, instead, provide a strategic system that frames and guides daily work. To assure that the teams will make the right decisions, the current system of strategy making must be changed.

MACHCO has made good progress with functional concurrence, but they need to work out the design to the manufacturing link more clearly. In addition, the breakdowns between design and marketing show that there was still a tendency to lobby separately for one's own favorite technology or product appearance. To fix this problem, the teams need to be more clearly multifunctional from the very beginning. If marketing people continue to be located at headquarters, then they must participate actively in the conceptualization process from the outset. The whole team should own the product conceptualization and the product's overall integrity, not any specific function. The team needs to make joint visits with custormers throughout the process, no matter how familiar they think the market is. Indeed, if people knew so much about the market, then why did the old product start losing share?

MACHCO needs to start early on portfolio concurrence. A portfolio system is premised on a business strategy that provides a common sense of the firm's domain of operation and character. This strategy focuses attention on markets the organization wishes to compete in, the key factors of competition, and the technologies that the firm can leverage. Within this general strategic frame, managers must first select effective development performance targets for each project (for example, time to market, product performance, unit cost, price point). They then must allocate resources to manufacturing design and engineering technology to support innovation. In particular, MACHCO needs innovation-supporting manufacturing capabilities, which in itself would be a major change. They can, however, build on changes in manufacturing and engineering that have already been made. In addition, some firms find it useful to set up separate pilot production facilities to avoid conflicts with high-volume products. Experimenting with other kinds of manufacturing control systems (for example, Just-in-Time) could help to unfreeze the long-held standard cost system. MACHCO seems reluctant to "waste money" on such facilities, but they have surely spent in cost overruns or scrap parts at least as much as a true pilot process would have cost. Perhaps it is time to acknowledge this particular cost of innovation and include it directly on the books, rather than in variance. Other options, such as continuing to develop a better base of external suppliers or adding new capacities in molding and composite processing, can also be evaluated.

Several managers recommended other ideas that can be tried to develop a portfolio system, such as more flexible capabilities in tooling or manufacturing that can be deployed to support both innovation and mature products. Cummins Engine, for example, has developed an innovative product/process classification scheme, which accounts for the inherent conflicts associated with manufacturing new and old (as well as high-and-low volume) products within the same facility. Their solution led to the development of a series of alternative process layouts (including transfer lines, cellular and Flexible Manufacturing Systems) to accommodae this variety. In chapter six, the impact of product variety on manufacturing is explored for the case of the auto industry.

A number of the engineers at MACHCO recommended a more deliberate technology strategy. Instead of re-inventing motor enhancements for each product, for example, they could set out several target technology development projects that could be used across the product lines. We suggest that a more systematic look at other aspects of the value chain should also be carried out (for example, distribution purchasing, parts and after-sales service).

A portfolio system could combine these various functional developments to form a framework of decision criteria for each innovation effort. This framework cannot become rigid, but neither can individual product efforts proceed in a vacuum. Particular criteria to judge priorities for time to market, degree of innovativeness, relationships within and across product lines, and feasibility on technology, distribution, and/or manufacturing capabilities are needed to assess a given product's likelihood of success. The nature of the market and the product's strategy (aggressive, preemptive, or defensive) would dictate the particular time frame for each product. Of course, many new products might encounter new uncertainties during development if expected technologies do not materialize or unexpected competitors do materialize. Additional choices along the way might need to be made to change the plans or perhaps even shelve the product idea for the time being. Considering a particular effort within the context of the entire portfolio of products would help make these choices.

None of these changes would stay in place without better institutional concurrence. Leadership from the top should initiate the strategic dialogue and orient operating-level people in a given direction, and then let the operating levels determine how to move in that direction. MACHCO needs to break down its fundamental communication barriers between the strategic and operating levels. The people at the plant truly do not understand group management, while group management truly does not seem to appreciate the realities of operations. They need to develop a strategic conduit or medium of exchange that is capable of a rich, complex exchange of knowledge, not just bits of information. One place to start would be to build on Springton's networking ability and craftsmanlike orientation to work, which would emphasize the good qualities of the existing system. A second obvious fix is to align the performance criteria, reward systems, and the processes through which activities are evaluated and monitored to support innovation. A third fix would be to develop "metrics" that convey the same message from top to bottom, despite the very different sensemaking worlds at the different levels. Worrying about costs in the abstract ignores the context of investment and opportunity. These concerns need to be translated into operation-level activities that crystalize the firm's improvement of its value and ability to generate cash flow. Finally, a process of participatory strategy making is necessary. Here, strategic and operating people discuss possibilities for business domains or moves within those domains, and try them out.

As indicated in Table 5.1, all four projects failed to satisfy the three dimensions of concurrency simultaneously. As a result, each project encountered difficulties. The outcomes of these projects reflect these difficulties.

We suggest that unfreezing and changing all three dimensions of organizational action at once are necessary to transform a stable old firm into an innovative one. Together, the three concurrencies capture the configuration of issues that are important to innovation management, from team management to strategic guidance. Making complete changes in each dimension is not possible at once, but beginning to change each at once certainly is possible. The innovative organization is not a stable state, so managing innovation never stops. Moving along these paths together is a continuous process of making connections, trying new ideas, evaluating the outcomes and choosing next steps.

Notes

The authors would like to acknowledge the comments of Daryl Brewster of Campbell Soup Company.

1. The company and products are disguised.
2. For an analysis of how people in different departments think very differently, see Dougherty, Deborah. 1992. Interpretive barriers to successful product innovation in large firms. *Organization Science* 3:179–202.
3. Years ago, people wrote books about factories as institutions, with real live cultures and shared norms. See, for example, Gouldner, Alvin. 1954. *Patterns of industrial bureaucracy*. New York: Free Press; Crozier, Michel. 1964. *The bureaucratic phenomenon*. Chicago: University of Chicago Press. Recent works by Shoshana Zuboff, Larry Hirschhorn, and Robert Thomas also capture the institutional aspects of factories and work.
4. Along with literature mentioned in note 1, see Clark, Kim, and Takahiro Fugimoto. 1989. Lead time in automobile product development: Explaining the Japanese advantage. *Journal of Engineering and Technology Management* t:25–58; Cooper, R. 1983. A process model for industrial new product development. *IEEE Transactions on Engineering Management* 30:2–11.
5. For summaries of these problems see, for example, Cooper, Robert G., and Elko J. Kleinschmidt. 1986. An investigation into the new product process: Steps, deficiencies, and impact. *Journal of New Product Development* 3:71–85; Dougherty, Deborah and Trudy Heller. The illegitimacy of successful product innovation in established firms. *Organization Science* (forthcoming).
6. See discussion in Adler, Paul S. 1990. Shared learning. *Management Science* 36:938–57; and Majchrzak, Ann. *The human side of factory automation*. San Francisco: Jossey-Bass.
7. Westley, Frances R. 1990. The eye of the needle: Cultural transformations in a traditional organization. *Human Relations* 43:273–93.
8. For a summary of these kinds of problems, see Leonard-Barton, Dorothy. 1988. Implementation as mutual adaptation of technology and organization. *Research Policy* 17:152–267.

9. See Schein, Edgar H. 1961. Management development as a process of influence. *Industrial Management Review* 59–77; Schein, Edgar H. 1987. *Process consultation*, vol. II. Reading, Mass.: Addison-Wesley; Lewin, Kurt. 1947. Frontiers in group dynamics. *Human Relations* 1:5–41.

10. See note 9.

11. See Dougherty, Clark and Fujimoto, Leonard-Barton.

12. Chris Ittner and Bruce Kogut, in "How control systems can support organizational flexibility," describe different approaches to developing systematic control systems that also encourage flexibility, and point out that standard control process, in fact, discourages flexibility.

References

Adler, Paul. 1990. Shared learning. *Management Science* 36:938–57.

Clark, Kim B., and Takahiro Fugimoto. 1989. Lead time in automobile product development: Explaining the Japanese advantage. *Journal of Engineering and Technology Management* 6:25–58.

Cohen, Morris, Jehoshua Eliashberg, and T. Hua Ho. 1993. New product design strategy analysis: A Modeling Framework. *Design Management.*

Cooper, Robert G. 1983. A process model for industrial new product development. *IEEE Transactions on Engineering Management* 30:2–11.

Cooper, Robert G., and Elko J. Kleinschmidt. 1986. An investigation into the new product process: Steps, deficiencies, and impact. *Journal of New Product Development* 3:71–85.

Crozier, Michel. 1964. *The bureaucratic phenomenon.* Chicago: Chicago University Press.

Dougherty, Deborah. 1992. Interpretive barriers to successful product innovation in large firms. *Organization Science* 3:179–202.

Dougherty, Deborah. 1992. A practice-centered model of organizational renewal through product innovation. *Strategic Management Journal* 13:77–92.

Dougherty, Deborah, and Trudy Heller. 1994. The illegitimacy of successful new products in large firms. *Organization Science.*

Gouldner, Alvin W. 1954. *Patterns of industrial bureaucracy.* New York: Free Press.

Ittner, Christopher, and Bruce Kogut. 1994. "How control systems can support organizational flexibility." *Redesigning the firm.* New York: Oxford University Press.

Leonard-Barton, Dorothy. 1988. Implementation as Mutual Adaptation of Technology and Organization. *Research Policy* 17:251–67.

Lewin, Kurt. 1947. Frontiers in group dynamics. *Human Relations* 1:5–41.

Majchrzak, Ann. 1988. *The human side of factory automation.* San Francisco: Jossey-Bass.

Schein, Edgar H. 1961. Management development as a process of influence. *Industrial Management Review* 59–77.

Schein, Edgar H. 1987. *Process consultation,* vol. 1. Reading, Mass.: Addison-Wesley.

Westley, Frances. 1990. The eye of the needle: Cultural transformation in a traditional organization. *Human Relations* 43:273–93.

6

Strategies for Product Variety: Lessons from the Auto Industry

MARSHALL FISHER,

ANJANI JAIN, AND

JOHN PAUL MACDUFFIE

Driven by the market's "pull" for increasingly differentiated products and by manufacturers' "push" to seek finely targeted niche segments, the variety of products offered in most industries has increased steadily over the last several decades. The "pull" comes from customers who seem to reward companies that can offer high variety while matching the price and quality of competitors with narrower product lines. Modern marketing methods accelerate this trend by identifying once-obscure specifics of consumer preferences. As more companies compete internationally, product markets become more crowded and product differentiation more important, both to make a product stand out in a popular product category and to help tailor a product to niche markets. The "push" comes from new firm capabilities as the increased sophistication and declining price of flexible, programmable automation bring the opportunity for greater product variety within the grasp of many more companies.

The U.S. auto industry nicely illustrates the events and forces that steadily increase product variety. Early in this century, Henry Ford achieved unprecedented productivity gains with a strategy based on low product variety, well-characterized by his famous quote, "my customers can have any color they want as long as it is black." Some years later, Alfred P. Sloan's rejoinder "a car for every purse and purpose" articulated General Motors' (GM) variety strategy of differentiated price and value embodied in GM's well-known "ladder" of product offerings from *Chevrolet* to *Cadillac*. Using this strategy, GM grew steadily to become the largest enterprise in the world, stealing enormous market share from Ford along the way. Ironically, the American auto industry would lose that market share, starting in the 1960s, to another group of "variety competitors"— Japanese and European firms offering compact and specialty cars. This competition led to increasing product differentiation based on size and features. It also began the globalization of the U.S. auto market, leading to today's situation of nineteen global competitors, each targeting the U.S. market with its own distinct portfolio of product offerings. Innovations in technology have also steadily increased the versions of cars available by introducing new features (automatic transmission, front-wheel drive, disk brakes, and so forth) that never completely replaced the old features (manual transmission, rear-wheel drive, drum brakes). Finally, there has been dramatic growth in the sales of specialty vehicles like sports cars, minivans, utility vehicles and, soon, electric cars. Nothing so symbolized for us the state the auto industry has reached as a statistic we learned during one of our visits to the Mazda Hiroshima plant. The Mazda 323 is produced in this plant for worldwide markets in 180 different colors, including four shades of black, an ironic twist on Henry Ford's original offer of any color, as long as it was black.

While many companies struggle with variety, suffering reduced productivity and quality, we found some auto plants that organize their production in a way that allows them to absorb high levels of product variety without compromising productivity or quality. The obvious question at this point is, how do some plants manage to insulate themselves from the effects of product variety? In pursuit of answers to this question, we have spent the last two years visiting more than twenty auto plants worldwide, studying their approaches to manufacturing flexibility. Besides observing the manufacturing processes in these plants, we have interviewed engineers and managers and examined company documents on the technology, systems, and concepts used to achieve flexibility.

This chapter reports what we have learned about successful approaches to manufacturing flexibility. Although our focus will be on the auto industry, we believe the principles of flexibility we have learned would apply to many other industries. Briefly, we have seen that achieving truly effective flexibility is a challenging and elusive goal. Clearly, technology is part of the answer, but technology by itself will not create flexibility. All auto companies can buy and have bought flexible automation, but few have added to this the style of human resource management and organizational structure that are needed to use the flexible equipment effectively.

Two examples illustrate just how deeply inflexibility can be woven into an organization. The first example concerns the accounting system. In many auto companies, the unit of analysis for capital investment accounting is the new car model program. The program manager for a new model project is given a budget with which to purchase tooling such as stamping dies, welding equipment, and molds for plastic parts. The goal under this system is to maximize the market value of the new model subject to the capital budget constraint—a goal that provides no incentive to spend more for flexible tooling than would have useful value beyond the immediate car program or what could be shared with other car programs. Indeed, new model program managers often delay or avoid investments in equipment that could be shared across several car programs in the hope that some other program manager will make the investment and give them a "free ride." Even if top management injects flexible automation into the organization outside of the normal capital budgeting process (as happened at GM in the 1980s under Roger Smith), the flexible equipment often does not get used to its full capability. This can happen if the profit accounting system for a proposed new model assumes that all production tooling is dedicated to the new model, which must then bear all equipment depreciation charges. This results in an estimation of break-even for the model that is too high, given that tooling is flexible and can be shared across models, so a niche model can be rejected when it would have been profitable.

We have also seen a mismatch between the *manufacturing* and *distribution* capabilities in many companies. We performed a small experiment to test the ability of an auto distribution system to handle product variety. One of us visited a dealer and inquired about purchasing a popular sports coupe. We learned from the sales literature that the car could be purchased in twenty million versions of color, interior combinations, drive train configurations, and option choices. But, as ordering a car necessitated a six-week wait for delivery, almost everybody bought from the dealer's stock. The dealer told us he had two such cars in stock on his lot, but if these did not exactly match our ideal specifications, we need not worry; he would get us a car from another dealer in the Philadelphia area. Checking the phone book we found ten dealers in the Philadelphia area. Assuming that other dealers had only two of the car in stock, we were buying from a stock of twenty for a car that came in twenty million versions.

Clearly the ability of the assembly plant to supply variety had greatly outstripped the ability of the distribution system to pass that variety on to the customer. But the assembly plant faces the worst of two worlds in this scenario. It must be able, if requested, to build any of the twenty million variants. Yet in practice, it so rarely faces a consistent demand for this product variety that it has continued to organize production for a high-volume standardized product sold mostly to fleet customers.

In this chapter, we first discuss some anomalous results from our statistical research that caused us to rethink our view of product variety. We next provide a foundation for understanding product variety and flexibility in the auto industry. We describe the production process, how variety complicates this process, and some common devices used by all auto manufacturers to cope with these complications. In the third section, we will look at different ways of coping with product variety under the three production paradigms that have characterized the auto industry historically—craft, mass, and lean production. This framework will set the stage for our final two sections: one that explores the potential *gains* from variety, not only from the marketplace, but also in terms of capacity utilization, cost reduction, and flexibility; and one that explores the current dilemmas and opportunities facing automobile companies as they develop their product variety strategy.

The Variety Paradox

Despite the forces promoting higher product variety, many companies still view variety as a "necessary evil." They must accommodate "product proliferation" to satisfy increasingly demanding customers, but they see it as a force that complicates their operations, increases costs, and exerts a steady downward pressure on profits. The "focused factory," streamlined to produce a few carefully chosen products with high efficiency, remains the ideal for most manufacturing managers. This mentality leads to a "tradeoff" view of product variety. More variety is "good" because it increases revenue, but "bad" because it drives up production costs. Somewhere between Ford's vision of black for everybody and a fully customized product for each buyer lies the "optimal" level of product variety that trades off these good and bad effects.

This viewpoint was uppermost in our minds when we embarked on a program of research to measure the impact of product variety on productivity and quality in automotive assembly plants. We felt that developing a methodology for quantifying the cost side of product variety would be a useful contribution to help firms better make the tradeoff between market benefits and production costs of higher product variety. But along the way, we encountered a "surprise." That surprise, and the discoveries we have made in understanding it, are the subject of this chapter.

Our first research effort was a study of a single plant over time in which we correlated plant productivity each month with measures of variety in the product mix produced in that month. The results of this study fit the pattern we had expected. Greater variability in product mix within a month correlated with lower plant productivity.

We then embarked on a broader analysis that correlated the productivity of sixty-two assembly plants worldwide with several measures of product variety (MacDuffie, Sethuraman, and Fisher 1993). Here came the surprise. This study showed no correlation between plant productivity and most measures of product variety. Apparently, some plants were able to combine a high level of product variety *and* a high level of productivity.

As we compared our studies with those of other researchers in different industries, we saw a similar pattern. For example, one study of a single head- and tail-light plant over time showed that product complexity resulted in higher costs (Banker et al 1990; Datar et al 1990), while a multiplant study based on the Profit Impact of Marketing Strategies (PIMS) database found that high variety was uncorrelated with high production costs (Kekre and Srinivasan 1990).

How are we to understand these studies that seem, at least partially, to contradict conventional wisdom about product variety? It will be helpful to draw a parallel with the evolution of thinking on product quality over the last couple of decades. Not so long ago, most managers thought of quality as a good thing, but something that came at a cost. Higher product quality meant higher manu- facturing cost, and the goal of most production systems was to reduce cost subject to the constraint of "good enough" quality. Then came evidence from the marketplace that did not fit this model. Japanese competitors started offer- ing higher quality products at lower prices. These apparent anomalies prompted some rethinking on quality. It became clear that it costs the same to produce a defective unit of a product as to produce a good one. Consequently, a focus on minimizing the cost per unit processed may not lead to the lowest cost per unit of good product produced.

For example, suppose a company is spending $100 per unit to produce a product with a 10 percent defect rate. Then their actual cost *per good unit of product* is $100/.9 = $111.11. Investing in a process improvement that *raises* the cost per unit produced by $5 but lowers the defect rate to 1 percent actually *reduces* the cost *per good unit of product* to $105/.99 = $106.05. If inspection were perfect, so that all defective units were detected and removed, then the quality of product received by customers would be unaffected by the change. But the large number of product defects encountered in the marketplace suggests that inspection is rarely perfect, so fewer defects produced means fewer defects going to customers. As a result, the process improvement that raised the cost per unit processed actually lowered the cost per good unit of product and increased the quality of products received by customers. As this example illus- trates, while there may be a tradeoff between cost and the level of specifications we design into a product (design quality), when it comes to the ability of a process to conform to those specifications (conformance quality), quality can be free.

What is the analogy between quality and variety? Just as it costs the same to produce a defective product as a good one, it costs the same to produce a unit of a product that nobody wants to buy as it does to produce a product distinctively tailored to the needs of an individual customer. A product nobody wants to buy is a "market defect" and, like quality defects, market defects are expensive. For example, an auto company with limited product lines and inflexible plants may be forced to produce more of a model than can be sold, and these "market defective" cars must be pushed on customers with rebates or sold to rental agencies at a loss. Just as with quality, an investment in flexibility and an enriched product line can be more than recouped by the savings in "market defects." Also, as the breadth of a manufacturer's product line grows, it is forced to invest in systems for coping with complexity (for example, programmable automation, computerized scheduling, material requirements planning (MRP), and worker training). Once these systems are in place, further increases in product line breadth and associated complexity can be handled with little or no incremental cost.

This logic is captured in Figures 6.1 and 6.2. Figure 6.1 depicts a company operating with an existing process at a particular level of cost and quality and facing a tradeoff curve in which higher quality implies higher cost. The company can lower this tradeoff curve by investing in process improvements that increase the ability of the process to conform to specifications. The company still faces a cost/quality tradeoff, but the process improvements allow it to move to a new operating point where it has both higher quality and lower cost. If the (present value of) reduction in operating cost exceeds the investment in process improvement, the company has achieved quality for free. There is ample evidence from industrial experience of cases where this has been done.

Figure 6.2 shows curves for product variety analogous to Figure 6.1. Consider two plants, each of which faces a cost/variety tradeoff as shown in the figure. Suppose that the second plant has invested in process improvements that

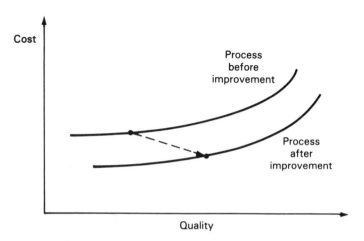

Figure 6.1.   Shifting the Quality-Cost Tradeoff.

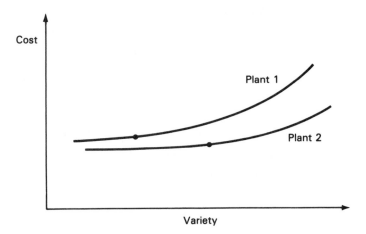

Figure 6.2.   Plant Differences in Variety Productivity.

have lowered its cost/variety tradeoff curve. Then this plant can be operating at a point that has both higher variety and lower cost than the first plant. Note that this model explains the apparent contradiction between our single plant and multiplant studies. The single plant study showed a significant cost/variety penalty within a plant, and that agrees with Figure 6.2. But Figure 6.2 is also consistent with the multiplant study if the sample of sixty-two plants contained some plants like the first in Figure 6.2 and some like the second.

Product Variety in the Auto Industry

The automobile industry is a good place to explore the relationship between product variety, productivity, and quality because this industry has seen an explosion of product variety at the same time that competition in productivity and quality has intensified. Also, various manufacturers have followed different strategies in their management of variety, which provides the opportunity to compare the effectiveness of alternative approaches to variety.

Key Dimensions of Variety

Figure 6.3 shows the way auto manufacturers organize their product offerings. Most firms have five to ten basic *platforms* off which they can produce a number of different models (for example, Ford's *Taurus* and *Sable*) and body styles (for example, two-door and four-door). The various models and body styles within a platform typically share many parts, usually including the floor pan and many

Platform

Models and Body Styles

Packaged Options

Stand Alone Options

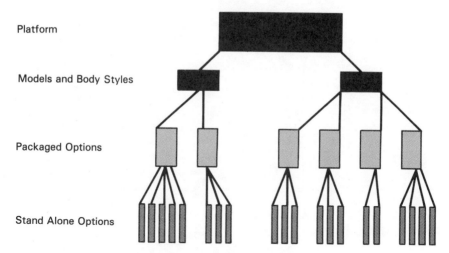

Figure 6.3. Product Hierarchy.

interior body parts. In addition, manufacturers offer a number of options from which the buyer of a particular model can choose. Common options include air conditioning, sunroof, power windows and door locks, as well as a choice of engine, transmission, and interior and exterior colors. Product variety in the auto industry is often classified as *fundamental variety* (different platforms, models, and body styles) and *peripheral variety* (different options). In our research we have also discovered that an intermediate level of *parts variety* (for example, number of engine/transmission combinations, number of interior/exterior color combinations) has become increasingly important in product differentiation. Parts variety also appears to have the greatest negative impact on assembly plant productivity (MacDuffie, Sethuraman, and Fisher 1995).

U.S. and Japanese producers have followed different strategies in providing their customers with product choices. The Japanese have typically competed on fundamental variety, offering more choices of models and platforms than their U.S. counterparts. At the same time, a Japanese model sold in North America usually has very few option choices, often just a selection between three trim levels. By contrast, the U.S. producers have had less fundamental variety but an enormous amount of peripheral variety, with millions of potential "build combinations" for a single model.

How Variety Complicates the Production Process

Let us start by walking through how a car is built. Then we will look at how variety complicates this process. Figure 6.4 shows the different steps in produc-

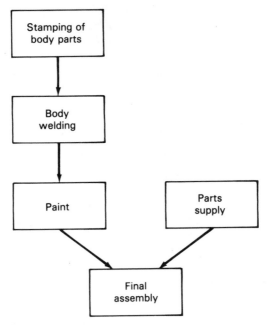

Figure 6.4.   Auto Production.

ing a car. First, the body parts of the car are stamped out of sheet metal using heavy steel dies driven by massive stamping presses. These parts are welded together to form the body of the car, which is painted. The last step is to install engine, transmission, and other parts on an assembly line.

The different steps in the process present different kinds of challenges to achieving flexibility. The upstream stamping and welding stages are highly capital intensive. For example, a full set of dies for a model will typically cost about $300 million, as will tooling for body welding. Traditionally, these dies have tended to be model specific, so high model-lifetime sales were required to break even on the huge capital investment. As product variety grows, it reduces model volumes, making it hard to recover capital investments.

Final assembly and parts supply are labor intensive rather than capital intensive. The challenge here is coordination of numerous small steps as tens of thousands of parts come together to form a car. The whole premise of an assembly line is to achieve efficiency by reducing variability to the absolute minimum. Ideally, each worker requires exactly the same amount of time to perform his or her task on a car, so no worker is forced to remain idle waiting for others to complete their tasks. Even if all cars produced on a line are identical, a perfect balance is generally unattainable. But as the variety of cars produced on a line grows, particularly when the total labor content of various cars differs, balance losses can increase sharply, resulting in reduced labor utilization. In extreme cases, tasks requiring extra time may not get finished on the line and require expensive rework to complete. (We will see some exceptions to this later.)

Product variety complicates the parts supply process because more parts require a greater coordination effort to get the right part into a worker's hands at the exact instant a car approaches the worker's station on the assembly line. Traditionally, if different cars required different parts at a production step, an inventory of each part type would be stored "lineside" by the worker who was responsible for selecting and installing the right part for each car. The cost of variety under this system is the time for the worker to walk among the stock points and a risk of getting the wrong part, particularly with hard-to-distinguish parts like wire harnesses. Recently, manufacturers have been working to improve the "presentation" of parts to line workers. For example, large parts like seats and fascia may be sequenced off-line and delivered via a separate conveyor at exactly the right time. This reduces the assembly line cost of variety, but adds the overhead of performing the sequencing function.

Having more part types also reduces the production volume per part, thus eroding economies of scale. It is also harder to perform statistical process control on parts with a limited production history, so conformance quality suffers.

Building Blocks of Flexibility: Hardware, Software, and Human Skills

The most conspicuous and readily acquired building block of flexibility for product variety is hardware. In automotive manufacturing, flexible programmable automation is heavily applied in the capital-intensive body welding and paint shops. Flexible automation can also be found in the labor-intensive final assembly process, but this is a relatively recent trend and opportunities for automation are still relatively limited. When hardware is flexible, the amount of capital investment that is model-specific is limited, allowing capital costs to be spread across multiple models.

A second building block is software. Interpreted narrowly, software includes coordination systems like sequencing algorithms to control balance losses and materials requirement planning (MRP) software to coordinate parts supply. More broadly, "software" can embrace procedures and decision processes and would include faster setup routines, Kanban systems for controlling work-in-process, or revised accounting procedures to better measure cost in a world of shared flexible capital.

The way that human skills are organized is the third important building block for flexibility. Organizational and human resource capabilities play a dual role in handling product variety. First, the effective utilization of flexible hardware and supporting software tools often depends on the existence of a broadly skilled work force that can carry out maintenance and programming tasks, managers and engineers who are skilled at cross-functional coordination, and a process of organizing work tasks and allocating people to tasks that can be easily modified in response to changing conditions. Second, these same skills and organizational processes can exhibit flexibility in dealing with the many aspects of product variety for which there are no easy hardware solutions, for example, insuring the correct installation of parts on a high variety assembly line.

Strategies for Variety in the Auto Industry

Auto manufacturers around the world face similar challenges from product variety, and all have similar access to hardware and software that can increase their production flexibility. But different companies put the building blocks of flexibility together in very different ways—particularly with respect to the organization of work and the utilization of human skills—with very different consequences for how product variety is handled. In this section, we take as starting points the three types of manufacturing that have characterized the automotive industry historically—craft production, mass production, and lean production. We describe both the challenge that each manufacturing approach faces with respect to product variety and the technical and organizational capabilities that each brings to this challenge—and the associated problems and dilemmas. We focus in this section on how the three types differ in their ability to *absorb* variety-induced complexity and return in the next section to the proposition that high product variety can be a direct source of *gains* to manufacturers who acquire flexibility.

Mass Production

THE VARIETY CHALLENGE

Mass production has been the dominant manufacturing approach in the automobile industry for most of this century, making it a good starting point for our discussion of different approaches to product variety. It also occupies the "low variety" end of the spectrum, in contrast with craft and lean production, both of which are organized to produce high variety. Indeed, mass production is virtually defined by its twin reliance on high economies of scale and a standardized product, which together allow a finely detailed division of labor for both people (narrow, highly rationalized production jobs and a hierarchy of specialists) and technology (equipment totally dedicated to a single product). The "logic" of mass production with respect to product variety is, essentially, to eliminate it. Henry Ford's "any color, as long as it's black" quote about the *Model T* captures this logic quite well.

This "pure" form of mass production—one truly standard product made in massive quantities—was largely superseded by Alfred Sloan's innovation of providing a product for every market segment. From the manufacturing point of view, however, this change had a modest impact, since most of the variation Sloan offered customers was "cosmetic," in the sense that core design features remained the same, while body styling and peripheral features were modified on different models. Over time, this strategy of product differentiation advanced to the point where the sheer number of peripheral features (commonly referred to as "options") came to pose a substantial problem of manufacturing complexity. But the underlying premise of a small number of core or fundamental designs, with each design matched to a dedicated manufacturing plant, remained unchanged.

Today's international automotive market no longer conforms to this mass production ideal. As competitors offering many different core designs gain market share, companies with more dedicated facilities and a mass-production orientation toward minimizing variety are put at a disadvantage. Thus, the challenge for companies using the mass-production model has been how they should cope with market demand for more variety without sacrificing the advantages of "focused factories."

TECHNICAL CAPABILITIES

Mass-production companies have developed three technological responses to this challenge. The first is the use of parts sharing to maximize the variety that the customer sees while minimizing the complexity that the manufacturing plant faces. The second is the increased use of flexible automation. The third response is designing production facilities to combine some high-volume, dedicated production lines for standardized products with some flexible lines for handling a variety of products.

Parts sharing. Through parts sharing, companies hope to maximize the number of common parts across models that are invisible to the customer, thus minimizing manufacturing complexity, while still preserving the styling and peripheral features that are attractive to consumers. The simplest gains from parts sharing can come from standardizing fasteners and other commodity parts to minimize purchasing, inventory, and delivery complexity. But parts sharing can also include complex mechanical and electrical components, interior instrumentation and trim, and even certain stamped or molded body parts.

The emphasis on parts sharing has been spurred on by several developments: product development teams organized to coordinate design decisions for components across multiple products (Nobeoka and Cusumano 1993); the increasing use of Computer-Aided Design (CAD) databases to record and communicate part designs; and the incentive of global economies of scale as a means to cost reduction in stagnant market conditions. For companies traditionally strong in mass production, this approach offers a way to reestablish the conditions under which they can use their manufacturing expertise most effectively.

However, parts sharing has proven to be both difficult to coordinate and costly, at least when attempted on a broad scale. Ford attempted in the early 1980s to make the *Escort* a "world car" with a common design in the United States and Europe; in the end, there were two separate designs and almost no parts were shared. Ford's more recent "world car" project, introduced first as the *Mondeo* in Europe and targeted to replace the *Tempo/Topaz* in the United States, has a relatively high percentage of parts shared across the European and American models—about 60 percent—but the overall project cost an estimated six billion dollars, nearly double the cost of a conventional project (*The Wall Street Journal*, March 23, 1993).

Flexible automation. The use of flexible automation by mass producers is also motivated by the desire to minimize the complexity experienced by the manufacturing plant. High-speed transfer presses in the stamping area, automated for rapid die change, eliminate much of the downtime penalty associated with changing models. Robots in the weld shop can be programmed to change the number, sequence, and placement of welds from model to model without requiring separate body lines. Even body framing, the process of bringing together the roof, floor pan, and two sides of the car to form its body, can be made flexible with a "robogate" framing station, originally developed by Comau (a Fiat subsidiary), that uses model-specific fixtures to hold body panels in place while an array of programmable robots applies welds. Paint robots and other programmable automation allow for instantaneous changes of color and painting pattern, even from one vehicle to the next.

Despite major investments in flexible automation, many mass production companies do not substantially boost the amount of product variety they can handle in a given assembly plant. This is partly due to their failure to reorganize the production process and train the workforce to take full advantage of the capabilities of flexible automation, as discussed below.

It also reflects a different strategy for capital investment than in the past. Many auto companies have begun investing in flexible automation for its advantages in making multiple model changes of a given product over time, rather than for multiple products being manufactured simultaneously. As the costs of programmable automation have dropped, companies find it is cheaper to install flexible rather than fixed automation, even if they only intend to produce one model at a time on the equipment, because the model changeover process (typically five to eight years for mass production companies) can be much shorter and cheaper. However, while this reduces the capital investment associated with model changes, it does not substantially boost the product variety a company can produce, since with single-product loading of each plant, variety is limited by the number of available plants.

Mixing dedicated and flexible production lines. A final strategy for mass production companies now appearing in Europe is to segment demand into the high volume, low variety portion, which is produced on lines with dedicated automation following traditional methods, and the low volume, high variety portion, which is assigned to flexible automation "islands" or separate lines. One problem with this strategy is that it requires fairly accurate forecasting of demand for the core, standardized product and for the more customized product variants in order to keep the capacity of these separate facilities fully utilized. As such, this approach is simply an accommodation of a traditional mass-production strategy—allocating models to dedicated plants in accordance with projected demands—to the realities of lower volume per model, without affecting the way most production lines are configured.

ORGANIZATIONAL CAPABILITIES

Common to these technical responses to the variety challenge is the goal of maintaining or recreating the conditions that allow high-volume, standardized production to occur. This is reflective of powerful organizational tendencies in mass-production companies to continue minimizing and eliminating product variety, and means that flexible technologies are often underutilized. As Jaikumar (1986) found in his study of flexible manufacturing systems (FMS), U.S. companies with a legacy of mass production tended to use their equipment to produce high volumes of a relatively small number of parts, in comparison to European and Japanese competitors. This was partly driven by high thresholds for return-on-investment for new equipment and other accounting conventions that favor economies of scale for single products, and partly by habit and organizational routines.

As noted above, mass production companies rarely make changes in organizational or human resource capabilities to match their investment in flexible automation. They adhere to a narrow division of labor in the production process, staffed by low-skilled production workers and a hierarchy of technical specialists whose job is to minimize disruptions to the meeting of daily production goals. In this context, technical strategies for product variety can face several problems.

Various empirical studies now suggest that the net effect of new automation is often to raise the average skill requirements of jobs, since the jobs eliminated by automation are often low-skilled jobs, and because programmable equipment has different set-up and maintenance requirements than fixed automation (Adler 1988; Attewell 1987; Cappelli 1993). Yet mass-production companies tend to offer relatively little training to their employees, either because they do not believe it is necessary, or because of concerns about a loss of training investment due to worker turnover, or because of a low-level of basic reading and math skills among their employees (MacDuffie and Kochan 1995). Furthermore, it is not necessarily easy for firms to lay off existing lower-skilled workers while hiring replacements for the new, more skilled machine operator jobs, because of union agreements, a shortage of applicants with the necessary skills, or a reluctance to lose the job-specific knowledge of experienced employees.

Under mass production, workers are viewed as an adjunct to the production line, a variable input that should be adjusted routinely with volume swings. Workers are only expected to contribute effort and have little motivation to think or solve problems on the job. Yet new technologies often require an extensive period of debugging to work effectively. Furthermore, any piece of production equipment has idiosyncrasies that must be learned before it can be operated at its full capacity. The machine operator is the most likely to learn about those idiosyncrasies, but under mass production, he will rarely have any incentive to use that knowledge to improve the productive output of the equipment. When staff specialists, such as industrial engineers, try to incorporate the presumed advantages of new equipment into work standards and cycle times, the stage is set for one of the oldest struggles in the industrial workplace: to discover (for the industrial engineer) or conceal (for the worker) the true content of the job.

The European trend towards separate lines for standardized vs. high-variety production within the same facility poses other problems on the organizational front. If the flexible line requires higher skill and motivation from its workers than the dedicated, high-volume line, management must cope with the complexities of selecting workers from two different labor pools and then training and compensating them differently to match the different job requirements. This dual workforce within a single facility can create potentially serious problems of equity, not to mention the managerial challenges of overseeing two very different kinds of employees. The organizational culture that develops around these different parts of the plant could differ greatly as well, leading to a dysfunctional "culture clash" of the sort that can often be found across plants or divisions in a given company—witness the tensions between Saturn and more traditional General Motors plants.

SUMMARY

A company using the mass-production approach may be able to accommodate modest increases in product variety through the technical mechanisms described above: parts sharing, flexible automation, and mixing fixed and flexible lines within the same facility. But the basic logic of mass production still points towards a minimization of variety. Furthermore, mass-production companies find it harder to match changes in technology with corresponding changes in organizational and human resource capabilities, since they have traditionally relied on a narrow division of labor requiring minimal skills from production workers and a hierarchy of experts trained (and rewarded) to focus on economies of scale and reductions in direct labor costs. Thus, we expect distinct limits to the amount of product variety a mass-production company can absorb without adverse impacts on cost and quality.

Craft Production

THE VARIETY CHALLENGE

At its essence, craft production is about infinite product variety—"one of a kind" creations where the uniqueness of each product emerges from the idiosyncrasies of the craft itself and enhances the product's value. The early automotive industry deserves to be classified as "craft production" not only because the initial automobiles were built-to-order for wealthy patrons with distinct ideas about the product, from decor to engine design. It was also the case that products were literally unique because of the absence of standardized parts, with the resulting "dimensional creep" and need for skilled "fitters" in the assembly process. (Hounshell 1984; Womack, Jones, and Roos 1990) Today, the carriers of this craft tradition are the small makers of expensive sports cars, such as Porsche, TVR, Lotus, Maserati, Lamborghini, and Ferrari.

While craft producers benefited from mass production's achievements in the standardizing of parts, many of the other dimensions of craft production remain relatively unchanged: very low volume (often only a few cars per day); simple but flexible tools; job-shop scheduling, with buffers to mitigate bottlenecks at key processes; highly skilled workers trained through long on-the-job apprenticeships, during which much firm-specific knowledge as well as craft knowledge develops; craft standards of quality oriented towards post-process "tuning" of each product; and a broad division of labor, with craftsmen involved in both design and manufacturing issues.

The "variety challenge" that interests us for craft production is how this approach to manufacturing can maintain high variety and quality while achieving enough efficiency to bring product costs within the reach of mass-market consumers. Thus we are less concerned with the small "pure" craft producers of expensive sports cars, and more with how certain craft philosophies and practices have affected the production systems of larger automobile companies. We will examine the emergence of a "neo-craft" approach that seeks to provide low-volume production of mass-market products with craft levels of variety and quality, focusing on two examples reflecting different production processes: the body-welding shop of Kurata Corporation, an affiliate of Mazda in Japan, and the assembly shop at Volvo's Uddevalla plant.

TECHNICAL CAPABILITIES

Kurata, the Mazda affiliate, has developed an innovative approach to handling the welding requirements of a low-volume, high-variety plant. Rather than a moving line that carries the various stamped parts and subassemblies past long rows of welding robots, the Kurata system has essentially one work station. The body is held on a pallet, and there is a short section of track adjacent to the work station, shaped like a T. One set of welds are applied while the pallet is held stationary, with robots moving around the vehicle. Then the pallet moves down the track, out of the way, and the robots move around the work station to reset the jigs that will hold the body for a new set of welds. The pallet returns to its position in the work station, the jigs move in to hold the body, and the robots apply another set of welds. After a few iterations of this process, all welds are completed. The entire welding area takes up about one-tenth the space of a conventional body line.

Uddevalla is the most recent of Volvo's experiments in innovative work redesign. From the start, Uddevalla was seen by proponents of both union and management as an opportunity to test a new technical design that would free automobile workers from the tyranny of the moving assembly line. As such, it marked a substantial step beyond Volvo's first famous experimental plant at Kalmar, where job cycles were lengthened to four-to-six minutes during which teams of workers carried out multiple tasks on a stationary vehicle. At Uddevalla, the line would be completely eliminated, and a work team, starting with a painted body sent from Volvo's main plant in Gothenburg, would assemble an entire car from start to finish.

The technical innovation of "no moving line" was the core feature of Uddevalla, from which its other design parameters emerged: one completely flexible work station at which all assembly tasks could be carried out by a single team; six physically distinct "minifactories," each containing eight-to-ten teams; very long cycle times (up to 3.5 hours); and automated routing of materials from a central warehouse to each "minifactory."

One area of potential difficulty with this approach is material handling, as was most apparent at Uddevalla. With the vehicle built at a fixed location, and hence limited storage space adjacent to the work station, all parts must be routed in sequence from a central warehouse. This is a relatively complex task even when only a single model is being built, but becomes much more complex as variety increases.

Thus the technical features, broadly described, of Kurata and Uddevalla are quite similar. The moving line is eliminated, in favor of a very flexible work station at a fixed location. Little physical space is required. Work cycles are very long. Materials must be routed flexibly to the fixed work station, with precise timing to match the sequence of activities carried out there. Each work station can hypothetically handle a variety of models, or variety can be generated by assigning separate models to different work stations or "minifactories."

ORGANIZATIONAL CAPABILITIES

The organizational and human resource characteristics of these two examples are quite similar. Kurata had a flat organization, with a team of multiskilled workers supporting each flexible work station and handling maintenance and quality inspection, as well as some of the programming. Uddevalla also had very few organizational layers, with team leaders reporting directly to the manager of each miniplant, completely autonomous teams making decisions about hiring, schedule, work assignments, and work methods, and a very high level of training to prepare teams to absorb staff (maintenance, quality control) as well as management functions.

One problem with the Uddevalla approach was the lengthy training period for work teams, who were required to learn all the assembly tasks for an entire vehicle. This made the cost of turnover extremely high. Despite Volvo's hope that turnover would be virtually eliminated because of the attractiveness of the Uddevalla jobs, it remained at around 10 percent—better than other Volvo plants but still high. Team efficiency was thus perpetually constrained by the lead-time needed to train new team members.

Also, it proved to be very difficult to design the warehouse jobs to offer the same kind of variety and autonomy as jobs on the self-managed assembly teams. The warehouse employees continue to be bound by the "moving line" of the materials flow. This created discontent because of perceived inequity in working conditions for different groups of employees.

Finally, the high degree of autonomy for each Uddevalla work team made it difficult for knowledge about work methods to be systematized and shared across teams. As Adler and Cole (1993) have noted, Uddevalla created ideal conditions for individual learning, but did not foster widespread organizational learning.

While we know most about these problems at Uddevalla, there is good reason to believe that they may be inherent in the "neo-craft" approach of fixed-location production combined with long job cycles and broad task assignments. Unfortunately, we have no way of knowing whether or not Uddevalla could have overcome these problems, because it is now closed. In 1992, Volvo found itself with a severe overcapacity problem due to stagnant or declining demand in the United States and Europe. As a result, it decided to close the Kalmar and Uddevalla plants, both "assembly-only" plants, rather than closing its fully integrated plants elsewhere in Sweden or in Belgium.

SUMMARY

In these examples, we can see the shape of a modern craft model, capable of greater efficiency in low-volume production than traditional craft methods, yet still allowing a high degree of customization in a complex product mix. Unfortunately, we have little data to assess the full variety-handling potential of such a model. Uddevalla made only one model in the years before it closed, although the variety of options was extremely high. Similarly, the Kurata system has not yet been applied to a high-level of product variety. Both of these low-volume production facilities suffered by being established just before the worldwide slump in auto sales in the early 1990s.

Nevertheless, this "neo-craft" model appears to have the potential for handling a considerable amount of product variety. Each flexible work station at Uddevalla or Kurata could potentially be devoted to a different product. Within the parameters of the low volume associated with niche products, volume fluctuations could be handled by raising or lowering the number of flexible work stations, making a certain product, given low capital investment requirements, very low changeover costs, and flexible labor.

The disadvantages of this approach are logistical complexity, as noted above, and overall efficiency. Although Uddevalla was reportedly more efficient than other Volvo plants, its efficiency was far from matching that of competitors at the time of its closing. Kurata's system was clearly quite efficient at very low production levels because of the low capital investment cost, but it is unclear whether that advantage would be sustained at higher volumes, given the investment and coordination costs associated with multiple welding stations.

Thus the "neo-craft" approach raises more questions than it answers. Can the products built in neo-craft facilities command a high-enough margin in the marketplace to offset the absence of scale economies and relatively high labor costs? Or can these systems multiply their production modules to handle higher volume products while achieving efficiency consistent with the lower margin these products may command in the market? These questions are particularly salient as we turn to examine the third approach to manufacturing—lean production. If lean production can produce similar levels of variety and quality as neo-craft systems at much lower cost, as we will argue, there is less chance that the neo-craft approach will survive and diffuse.

Lean Production

THE VARIETY CHALLENGE

Although lean production is best known for its ability to combine high productivity with high quality (Womack, Jones, and Roos 1990), it is also strongly associated with high-product variety, both historically and at present. The early innovations of lean production at Toyota in the 1950s—small lot production, quick die changes, Just-in-Time inventory systems, the switch from a "push" to a "pull" system of coordinating the flow of parts and vehicles—all emerged in the context of high-product variety. Japan's postwar market was small, the number of competitors high (in 1954, eight companies to serve a market of 70,000 vehicles, vs. four companies serving a market of 6.4 million vehicles in the United States), and the variety of vehicles (including trucks as well as cars) in demand was high. Indeed, Cusumano (1988) has argued that Japan's market requirements for small-lot production of many models in the 1950s is what drove the development of other features of lean production. Product variety has also played a prominent role in the strategic thinking of Japanese companies. As Stalk and Hout (1990) note, product proliferation has often been used as a strategic weapon to win market share, once price and quality criteria can be successfully met by various companies.

As noted above, mass production thinking emphasizes an inevitable trade-off between cost and variety or quality and variety. For lean-production companies, the variety challenge has been to avoid such a tradeoff by developing the manufacturing capabilities to handle greater product complexity. To the extent that manufacturing investments—in both technical and organizational capabilities—allow lean-production companies to absorb higher complexity without penalty, these companies gain more degrees of freedom for strategic decisions to increase product variety. Still, strategic decisions to boost variety may outpace a company's ability to handle complexity in its manufacturing plants. Recent reports suggest that Japanese auto companies are beginning to rethink the level of product variety they offer, concluding that they have allowed design engineers too much latitude in developing product variants in which customers have little interest (*Automotive News*, May 17, 1993). Thus, the current variety challenge for lean production may be avoiding *overinvesting* in flexibility.

TECHNICAL CAPABILITIES

Most lean-production companies follow a policy of making technology as flexible as possible. Heavy investments are made in purchases of robots and other programmable automation, in both new and older plants, so that the average level of flexible equipment in a lean company's plants is higher than in a mass production company, where such new equipment tends to be concentrated in newer plants only. In addition, great attention is paid to expanding the range of flexibility of key process technology to create the ability to handle very different platforms and models.

For example, both Toyota and Mazda have developed flexible body lines that allow for a very diverse product mix. While similar to the "robogates" developed by Fiat, they are based on a somewhat different design philosophy. Both Toyota and Mazda use a carrier for the body that has special jigs on its interior face that are customized to a specific model of a specific platform, but an exterior face that creates a fully standardized envelope. Any carrier can pass through a line consisting of completely general-purpose welding stations, with weld robots reprogrammed for each different model. The only model-specific development required is the interior jigs for the carrier, which can be fabricated separately and added to the storage pool of carriers as a new model joins the product mix. Parameters for maximum length and width are the only constraints to what can be built on such a line. While the investment cost for new carriers can be relatively high if the volume of a new product is high, the threshold investment for introducing a few units of a new model is minimal.

Savings from these flexible body lines can accrue in multiple ways. Since the life of the welding equipment is longer than the four-year product cycle, there is no need for expensive retooling when major model changes occur. Also, as demand for models fluctuates, the mix of products on a given line can be adjusted simply by changing the mix of model-specific carriers that circulate through the line. Products can even be moved from one line to another in this way. With this range of flexibility available, Toyota and Mazda rarely use the full variety-absorbing capacity of their body lines. They appear to value this system for giving them the ability to adjust product variety up and down, as appropriate to market conditions and product strategy.

ORGANIZATIONAL CAPABILITIES

While there are some differences between the automation strategies of lean-production and mass-production companies, a far greater difference exists in how these two systems approach the organization of work and the management of human resources. Rather than layers of staff specialists to deal with the ramifications of manufacturing complexity, lean production relies on teams of multiskilled workers to play a major role in absorbing product variety. Workers in a traditional mass-production plant are trained in one simple task and conditioned to avoid any activity that might imperil reaching production targets. If a problem occurs, such as a mixup of parts, these are remedied not during regular production but in postprocess repair. In this situation, any increase in product variety is risky, for it requires both additional skills and a higher level of attentiveness from workers not accustomed to changes in the production routine; hence, higher product variety is likely to raise supervision, inspection, and repair costs in the traditional mass-production operation.

In contrast, workers who are members of work teams are explicitly trained in multiple skills, both off-the-job and on-the-job through job rotation. Because teams are responsible for overseeing their own quality, workers are accustomed to a more proactive, attentive stance towards production and are authorized to stop the line, when necessary, to prevent passing a production problem downstream to other work stations. A worker already attentive for quality problems is better prepared to deal with the demands of higher product variety.

Furthermore, through *kaizen* or continuous improvement activities, teams can also improve their ability to handle product variety over time. In team meetings and quality circles, workers may suggest better methods of parts presentation. Through their standardized work activities, in which teams refine their work methods to eliminate waste and improve cost and quality, various sources of line imbalance may be minimized, thus limiting the balance losses associated with the variability of options from vehicle to vehicle.

SUMMARY

The ultimate advantage of lean production with respect to product variety derives from the fact that its technical and organizational capabilities reinforce each other. For example, take the well-known innovation of just-in-time (JIT) inventory systems. When the inventory of parts for each distinct model is kept extremely low, high product variety has a minimal impact on inventory holding costs. When lineside inventory is minimized, extra space is created for the staging and presentation of parts to workers, allowing for better layout and less walking time to get parts. Furthermore, when suppliers can package parts for JIT delivery in the exact sequence they will be used on the assembly line, parts selection is much less complex for workers.

Realizing these benefits of JIT requires team members who understand the logic of minimizing inventory buffers and are motivated to identify and deal with problem conditions that are revealed. A multiskilled and motivated workforce can also facilitate quick die changes—crucial to allow small lot production of stamped parts for different models—and improve performance through ongoing modifications of equipment layout, set up, and operations.

Lean-production companies can certainly benefit from parts sharing and other mass-production-derived techniques for minimizing manufacturing complexity, and indeed, they tend to emphasize this approach during periods of stagnant demand. But more distinctive is the willingness of lean-production companies to invest heavily in extremely flexible capabilities, both technical and organizational, often far beyond what may be utilized at any given point in time. The question this raises is whether lean production actually tends to *overinvest* in flexibility. We will address this below, in our discussion of the current efforts of the Japanese auto companies to reduce product variety.

Variety and Flexibility as Sources of Productivity Gains

Gains in the Marketplace

The market benefits of product variety derive from customers who have diverse, changing, and unpredictable needs. Such an environment rewards a manufacturer who can offer a diverse portfolio of products and whose operations are flexible enough to allow rapid adjustment of product mix as customer requirements change. For example, the popularity of small cars tends to ebb and flow with the price of gasoline. Soon electric cars will enter the scene and their sales should also be strongly correlated with the cost of various types of energy, as well as with pollution regulations. The development time for a car model is too long to allow one to predict when development is started what energy prices will be when the car is launched. But if a manufacturer's lineup includes both small and large cars, as well as electric cars, and if it has the flexibility to move production among these various types, it can insulate from the loss of sales and market share that can result from changing customer tastes.

By contrast, a manufacturer with a limited product selection or inflexible plants dedicated to individual models may be forced to produce more of a particular model—just to keep the plant running at close to capacity—than the market is willing to buy. The manufacturer is then led to follow a philosophy *The Economist* (December 12, 1992, 79–80) calls "Pile them high and sell them cheap." Price discounts are offered in the form of rebates to induce customers to purchase the unwanted production. One form this practice takes is manufacturers selling cars at deep discounts to rental agencies. General Motors has recently received favorable publicity for taking the bold step of abandoning this policy: "Under the eye of the Strategy Board, GM abolished its policy of flooding the daily rental market with cars in order to balance production schedules. 'We figure that decision is worth $300 million to $400 million' in profits this year, Losh says. (Mike Losh, GM's vice-president and group executive of North American sales, service, and marketing)" (*Automotive News*, May 17, 1993).

The two modes of operation stand in sharp contrast: the first relies on flexibility and product variety to adapt production to consumer needs; the second uses price to adapt consumer purchases to production requirements. Shunji Koike, a Japanese entrepreneur who had perfected the first approach summarizes his philosophy as "we don't sell what we produce; we produce what sells," a stark contrast to Henry Ford's "any color as long as it's black" philosophy.

Another benefit of producing what sells is that your sales then become a much better indicator of true customer preferences. National Bicycle has exploited this benefit to great advantage in their custom-made bicycle operation that sits beside their much larger mass-production plant (*Fortune*, October 22, 1990, 132–35). They use the colors ordered in their custom-production facility, where they offer essentially infinite color variety, as a gauge of customer's color preference. The most popular colors are then scheduled for production in the mass-production facility.

Increased Capacity Utilization

As we have mentioned above, the growth in product variety makes it imperative that manufacturing processes become flexible. Once acquired, however, process flexibility becomes not only an important competitive weapon in the variety-driven marketplace, it also becomes a strong hedge against uncertainty in demand volumes.

The demand for many products is notoriously hard to forecast, even over a short horizon. In the auto industry, some firms have experienced an average difference of about 40 percent (both positive and negative) between forecasts one-to-three years in the future and actual sales for individual nameplates (Jordan and Graves 1991). These forecasts are crucial because they form the basis for decisions on capacity investment and tooling, which must be made one-to-three years before start of production. As product variety increases, so does the uncertainty in demand for individual models.

There are two points that need to be emphasized in this context. First, compared to dedicated processes, flexible processes can provide a big improvement in capacity utilization when demand is uncertain. When plants are dedicated to specific models, then a downturn in demand leads to underutilization of capacity, and an upturn in demand, if it exceeds capacity, can lead to lost sales. When plants have the flexibility to coproduce different models, then the excess demand of a model can be shifted to a plant that is experiencing low sales of another model; and the system as a whole minimizes both capacity underutilization and lost sales. During fieldwork in the auto industry, we encountered numerous examples where flexibility, necessitated originally by the need to accommodate multiple models in the same plant, has also proven to be an effective way to absorb demand fluctuations without incurring low-capacity utilization. For example, Mazda now bases its plant configuration and process-design decisions explicitly on how demand variability will affect utilization.

Second, a little bit of flexibility can go a long way in hedging against the uncertainty of demand—one does not need full flexibility (that is, all processes capable of producing all the products) to get almost all the benefits of full flexibility. If each assembly line can produce a few different models, which overlap sufficiently, then the system as a whole can absorb a high-demand volatility by sharing capacity. The same logic applies to processes within the assembly line; for instance, in body framing and welding—where it is difficult and expensive to achieve full flexibility—can consist of two or more parallel lines, each capable of handling two or more models. Several auto companies we studied have implemented, to varying degrees of sophistication, their version of this concept. Toyota's FBL (Flexible Body Line), Nissan's IBAS (Intelligent Body Assembly System), and Mazda's C-BAL (Circulation Body Assembly Line) are among the most flexible systems for body welding. The investment in these systems has been rewarded by the firms' ability to keep capacity utilization high and to respond quickly and profitably to the emergence of small niche markets.

It is important to recognize that the *configuration* for achieving flexibility must be chosen carefully. Jordan and Graves (1991) demonstrate through an analytical model that with a configuration that requires barely 10 percent of the investment of full flexibility, firms can achieve more than 90 percent of the benefits of full flexibility. Under the assumptions of their model (e.g., that demands for different products are uncorrelated), they show that the "chain" configuration achieves the best results. Plants are in a chain configuration when each plant is capable of producing two distinct products and each product can be made by two distinct processes. Figure 6.5 is an example of a chain linking ten products and ten processes (the line segment between a product and process means that the former can be made by the latter).

Throughput Gains from Product Complementarity

In this section we present the argument that in the presence of flexible manu-facturing processes and multiskilled workers, product variety can be a source of

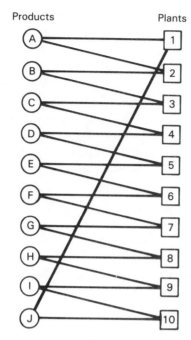

Figure 6.5.   The "Chain" Configuration.

improvements in productivity. This view is contrary to the "focused factory" argument for limiting the scope of plants (and of processes within plants) to a few closely related products. While our argument is motivated partly by analytical models, our fieldwork in the auto industry also suggests that world-class firms benefit from high product variety by exploiting the opportunity that variety offers for improving productivity, capacity utilization, and lead-times in operations.

The introduction of variety on an assembly line—with different models presenting different processing requirements to the workstations—can upset the "balance" established for a line originally dedicated to a single product. In balancing an assembly line, industrial engineers attempt to minimize the unproductive time spent by workers (or machines) waiting for the next job. If it were possible to subdivide the total assembly task into equal segments, then balancing would be trivial and worker (or machine) utilization would be 100 percent. However, due to the discrete nature of many assembly tasks, equal subdivision is usually not possible. In auto assembly lines, it is often hard to achieve anything less than 15–20 percent forced idleness (or "balance loss," as it is called).

Adding variety to an assembly line would seem at first glance to exacerbate the balance loss. However, variety also provides the opportunity to *reduce* balance loss by judiciously mixing in jobs that complement each others' processing requirements. To see how "product complementarity" works, consider a simple example. Suppose that a manufacturing process consists of two operations carried out at two work stations (labelled W_1 and W_2 in Figure 6.6 below).

Suppose that no work-in-process (WIP) is allowed to accumulate between the two workstations (as is the case in most assembly lines). Consequently, if W_2 happens to be busy with a job when W_1 gets done with its job, then W_1 must wait for W_2 to finish before the former can begin the next job (since there is no in-process buffer). In this situation, W_1 is said to be *blocked*. Conversely, if W_2 gets done with its job (which leaves the process as a finished unit) while W_1 is still busy, then W_2 is forced to be idle until W_1 finishes the job and moves it down to W_2. In this situation, W_2 is said to be *starved*.

Suppose that the above process is used to produce product X, which, due to the indivisibility of its tasks, has uneven processing requirements at the two work stations: As indicated in Figure 6.6, a unit of product X requires five minutes at W_1 and one minute at W_2. This process produces one unit of X every five minutes (twelve units/hour), with W_2 starving four minutes in every five-minute cycle.

Consider now the introduction of product variety to this process. Suppose that another product—let us call it Y—can be coproduced on our process without any loss of time at a work station to change over from one product to the other. Suppose product Y is "complementary" to product X in its processing requirements at the two work stations: It requires one minute at W_1 and five minutes at W_2. Now if products X and Y are produced in *alternating sequence*, we observe the following (see Figure 6.7). In steady state, when W_1 is processing product X, W_2 processes product Y. Upon completion of the respective jobs, product X moves down to W_2 and W_1 begins work on the next unit of product Y. We notice that there is a *six-minute cycle* during the first five minutes of which

Single Product

Product X

Throughput = 12 units/hour

Figure 6.6. The Single Product.

Mixed–Model Line: Two Products

Throughput: 2 units every 6 minutes
= 20 units/hr.

Figure 6.7. Mixed-Model Line, Two Products.

product X gets processed at W_1 while product Y gets finished at W_2 (each requiring five minutes). Then it takes one more minute for product X to move down to W_2 and receive processing while the next unit of product Y gets done at W_1. Thus, every six minutes we get one unit each of products X and Y, giving us a throughput rate of twenty units/hour. This improvement over the original throughput is achieved by combining two complementary products to eliminate the unproductive idle time at workstations.

Data from the Harvard Business School case *Okuma Machinery Works Ltd.* (A) (1989) illustrate how complementarity can lead to productivity gains in a realistic setting. The case describes technological choices faced by a Japanese developer of flexible manufacturing systems (FMS). One of the issues in the case is the estimation of the benefits of *mixed-model* capability in a proposed FMS. While the existing system requires set ups to switch between families of parts, the mixed-model FMS would allow parts of *any* family to be processed— in arbitrary sequence and in arbitrarily small lot sizes—without tool or fixture set ups. The mixed-model FMS clearly provides savings in set-up cost and the ability to produce small lots of parts on a JIT basis for downstream requirements, thus reducing WIP inventory of parts. However, a more substantial (and less apparent) source of benefits is the productivity improvement through greater capacity utilization achieved by exploiting the complementarities that exist across different part families.

The FMS consists of five numerically controlled machining centers, which perform different operations on each part as it proceeds through the system. The processing time required by a part at each machining center varies from one part family to another; Table 6.1, reproduced from the case, contains data on the processing times needed by the existing 16 part families at the five machining centers (labelled M1 through M5).

On the existing FMS, parts within the same family are run in large batches for each set up of the system, and the throughput rate is determined by the bot-

TABLE 6.1. Processing Requirements

Machine	Processing Time in Minutes for Part Families															
	1	2	3	4	5	6	7	8	9	10	11	12	13	14	15	16
M1	1.6	1.8	1.8	2.5	2.2	3.0	3.0	2.6	3.2	2.5	3.4	1.7	1.8	3.0	2.5	1.8
M2	2.5	1.7	2.7	2.2	2.8	3.3	2.6	2.8	2.5	2.2	2.6	2.7	2.6	2.5	2.4	2.4
M3	1.9	1.7	1.8	2.4	2.2	3.1	2.9	2.7	3.0	2.4	2.5	2.6	1.7	3.2	2.4	1.4
M4	2.6	1.8	2.0	2.4	3.2	3.2	2.0	2.7	2.0	2.4	2.2	2.9	3.0	1.4	2.3	3.2
M5	2.3	1.6	3.0	2.3	3.1	3.0	2.2	2.8	1.6	2.3	1.8	3.3	3.4	1.7	2.4	3.0
Total	10.9	8.6	11.3	11.8	13.5	15.6	12.7	13.6	12.3	11.8	12.5	13.2	12.5	11.8	12.0	11.8

Source: From Okuma Machinery Works Ltd. (A) Case (1989).

144

tleneck operation. For instance, when the system is running part family 13, finished parts are produced once every 3.4 minutes, with machines M1 through M4 being underutilized. The proposed mixed-model FMS would allow part families to be "interleaved" to take advantage of complementarities. For instance, if parts of families 13 and 11 are produced in an alternating sequence as opposed to running large batches for each, the average time per part goes down from 3.4 minutes to 3.2 minutes, a 5.9 percent improvement. In general, the potential for productivity gains improves as more parts are added to the mixed-model sequence. Our analysis shows, for example, that combining part families 13–5–14–7–11–13 (and running them in that cyclic sequence) would bring down the average time per part by almost 10 percent compared to running large batches (see Jain (1993) for details). This gain is purely due to complementarity and does not include savings in set-up time on the proposed FMS. Figure 6.8 shows how the throughput rate improves as more families are added to the model mix on the FMS.

The idea of complementarity can be generalized to assembly lines with an arbitrary number of work stations and products and with or without intermediate buffers (Jain 1992). Determination of the grouping and sequence of products that maximizes complementarity in the general case becomes a nontrivial optimization problem that can be addressed through mathematical programming methods. As we noted above, greater product variety brings better opportunity for finding complementarities (though it also adds greater complexity to the mathematical optimization).

Throughput gain from complementarity also depends upon the mechanism

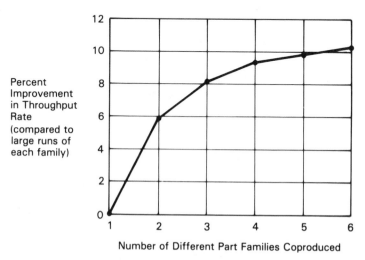

Figure 6.8. Throughput Gains from Complementarity.

governing the flow of jobs on the assembly line. The gain is highest when jobs on the line can move *asynchronously* of each other. The job flow is called *asynchronous* when each job, upon completion at a work station, can move to the downstream work station, unless the downstream work station is busy (in which case the job blocks the current work station). A *synchronous* flow places a restriction on the asynchronous discipline: the movement from one work station to the next must be simultaneous for all jobs. The most restricted case is that of the *constant-pace* line, where each job gets the same "window" of time at each work station.

Traditionally, most segments of auto assembly plants have a constant-pace line. Recognizing the benefits of asynchronous flow, however, some modern plants have begun to abandon the moving conveyor line. Their place is taken by automated guided vehicles (AGV) carrying the jobs and moving asynchronously from each other. Nissan's new assembly plant at Kyushu, for instance, has attracted much attention lately for using AGV's throughout the assembly process. Nissan's executives expect this and related innovations to make Kyushu 30 percent more productive than their other plants (*The Wall Street Journal*, July 6, 1992). Other plants have also adopted this concept. For example, the Volvo BV plant in the Netherlands also uses AGV's, which stop at work stations where teams of workers perform roughly an hour of assembly tasks before routing the AGV to the next station.

Organizational Gains

A manufacturing environment of high product variety can provide a very effective "learning system" for the organization. The organizational capabilities needed to operate effectively in a high-variety environment are also useful in dealing with many contingencies. The acquisition of multiple skills by workers in a high-variety plant can serve as an organizational "buffer" to avoid disruption in the face of problems and breakdowns. Organizations with these capabilities also absorb more effectively the discontinuities caused by volume swings and new product launches.

Organizational flexibility also leads to better utilization of "human capital" and work time. Workers who are multiskilled across different *products* will better absorb demand variability in the same way that "chaining" allows different plants to share capacity. Workers who are multiskilled across different *processes* mitigate the need for in-process buffers that are used as insurance against breakdowns. Indeed, it could be argued that the flexible skills and capacity for improvement of the work force *become* the new buffer that allows the organization to absorb contingencies. This is why Japanese companies pay more attention to labor utilization and worker skill enrichment than to equipment utilization.

Flexibility with respect to product mix and volume changes can have unexpected benefits for issues that appear to have little to do with variety. Production of the *Miata* sports car was at one point moved from Mazda's main production complex at Hiroshima to the Hofu plant eighty miles (a two-hour drive) away. The reason was Mazda's lifetime employment policy. Demand was very low for products made at Hofu, so the plant was operating at half capacity, while demand was still high at the Hiroshima plant. With a "no layoff" policy and no easy way to move workers between plants, it was easier for Mazda to balance the utilization of the work force by moving the product, even though this meant that a niche sports car had to be integrated into the production mix with the Mazda 626, a midsize family sedan. Since the mass production practice of using layoffs and hiring to adjust labor inputs to capacity was unavailable, Mazda derived considerable organizational benefit from its ability to handle changing levels of product variety at all of its plants.

Finally, the coupling of broad production knowledge, employee motivation, and a flexible system of work specification and task allocation at lean production companies creates a fertile environment for experimentation with new products and processes—something that generates invaluable feedback for product designers and improves design-for-manufacturability. For example, pilot vehicles are often built in regular assembly plants at lean production companies, with workers involved in developing task specifications for upcoming models, compared with mass production companies that utilize a specialized pilot plant with a separate work force. This willingness to use the assembly plant as a locus of learning is antithetical to the mass production view of manufacturing as a domain of standardization and not-to-be-interrupted production, and provides the most significant organizational gain from pursuing a high flexibility/high variety strategy.

Conclusions

In this closing section, we summarize our recommendations for handling product variety and look ahead at future trends for product variety in the international automotive industry.

Handling Product Variety

While effective management of product variety can provide important competitive advantages for a company, a high-variety strategy also creates some management challenges. Our first observation is that companies need a market strategy to successfully minimize "market defects," that is, product varieties that customers simply do not want. Two things are needed as part of such a strategy:

1) periodic housekeeping to get rid of dysfunctional variety in the product line that may have served a purpose once, but no longer does.; and 2) basing the introduction of new variety on true customer needs and preferences. This is hard to do because these needs and preferences are often unknown. But many companies are finding ways to encourage a high level of interaction with customers to obtain their reactions to various products, and to elicit ideas for new product development. Developing the right sort of information from customers is clearly crucial to avoiding "market defects."

Some of the difficulties of Japanese auto companies in the early 1990s can be attributed to a period in the late 1980s when designers were given free rein to develop any product variant that customers might conceivably find appealing. Many of these variants simply did not sell, not even when the market was relatively strong, and the subsequent recession and collapse of demand has worsened the impact of these design choices. Whatever the capability of "lean" assembly plants to absorb high levels of product complexity in support of a "high-variety" strategy, the best manufacturing plant cannot remedy the problem of unwanted products.

Our second point takes issue with what is becoming conventional wisdom about handling product variety: parts sharing across models. United States, European, and Japanese companies alike have announced ambitious programs to increase the share of common parts to 30 percent across models on the same platform. We recognize the allure of a solution that promises to minimize complexity for the manufacturing plant while still allowing a wide array of variants and options for any given product. Nevertheless, we believe that the consequences of variety-reducing designs need more careful investigation before they are embraced wholeheartedly. No company seems to have a clear strategy for avoiding the "Achilles' heel" of parts sharing: products—across niches or segments differentiated by price—that look alike. Moreover, the coordination costs of parts sharing are not trivial, as past unsuccessful efforts to design a "world car" have shown. Similarly, "design for manufacturing," particularly when focused on such variety-related goals as reducing total parts count, can be accompanied by considerable costs, particularly in lengthened product development time (Ulrich et al 1993). Mass production companies may bear the greatest risk here, because their strong inclination to minimize variety makes them vulnerable to seeing parts sharing and design-for-manufacturing (DFM) as a panacea.

Third, our analysis of different company strategies with respect to product variety supports the wisdom of investing heavily in flexible manufacturing capabilities—including technology, organizational systems, and human skills.

Combined, these flexible capabilities offer far more than the ability to make multiple products simultaneously. They also offer the benefits of reduced changeover costs across product generations, the ability to adjust product mix in the face of uncertain demand, even at volumes that would be unprofitable for a more rigidly organized facility, and the ability to use the factory as a testing ground for new products and production processes.

Indeed, it is important to note that a plant's flexibility does not need to be in use at all times to justify investing in it. The ability to avoid costly underutilization of capacity and to minimize the time and cost of a major retrofit are benefits that can easily outweigh the cost of such an investment. However, increasing investments of this kind, whether in robotics or in worker training, can be difficult in the face of accounting systems that overstate the costs and understate the benefits of flexibility. Changing the accounting mindset about flexible technical and organizational capabilities may therefore be a necessary precondition to boosting investments as discussed in chapter seven of this book.

The human resource aspect of flexibility is often overlooked because of mass production assumptions about the benefits of narrowly skilled, interchangeable employees for the standardization of production. Work force flexibility with respect to product variety is not simply a matter of more training for cross-skilling. When the problem-solving abilities of the work force are developed in the context of a plant culture that emphasizes constant experimentation with production processes, the plant has a new sort of "buffer" available. In place of the "just-in-case" buffers of inventory that provided a way to deal with various unexpected contingencies in mass production, an attentive, skilled, and motivated work force that is accustomed to rethinking work processes and respecifying work can absorb contingencies in a different way: resolving rather than hiding problems.

Finally, we urge companies to take a broader view of the potential gains from product variety. In part, this requires an "economies-of-scope" way of thinking that seeks out efficiency-enhancing complementarities across products. In part, it may require yet again more investment in flexible capabilities than is indicated by a firm's product strategy. The greatest payoff to a broader view of product variety and manufacturing flexibility may come when investments in flexibility are coupled with "quick response" strategies of distribution (Fisher and Raman 1992). This approach to distribution helps to generate a tremendous amount of valuable data for product designers and manufacturing planners. The more companies "produce what sells" rather than "sell what they produce" the lower the rate of "market defects" and the greater the market gains of variety.

Looking Ahead: Variety in the Automotive Industry

Each of the primary auto-producing regions—the United States, Europe, and Japan—has a different history with respect to product variety and appears likely to follow a different trajectory in its future approach to variety.

For the "Big Three" in the United States, decisions on variety still seem to be guided by a mass-production logic. While recognizing increasing consumer demand for variety, the Big Three have largely tried to accomodate this demand without altering their practice of high-volume production of core models in plants mostly dedicated to single platforms. When choices about variety strategy have needed to be made, the Big Three have increasingly opted for variety reduction, partly as a consequence of their determined drive to match or exceed Japanese levels of productivity and quality.

One example of this trend was the "option deproliferation" drive that swept through the Big Three during the mid-1980s. This effort sought to remedy a situation in which manufacturing plants had to be ready to make vehicles with any one of millions of possible option combinations, regardless of whether customers showed much interest in the vast majority of these combinations. Although such pruning was needed, it was linked to other efforts to consolidate platforms, reduce models and generally return to "focused factories," and hence represented a step away from variety.

A more recent example is General Motors' drive to regain profitability after an alarming loss of market share in the 1980s. Central to this effort is a steady cutback in platforms and product variants. CEO Jack Smith has established a policy that GM will focus on "core products that have the potential of leading their class in sales while delivering the best customer attributes, price, quality, and features" (*Automotive News*, May 17, 1993). The number of car platforms will be reduced to five and the number of product development teams to just three for small cars, mid-sized and rear-drive cars, and large, front-drive luxury cars. Models are being trimmed each year. In 1991, GM offered 144 car model selections (including captive imports manufactured by other companies), a number reduced to 126 in 1992 and 117 in 1993. This reduction targets variants of popular models that have not sold well.

GM's actions in reducing product variety are significant, because in relative terms, GM has been the high-variety producer of the Big Three as a consequence of Alfred Sloan's product differentiation strategy. On the whole, the Big Three's strategy toward variety in the past ten years has been to reduce it, even at a time when the number of product offerings in the U.S. market has exploded. Only recently has Ford begun to break from this pattern by offering more variants of its popular truck and sport utility models.

European companies have had a very different approach to product variety, partly out of necessity as they rebuilt their industry on an export-oriented strategy of low-volume niche products. Since many of these were luxury/specialty products, they typically contained high levels of option content, with customers being given wide latitude in custom-ordering option combinations. Because these products were exported to many countries, European companies have long had to face export-driven variety based on different regulatory requirements, for example, catalytic converters for the U.S. market but not for Europe. As a result of these conditions and a strong tradition of craft production dating back to the early days of the industry, European companies have long been accustomed to dealing with variety.

This experience does not, however, mean that European companies have had a "no tradeoff" view of variety. Higher-cost products have long been accepted as the price European customers must pay for a wide array of product and feature choices. Furthermore, European companies have long felt the pull of scale economies and mass-production logic. Ironically, European companies moved away somewhat from a high-variety strategy in the 1980s when the sales volume for popular models from Fiat, VW, and Renault reached historic levels, with plants increasingly dedicated to these products. Nevertheless, to the extent that company capabilities to handle high levels of product variety remain competitively important in the 1990s, European companies should be well positioned. The dilemma these companies face is how to increase their productivity and quality levels to world standards while maintaining their traditional strengths in handling high product variety.

The situation for Japanese companies is particularly fluid. With the bursting of the "bubble" economy and stagnant sales, compounded by overinvestment in new plants, Japanese companies have been forced to cope with financial losses and severe underutilization of plant capacity. In 1993, Nissan decided to close its Zama plant, the first plant closing in Japan in the postwar era. Against this backdrop, the rapid proliferation of product variety in Japan in the 1980s has become a highly visible problem. Many companies have announced ambitious programs to trim model variants and to increase parts sharing in an effort to bring product variety under control. For example, Toyota has announced that it will reduce varieties of the *Corolla* model from eleven to six; Mazda has eliminated seventy-six variations of its *929* model; and Nissan has announced it would reduce its number of engines by 40 percent over the next five years (Stalk and Webber 1993).

The crucial question from our perspective is whether the current problems of too much variety in Japan should be interpreted primarily as "market defects"—versions of products that suited the fancy of designers but did not interest consumers—or as evidence that manufacturers had exceeded their ability to handle variety. In the former case, product variants may be trimmed and rationalized, but manufacturing capabilities to absorb variety would remain unchanged. In the latter case, we might expect to see companies moving their production systems back along the continuum toward mass production of more standardized products.

Early indications from our interviews suggest that Japanese companies still place an extremely high priority on manufacturing flexibility. There is little sign that they will back away from their investment in flexible capabilities, whether technological or organizational. We have heard of no plans for cutting back on the number of platforms—not surprising, since multiproject coordination of product development for rapid design transfer across platforms has become the norm across Japanese companies (Nobeoka and Cusumano 1993)— nor of plans to trim option content. There will be trimming in the intermediate category of product complexity—fewer different body styles per model, offered with fewer engine/transmission combinations, for example. We see the current pruning of product variety as more an application of "lean" principles to the "waste" of market defects than as any retreat toward the low-variety, mass-production model.

Nevertheless, Japanese companies may continue to face difficulties in their manufacturing plants that make it difficult for them to maintain high variety without some cost or quality penalty. Labor shortages at the assemblers reduces the skill and experience base of the work force and increases the training requirements needed to achieve multiskilling. Labor shortages at suppliers can threaten parts quality at the assembly plant and supplier capabilities for in-sequence delivery to the assembly plant. If more defective parts reach the assembler and in-sequence delivery drops, the burden of variety on the assembler work force will be greater than ever.

Thus, while a "variety/flexibility" gap continues to exist between Japan and the United States, there is a great opportunity for American auto companies to move beyond their legacy of low variety. If the American Big Three could close the *variety* gap as quickly as they have been able to close the cost and quality gap with Japan, they could be even more formidable competitors. At the present time, however, the current trend of American companies toward variety *reduction* suggests that the "variety gap" will continue.

This suggests a broader conclusion. Growth in product variety seems to be an inexorable trend in many industries as customers get more discriminating and marketers become increasingly focused in their search for niche markets. Minimizing variety may not be a viable choice in such circumstances. Firms will be forced to cope with variety. Thus, the strategic stance of the firm toward variety becomes critically important. Firms that acquire and develop the building blocks of flexibility proactively can win by making product variety a source of competitive advantage. Those that get trapped in the variety/cost tradeoff stand to lose.

Note

The work of the first and second authors was supported in part by the National Science Foundation and General Motors under industry/academia collaborative grant NSF SES91-09798. The work of the third author was supported by the International Motor Vehicle Program at MIT, one of the Sloan Foundation-funded projects on industrial competitiveness. We are also grateful to Mr. Denis Hamilton, Director of Quality Management and Customer Satisfaction at the Johnson & Johnson Quality Institute, for his insightful comments on an earlier draft of the paper.

References

Adler, Paul. 1988. Managing flexible automation. *California Management Review* XX:34–56.

Adler, Paul, and Robert E. Cole. 1993. Designed for Learning A Tale of Two Auto Plants. *Sloan Management Review* 34:85–94.

Attewell, Paul. 1987. The deskilling controversy. *Work and Occupations* 14:323–46.

Banker, Rajiv D., Srikant M. Datar, Sunder Kekre, and Tridas Mukhopadhyay. 1990. Costs of product and process complexity. In *Measures of manufacturing excellence*, edited by R. Kaplan. Boston: Harvard Business School Press.

Cappelli, Peter. 1993. Are skill requirements rising? Evidence from production and clerical jobs. *Industrial and Labor Relations Review* 46(3):515–30.

Cusumano, Michael. 1988. Manufacturing innovation: Lessons from the Japanese auto industry. *Sloan Management Review* 30:29–40.

Fisher, Marshall L., and Ananth Raman. 1992. The value of quick response for supplying fashion products: Analysis and application. Working Paper 92-10-03, Operations and Information Management Department, the Wharton School.

Hounshell, David A. 1984. *From the American system to mass production 1800–1932.* Baltimore: Johns Hopkins.

Jaikumar, Ramchandran. 1986. Postindustrial manufacturing. *Harvard Business Review* 64:69–76.

Jain, Anjani. 1992. Batching and sequencing in mixed-model assembly lines. Working Paper, Department of Operations and Information Management, the Wharton School.

Jain, Anjani. 1993. A case analysis of *Okuma machinery works.* Teaching Note, Department of Operations and Information Management, the Wharton School.

Jordan, William C., and Stephen C. Graves. 1991. Principles on the benefits of manufacturing process flexibility. Research Paper, General Motors Research Laboratories.

Kekre, Sunder, and Kannan Srinivasan. 1990. Broader product line: A necessity to achieve success? *Management Science* 36:1216–31.

MacDuffie, John Paul, Kannen Sethuraman, and Marshall L. Fisher. Product variety and manufacturing performance: Evidence from the international automotive assembly plant study. *Management Science* (forthcoming).

MacDuffie, John Paul, and Thomas A. Kochan. 1995. Does the U.S. underinvest in human resources? Determinants of training in the world auto industry. *Industrial Relations* (forthcoming).

Nobeoka, Kentaro, and Michael Cusumano. 1993. Multiproject management: Strategy and organization in automobile product development. Working Paper, International Motor Vehicle Program, MIT.

Okuma machinery works (A). 1989. HBS Case #687-038. Boston: Harvard Business School Publishing.

Stalk, George, and Alan M. Webber. 1993. Japan's dark side of time. *Harvard Business Review* 71:93–102.

Stalk, George, and Thomas Hout. 1990. *Competing against time: How time-based competition is reshaping global markets.* New York: The Free Press.

Womack, James P., Daniel Jones, and Daniel Roos. 1990. *The machine that changed the world.* New York: Rawson Associates.

Ulrich, Karl, David Sartorius, Scott Pearson, and Mark Jakiela. 1993. Including the value of time in design-for-manufacturing decision making. *Management Science* 39.

7

How Control Systems Can Support Organization Flexibility

CHRISTOPHER D. ITTNER AND BRUCE KOGUT

Ronald Dore, a sociologist at Cambridge University, once posed the question of why Japan should evidence a paradox of "flexible rigidities." Despite being a country marked by rigid restrictions on the lay off of workers and on the mobility of capital, the economic record of Japan shows a remarkable flexibility in coping with the major economic shocks of the 1970s. In comparison, the economic adjustment of the major Western countries progressed more slowly.

We are puzzled by the converse problem: why do firms find it so difficult to become more flexible? The advantages of flexibility are clear, ranging from the capability to tailor products and services for customers to the facility to expand rapidly when market opportunities suddenly open up. The creation of new information technologies and manufacturing systems has created the potential to achieve dramatically higher degrees of flexibility. The impact of these technologies is felt not only on the plant floor, but also in the way financial and retail services are provided and supply chains are managed.

The flexibility possible with current technologies is a qualitative change from past practice. Unfortunately, these technological investments, when implemented in isolation from organizational changes, have proven to be woefully inadequate. Here is the dilemma that makes flexiblity so difficult to achieve. Firms have long been described as designing mechanisms by which to buffer uncertainty in order to minimize risk.[1] Yet the development of flexible capabilities implies a contradiction of this learning. The value of flexibility lies in increasing an organization's ability to respond to changing and uncertain environments. Designing an organization that does not shield itself from this uncertainty requires fundamental organizational changes.

Harumo Shimada and John Paul MacDuffie, for example, have contrasted the "robust" concept of organizational design prevalent among Western manufactures with the "fragile" concept of their Japanese counterparts. A "robust" production system attempts to "buffer" itself against the uncertainties of sales fluctuations, supply interruptions, and equipment breakdowns through reliance on inventory stocks, large repair areas, and other forms of organizational slack. A "fragile" system, in contrast, attempts to avoid buffers in order to stay more responsive to environmental changes. With no buffers to shield the fragile system from uncertainty, flexible capabilities are required to permit rapid responses to unpredictable production contingencies and demand changes. These capabilities are embedded not only in hardware such as flexible manufacturing systems, but also in the organization's employees, or what they call "humanware". Chapter five in this book on cross-functional teams and chapter six on product variety provide examples of some of the methods available to increase workforce flexibility.

This chapter is intended to show why changes in the desired capabilities of a corporation require an alteration in control systems and the metrics by which performance is evaluated. Attempts to develop flexible organizations without first changing the way objectives are set and performance is measured are typically futile (Voss 1988 and Lim 1988). To examine why, we conducted interviews with three American firms in three industries: pharmaceutical, automobile production, and telecommunicatons. (The research design is summarized in Table 7.1) Each of these industries currently faces challenges to increase flexibility in order to respond to rapid changes in customer demands, regulatory environments, and product markets. The inferences from these interviews were checked against the extant literature and against interviews with managers from a European and a Japanese firm in each of the industries in order to evaluate the robustness of our findings.[2] Finally, we interviewed managers at firms that were cited as being industry leaders in particular control practices, or when the results from an interview required validation—as was the case with the practices of capital budgeting in Japanese firms.

Our work shows that existing control systems, many of which were developed to support the mass production strategies of the past, frequently provide

TABLE 7.1.   Summary of Field Research Design

Use of Flexibility	Industry
Flexible manufacturing	Automobiles
Research and development	Pharmaceutical
Strategic planning and joint ventures	Telecommunications

incentives that are inconsistent with the adoption of the organizational capabilities needed to meet today's strategic challenges. Some of the firms that we investigated were in the midst of major transformations, but had not thought through the consequences for their control systems. Other firms had instigated major changes in control systems by moving toward single financial measures of performance, even though their stated strategies contained multiple, often nonfinancial, objectives.

There were fundamental differences in whether companies viewed measurements as "incentives" to be used in performance evaluation or as "signals" to highlight the desired strategic direction of the firm. In reality, performance measures are both. Yet, the signals sent by the organizations' control systems often contradicted the firms' strategies; the concern with incentives dominated the internal discussion of many corporations, overlooking the role control systems can play in signaling the new skills and capabilities that must be acquired to achieve the organizations' strategic objectives. In times of change, a control system supports not only efficiency, but also exploration and experimentation.

Our recommendation is that the development of flexible capabilities requires performance measures that explicitly recognize the specific capabilities that the firm hopes to acquire. In doing so, companies must remember that control systems serve two related purposes—evaluating performance and signaling the actions and experiments that management considers desirable. To rephrase an old saying, you get what you signal. If the development of a specific capability requires actions that are incompatible with existing performance measures, it is unlikely that the capability will be acquired.

Since many strategic investments in the development of organizational capabilities resemble research and development (R&D) projects, they should be treated as such; they are risky on an individual basis but even when they fail, they contribute to the accumulation of experience and new skills that ultimately lead to organizational success. Individual investments in flexibility should therefore be measured in the same way as individual research projects, with greater emphasis placed on nonfinancial measures that reflect the extent to which the desired capabilities and learning are being achieved. Evaluating the achievement of overall strategic and financial goals should be performed at higher levels in the organization, much as a basic R&D laboratory limits financial measurements to broad research areas. By placing greater emphasis on nonfinancial criteria in the evaluation of individual projects, companies avoid penalizing managers for undertaking inherently risky investments that lead to the acquisition of valuable capabilities.

Our recommendation should be clear: we suggest multiple criteria and a change in the relative weights placed on financial and nonfinancial measures, not the elimination of financial objectives. Companies must recognize that control systems are an important signaling device. Managers are busy; their attention is limited. A control system provides powerful symbols with which to focus attention on strategic goals and the development of organizational capabilities.

Control Systems and Organizational Experimentation

One way to understand how control systems influence an organization's capabilities is to recognize that control mechanisms guide what is done in a firm by directing the behavior of people toward organizational objectives. Control mechanisms can take a variety of forms, including personal supervision, job descriptions, work rules, standard operating procedures, performance appraisals, budgets, incentive compensation schemes, and planning systems, as well as informal norms and expectations.

Formal control systems represent not only what information management will be evaluated on, but also signal *what is important* to the organization. Consequently, control systems have a strong influence on the priorities placed on alternate courses of action. For example, efficiency and effectiveness—that is, "doing things right" vs. "doing the right things"—represent two very different, and possibly contradictory, goals (Hrebeniak and Joyce 1984). A company that rewards performance based solely on efficiency measures will see greater emphasis placed on improving resource utilization than on determining whether the organization is producing the correct product mix or serving the appropriate markets.

The message that a control system sends regarding what an organization values is not isolated from how things are done. For example, the adoption of mass production strategies using Taylorist principles was accompanied by the implementation of standard costing systems which specified exactly how much labor and material should be expended for each product (Johnson and Kaplan 1987). The goal of these systems was to determine the "best" way to perform a task and to formalize these practices in labor and material standards, Performance was subsequently measured based on variance from standard. Standard costing systems allowed companies to use the accounting system to signal that good performance meant maximizing labor and material efficiency. This measurement made sense for the strategy of standardized mass production, where the control system's emphasis was on signalling the most efficient production techniques—that is "doing things right". However, in rapidly changing environments where opportunities for long production runs of standardized products are rare, "doing things right" no longer assures competitive success if the company is not "doing the right things" by quickly responding to changes in customer demands.

As this example illustrates, a company's articulated strategy and control systems send strong messages regarding the appropriate actions to consider and the appropriate lessons to be learned. A performance evaluation system that emphasizes efficiency over flexibility tells managers that short-term productivity takes precedence over building organizational capabilities, regardless of the organization's espoused long-term direction.

The danger is that a control system's value as a signaling device is easy to underestimate. Control and flexibility sound contradictory. They are not, once it is recognized that a control system can serve as a powerful guidance mechanism to support a company's development of organizational capabilities.

Firms are Rule Based

A simple reason why firms do not build or exploit flexible capabilities is the fact that management behavior is constrained by the "rules of the game" that are found in any organization. These rules appear not only in the policies, procedures, and measurements that make up the formal control system, but also in the informal norms, expectations, and "rules of thumb" that emerge over time.

In many cases, organizational rules are functional. They are the intelligence of a firm, much like the knowledge embedded in algebraic rules, which, if applied correctly, increase the knowledge and competence of a student. Rules have a bad reputation because their existence is typically acknowledged only when they do not work. but they are the backbone of all firms. Good rules and good firms are synonymous expressions.

Both formal and informal rules are the collected wisdom of experience and, occasionally, analysis. They work, and they frequently work well. Ned Bowman studied whether managers did better when they stuck to rules or when they tried to tailor their responses to the circumstance (Bowman 1963). Consistent rules produced better results, even though they were not optimal or "best" in a global sense.

But rules can also be dysfunctional. They are based on the repetition of learned behavior of individuals and coordination in and between groups. As learned behavior, they do not change easily. They become "believed" and are embedded in the distribution of power and authority. Rational responses from managers who view their behavior as consistent with objectives can be radically irrational in their consequences.

For example, a team of researchers in France analyzed the procurement activities of a large industrial firm. This firm established an inflation forecast for the year that set a precise target for permitted increases in the prices of procured parts. As this forecast never matched the actual inflation rate, the management responsible for procurement developed a policy that relied upon two suppliers for identical parts. The price paid to one supplier was 30 percent greater that that paid to the other. The inflation target, consequently, could be realized by changing the proportion purchased from the two suppliers, depending upon whether the inflation forecast was too high or too low. In many years, the firm wound up paying more than necessary for the parts due to the influence of the control system on the employees' actions (de Pourvourville 1981; Berry 1983).

Very often, the dysfunctionality of decision rules is not even noticed. Companies that have been successful in the past frequently believe that applying the same "formula" will ensure success in the future. All too often, however, the competitive environment requires a new set of capabilities that are not incorporated in the firm's current decision rules. By clinging to existing formulas, companies often lose the ability to compete in new environments.

Decision Cues and Performance Measurement

One problem with rules is that people do not make judgments based on all available information. Instead, individuals respond to what they consider "salient" or to how a problem is framed (Tversky and Kahneman 1973). By providing the framework that will be used to evaluate performance, control systems provide signals or cues for managers to follow when making decisions.

Japanese manufacturers, for example, typically allocate overhead expenses based on the amount of direct labor used in a department or product. This policy is enacted to drive plants towards further labor-reducing automation in order to avoid anticipated labor shortages (Hiromoto 1988). By allocating overhead based on direct labor content, the accounting system sends the message that reducing direct labor leads to significant reductions in overhead costs as well. The allocated expenses are clearly not an accurate measure of an operation's use of overhead resources, but do provide an important cue by which to direct managerial attention toward the goal of lower labor content.

The trick in designing an effective control system is providing cues that direct managers to take the appropriate action or apply the appropriate decision rule. The selected performance measures or cues, consequently, should be supportive of the strategy of the business and the corporation. Though simple in theory, developing the required linkages between strategy, performance measures, and decision rules can be extremely difficult.

Changes in performance measures may make obsolete the decision rules by which managers have learned to play. Japanese managers, for example, have traditionally ranked other goals ahead of profitability and shareholder value, a sensible choice in expanding, profitable markets (Kagono et al 1985). However, our interviews with Japanese firms indicated that there is currently increasing interest in profitability and return on capital measures. This interest is not surprising given the state of the Japanese economy. Capital costs more than before; profits are negative. For Japanese managers who have emphasized market share growth in their decisions, the change to financially oriented performance measures requires a fundamentally different set of decision rules for strategic decision making.[3]

Even more problematic is the difficulty in specifying the appropriate "benchmark" against which to compare performance. An easy solution is to measure performance based on financial results, such as profits or return on capital. But financial measures may not be appropriate or feasible in all cases. The short-term profit impact of a basic research laboratory, for example, may be impossible to ascertain. Consequently, the performance of scientific staff is typically evaluated based on nonfinancial measures such as the number of patents issued, the number of papers published, or the ability to meet project milestones. Similarly, long-term investments such as joint ventures typically produce poor financial results during their early years. Yet the investment may be making satisfactory progress toward longer-term goals, or meeting short-term goals that are not financial in nature. Evaluating the investment using financial indicators will in the short-term understate its performance. Moreover, emphasizing financial results sends the message that managers should focus on maximizing short-term accounting returns rather than experimenting with longer term organizational capabilities.

William Ouchi distinguishes two types of performance measures that can be used to provide the appropriate decision cues to managers (Ouchi 1979). Output measures are indicators of results and include financial measures, such as profitability and return on capital. Input measures, in contrast, represent variables that should determine or create measurable results, such as the number of new products introduced or the percentage of employees trained in quality improvement techniques. Input measures, which are frequently nonfinancial in nature, are not themselves measures of the results that a company establishes as its ultimate goals, but rather are indicators of longer term health and vitality.

Erin Anderson provides a framework to guide the selection of input and output measures.[4] As shown in Figure 7.1, the two dimensions in the framework are the extent to which managers understand the transformation process (that is, how inputs become outputs) and the ability of the firm to assess, measure, and judge outputs or results.

Dimension 1:
How well do you know the "transformation process"?
Do you know how inputs get transformed into outputs?
Do you know what people should do?

		Understood Poorly	Understood Well
Dimension 2: How thoroughly and accurately can you assess outputs (results)?	Poorly	Evaluation performed informally, implicitly, seldom	Input measures heavily weighted Output measures lightly weighted
	Well	Output measures heavily weighted Input measures lightly weighted	Either inputs or outputs are valid Use both, weighting outputs more heavily

Figure 7.1. Should Evaluation Be Weighted Toward Inputs, Outputs, or Neither? (*Source:* Anderson 1990, adapted from Ouchi 1979.)

In cases where the process is well understood but results are difficult to assess, input measures should be more heavily weighted. This situation occurs in basic research, where a manager may be able to assess whether a scientist followed the right scientific and project management practices, but is not able to judge the potential financial returns from a new discovery.

Output measures should be more heavily weighted when a firm can measure results but the transformation process is not well understood. This case arises when top management is able to evaluate the profitability of a division but does not have the necessary, intimate knowledge of the division's operations to assess exactly what strategic moves the unit should have made.

Finally, when the transformation process is well understood and results can be accurately assessed, either input or output measures are valid indicators of performance. As we will discuss later in the chapter, the continuum of input and output measures provided in this framework can assist in selecting control mechanisms that support the development of organizational capabilities.

Cues for Flexibility?

The preceding discussion indicates that flexible capabilities cannot be built without putting in place the appropriate decision cues. To do so, a company must first identify the forms of flexibility needed to accomplish the organization's strategic objectives. Broadly defined, flexibility is a capability that gives managers the ability to respond appropriately to different contingencies.[5] A natural way to think about flexibility is in relative terms. A firm is more flexible if it outperforms another when the environment changes more rapidly.

Of course, if the environment is not especially volatile, then flexibility might be at best a useless capability; at worse, it raises the costs of the firm with no benefit. It is as though one has a set of serving china with no occasion for its use.

The specific form of flexibility adopted by a company will depend upon the capability or uses it provides. Sometimes its use is clearly known at the time of implementation. For example, a manufacturer might design a manufacturing process to have the flexibility to produce a car with five basic option packages. At the time the process is developed, the company does not know the exact mix of packages that customers will order, but it can resolve this uncertainty when the orders arrive at the factory. As long as customer orders are limited to the five option packages that the equipment is capable of producing, any mix of products can be accommodated by the system. Switching production between known options is an example of *static flexibility*.

Occasionally, however, we lose sight of Say's law that supply creates demand: having the capability to be flexible may generate new ways to capitalize on its use. Flexible capabilities may allow a firm to experiment with new production methods, to pick up experience in new technologies that provide a competitive advantage in the future, and to move into unanticipated market segments. If the investment in flexibility proves beneficial, it can be expanded. If not, then no further investment is required.

The ability to expand the use of new capabilities over time is an example of *dynamic flexibility*. In the static case, management knows that it can produce five kinds of options; the question at any given point in time is *which* mix of options will be manufactured. In the dynamic case, the issue is when or if to take advantage of existing flexible capabilities. For example, a company may decide to expand previous investments in flexibility because the capability has created opportunities to improve its position in new or expanding markets or provided experience in emerging technologies or products. At the same time, the company has the option not to expand and may even decide to abandon the investment altogether. The central question in the dynamic case is therefore *when* to make a decision to abandon, maintain, or expand an investment in flexibility.

The reader has the right to smile at our attempt to define flexibility as contingent upon knowing what capabilities or uses it provides. A rather "flexible" definition. Yet, knowing the potential uses of flexibility is a fundamental element in the design of the appropriate control systems.

The following three cases show how control systems can hinder or support the development and use of flexible capabilities, the first in a flexible manufacturing operation, the second in R&D planning for a pharmaceutical company, and the third in a telecommunications joint venture.

Static Flexibility and Mix Variances

Manufacturing plants increasingly look like restaurants. Customers place their orders, waiters transmit the specifications by computer to the kitchen, and a team of cooks rushes to assemble the product. And if the tomato sauce for the spaghetti is similar to that for the lasagna, we indeed can speak of a "modularized" production process that assembles and reassembles components to create variety.

A restaurant is an example of *static* flexibility. The menu is already printed and the hours of production are fixed. As in the automobile options example discussed above, the primary question in the restaurant is what to produce during a given period.

An interesting question is why manufacturers that have purchased flexible machinery have limited the "menu" that they offer to customers. Ramchandran Jaikumar, for example, found that "the average number of parts made by an FMS (flexible manufacturing system) in the United States was 10; in Japan the average was 93" (Jaikumar 1986). The U.S. systems were flexible technologically, but rigid in practice.

A team of researchers at Wharton has found that the decision cues provided by control systems are a major reason why high levels of flexibility are not being achieved at many U.S. manufacturing sites.[6] The Wharton team is investigating the interaction between control systems and capital investments in one of the American big three automakers. The company has recently established a manufacturing strategy that places significant emphasis on the development of flexible capabilities that will allow more rapid introduction of new products and the production of multiple models on the same assembly line. Even though this strategy focuses on the *effective* use of flexible automation, the primary plant-level performance measure continues to be direct labor utilization rates, an *efficiency* measure.

This measurement system has had two significant effects on the adoption and utilization of flexible machinery. First, some plant managers are wary of the training costs and teething delays involved in moving from traditional hard automation to robots, as well as of the additional ongoing maintenance requirements of the new technology. Because performance is evaluated based on direct labor utilization, these managers prefer to use technologies that maximize direct labor productivity, regardless of the stated manufacturing strategy of the company.

More important, direct labor measurement provides no incentive to *use* the flexibility once the new equipment is purchased. As one manager stated, "We focus on direct labor utilization because once you buy the equipment, you just depreciate it over time. But labor you have to deal with every day." It is not surprising that, unlike many Japanese automakers, none of the company's plants produces more than one platform on a production line. Plant managers view flexibility as the ability to reuse the same equipment after discontinuing the current model (with each product generation lasting roughly five years) and to adapt to minor, annual trim changes. Under the existing control system, assembly plants have no incentive to seek ways to take advantage of the robots' full capabilities, and consequently use flexible machinery in much the same way as existing hard automation. Taking advantage of the flexible equipment's capabilities will require a radical change in the measures that are used to evaluate plant-level performance.

One solution that has been suggested in the flexible manufacturing literature is the use of "flexible budgets." Traditional static budgets are developed based on the capital, labor, and material required to produce the forecasted product mix. As a result, static budgets indicate that productivity is poor when the inputs required to manufacture the actual product mix are greater than those required for the forecasted mix, even though the plant may be operating efficiently.

This false signal can be a significant problem in flexible manufacturing operations where the actual mix of products that will be manufactured is highly uncertain until orders are received. To alleviate this dilemma, the flexible manufacturing literature suggests that companies develop flexible budgets that are contingent on the mix of products actually produced. Flexible budgets are calculated *ex post* by multiplying the actual product mix by the standard costs for each type of model produced. A "mix variance" is then calculated to account for any differences between actual costs and the original static budget that are due to disparities between the forecasted and actual product mixes.

Does the flexible budget solve the control system problem? Clearly, comparing actual costs against a flexible budget has the virtue of capturing how well costs were managed, given that a certain level of flexibility was exercised. But it does not indicate whether the flexibility was exercised well, that is, whether the flexible *potential* was economically utilized.[7] In this respect, a performance measurement system using flexible budgets is no different from the control systems that are used to manage traditional manufacturing environments. Flexible budgets and mix variances do not measure the effectiveness of a flexible manufacturing system—only its efficiency. They provide no incentive for managers to do the things necessary to utilize the flexible machinery's potential (for example, to introduce new products or to make many products on the same machine).[8]

How, then, does a company develop performance measures that support the development and utilization of static flexibility in manufacturing? The answer depends upon the reasons for acquiring flexible capabilities in the first place. Robb Dixon and his colleagues (1990) identify four dimensions of flexibility that are available in manufacturing operations: quality-associated, product-associated, service-associated, and cost-associated. As shown in Table 7.2, each of these dimensions is characterized by an "ability" to be flexible in a certain area and each makes a different strategic contribution. To develop effective performance measures, companies must first determine which of these dimensions is required to support their organizational objectives.

While the need to develop capabilities that are consistent with overall business goals may seem obvious, S. H. Lim found that the types of manufacturing flexibility being implemented by most companies are incompatible with the strategic objectives of the firms (Lim 1988). For example, although most firms considered quick changeovers to new products to be an important use of their flexible equipment, few believed that the introduction of new products was an important strategy within their organizations. The incompatibility between the types of flexibility that companies implemented and their competitive strategies was due in large part to the fact that the firms' strategic and operational objectives were not linked.

TABLE 7.2.   Dimensions of Manufacturing Flexibility

Quality-associated flexibility dimensions	
Material:	Ability to accommodate variation in the quality of purchased materials.
Output:	Ability to make products with different quality requirements.
Product-associated flexibility dimensions	
New Product:	Ability to introduce new products.
Modification:	Ability to modify existing products.
Service-associated flexibility dimensions	
Delivery:	Ability to change the current production and/or delivery schedule to accommodate unanticipated needs.
Volume:	Ability to vary aggregate production volume from period to period.
Cost-associated flexibility dimensions	
Factor:	Ability to modify the mix of resources (materials, labor, and capital) used in the production process.

Source: Dixon, Nanni, and Vollmaun (1990).

Once a company determines the means by which flexibility contributes to the achievement of strategic objectives, the appropriate performance measures can be developed to provide the required decision cues. For example, a strategy focused on being first to market with state-of-the-art products requires managers to develop and utilize the flexibility to rapidly introduce new products and modify existing products. Performance measures, such as the number of introductions of new products and the speed of new product start-ups, signal that success is achieved by building the capability to introduce new products quickly. Note that neither of these measures is a short-term financial measure. Instead, they are indicators of long-term success—that is, the capability to meet the manufacturing requirements of the strategic plan. Our emphasis on nonfinancial measures of manufacturing flexibility follows the framework in Figure 7.1. Because flexibility is a capability rather than a result, output-oriented financial measures do a poor job of evaluating its effectiveness. If a company knows what uses are desired from investments in flexibility, nonfinancial input-oriented measures can be used to specify and assess the actions managers are taking to build and utilize the desired capabilities.

Dynamic Flexibility and Goal Setting

Imagine you are to take a trip, but you are not told the destination. What would you pack? You do not want to take too much, as it is painful and costly to move the bags around. An umbrella is always good, as the old line on benefits of diversification tells us, whether it rains or shines. But first you have to buy and pack the umbrella and then remember not to lose it along the way. The other choices may be more difficult. Do you bring a dark suit or dress? The probability of its use on a pleasure trip is low, but it might be handy if the destinaton is the casino at Monte Carlo.

Of course, you could follow another strategy. you could pack a few things now and bring along a credit card. But you might reget the decision if you find you are stuck on an island with exorbitant prices; the clothes you left on your bed at home would look like a bargain.

The cost of buying late is not unlike the experience of one telecommunications firm that had to make an acquisition to enter a market after its competitors were already there. The company had previously carried out a pilot R&D project in the area, but had abandoned it at the time when the technology became marketable. The cost of commercialization seemed too large for such an uncertain market. In retrospect, keeping the R&D project alive seems like a small price to have paid to retain the option to commercialize the product, just in case the market looked good in the future. Other firms did commercialize the product, and the market later looked good enough to cost the telecommunications company several hundred millions of dollars to reenter.

Investments in new products, technologies, or markets that provide a company with the option to expand if the endeavors look promising are examples of *dynamic* flexibility. More generally, dynamic flexibility is the creation of a capability to act in response to opportunities as they develop over time. A simple response is to abandon the project; another is to expand the project into a business. The use of dynamic flexibility poses the question of when to act given that you already have the capability to respond.

One industry where dynamic flexibility is extremely valuable is pharmaceuticals, where investments in risky projects are routine. Only about 5 percent of drugs that enter development get to the market. From the time development begins until final market entry, a number of discrete steps must be followed. Roughly three years into the R&D process, a compound goes through synthesis examination and screening, in which its chemical and biological properties are assessed. This is followed by two years of preclinical tests on animals. If the compound passes this hurdle at year five, it enters clinical tests on humans. The Federal Drug Administration stipulates standardized trials (phases I, II, and III) that the compound must pass to be marketed. Since each stage involves the commitment of tens of millions of dollars, there is a strong incentive to evaluate the selection of drugs in light of the flexibility to discontinue further development, known as the abandonment option, or to commit additional resources.

The company that we studied is widely regarded as one of the leaders in the evaluation of investment and risk.[9] In the early 1980s, the company began to develop risk assessments of its portfolio of research projects through the application of Monte Carlo techniques. The Monte Carlo model evaluates the current portfolio of products and development projects in order to forecast company performance over a twenty-year horizon. Inputs to the model include assessments of the probabilities of development success by an expert panel of research directors, sales forecasts from the marketing group, and cost forecasts from manufacturing. Assessments of project success are generally in the form of 10 percent probability, 90 percent probability, and most likely. The results from the Monte Carlo model are used to identify gaps in the company's product portfolio and to estimate the firm's long-term value for comparison to the firm's stock price.

Despite the importance of this methodology to overall corporate planning, post-completion analyses do not tie these projections to an assessment of managerial performance. In fact, scientists in the laboratories described an R&D planning process that does not rely heavily on financial and marketing simulations, especially in basic research and the early stages of product development.

Instead, the choice of research projects is guided by commitments to long-term drug programs in targeted therapeutic areas.

Financial analysis is not critical to the determination of the research portfolio. The decision to continue or abandon a project is made on the basis of screening and clinical trials. Work on a substance is killed if toxicity is found, not on the basis of financial assessment of earnings. Since outcomes are so unpredictable, there is no financial justification for a product until a substance is registered with the government.

The high risk of projects not coming to market creates a demanding environment for the evaluation of managerial performance. Senior management recognizes that with a 5 percent industry success rate, any project is a high-risk bet. The probability of failure attached to any single project is mitigated by investing in a portfolio of projects within targeted long-term drug programs, rather than by betting the company on specific projects or drugs.

The logic of this planning leads to a policy of hiring the best scientists in any given area and then committing substantial resources to developing knowledge in basic research. Even if a particular drug fails, knowledge of the general science related to the drug is achieved. In a sense, investing in research programs increases the probability that future drug projects will succeed. Although individual projects may fail, they contribute to the future success of the firm.

It may be for this reason that strict financial measures are not used for project selection. Projects in areas that are considered strategic are not subject to financial evaluation because they represent the generation of future opportunities rather than investments in any particular market opportunity. The project portfolio approach of this company is not merely a method by which risk is diversified, but also a long-term investment in a set of skills and capabilities that are useful to many markets.

William Brown's and David Gobeli's (1992) study of performance measurement in R&D environments supports the pharmaceutical company's emphasis on nonfinancial measures at the project level. Their research identified three levels of activities within R&D, each of which requires a distinct set of measures. These levels are mapped against the input-output continuum of performance measures in Figure 7.2.

At the lowest level of the hierarchy are the individual activities and processes within R&D. Since the output of individual research activities may be a poor indicator of performance due to the inherent risk in R&D and the inability of output measures to capture the development of organizational capabilities, input measures such as the percentage of key skill areas learned by R&D personnel or the number of publications predominate at this level.

At the project management level, more specific input measures such as timeliness in meeting project milestones are emphasized. As the project moves

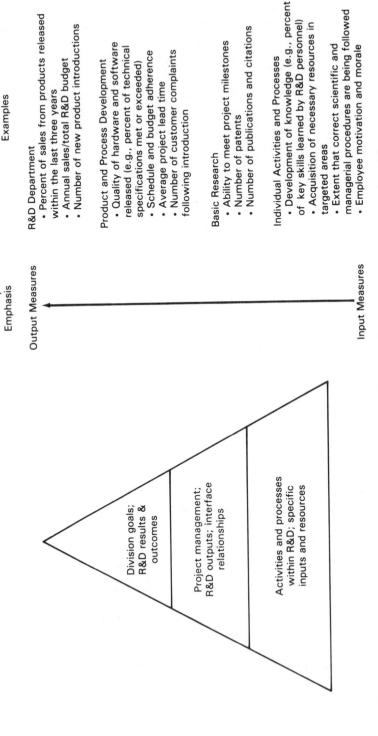

Figure 7.2. The R&D Performance Measurement Hierarchy. (*Source:* Adapted from Brown and Gobeli 1992.)

into the lower risk development stage, outcomes become easier to evaluate and performance measures move closer to the output end of the performance measurement continuum, focusing on factors such as project cost overruns, the number of engineering change orders caused by modifications to specifications, and the quality of the hardware or software released.

Finally, output measures move to center stage when evaluating the performance of the entire R&D organization. At this level, the risk inherent in individual projects is diversified away in the many projects that are ongoing at any point in time. Consequently, output measures become a valid measure of organizational success. Typical output measures for an R&D organization include the percent of sales from products released within the last three years, the contribution to gains in market share, and the ratio of annual sales to the R&D budget. By utilizing this performance measurement hierarchy, companies avoid penalizing managers for individual R&D projects that develop organizational capabilities but fail due to inherent risk.

The Case of Joint Ventures

The development of flexibility in high-risk environments is hard to value because performance is measured against a probabilistic and potential use, not an expected standard. But even in the case of flexible manufacturing, the measurement of performance using flexible budgets and mix variances only provides an illusion of control over the use of flexible capabilities. If the factory only solicits orders for one model, would we say that it has exploited its flexibility fully? A multibillion dollar investment in flexible machinery, yet there is no strategic use of the equipment.

If flexibility is an investment in a capability, then it must be evaluated in terms of its contribution to the development of the desired capability. Let us take a concrete example. One of the non-U.S. telecommunication firms in our study established a joint venture in the United States for the adaptation of its digital exchange switch. This switch serves to direct incoming and outgoing telephone calls and was to be expanded to handle both voice and data (for example, transfer of computer files). From the European firm's perspective, the primary reason for creating the joint venture was to utilize its partner's technological capabilities to adapt a product designed for the European market to unfamiliar American standards. The venture proved to be a technological success, but the product failed when the anticipated markets did not materialize. The joint venture was terminated within five years.

Normally, this business venture would be interpreted as a failure. The firm designed a tight functional plan; from a product design perspective, the joint venture ran perfectly. Yet the business strategy to enter the anticipated market leaked like a colander.

However, the termination of the joint venture does not end the story. The venture was not dissolved; it was acquired by the non-U.S. company, which had negotiated the right of first refusal should the operation be put up for sale. Although the venture was not profitable, it provided the European firm with two key capabilities: the technology required to meet U.S. specifications and knowledge of the U.S. market. These capabilities gave the company the flexibility to expand their U.S. presence beyond the market that had originally been anticipated. Since the joint venture was acquired, it has been expanded into one of the company's global research centers and has successfully supported the adaptation of the firm's larger and more profitable products to the U.S. market. The decision to acquire the joint venture is an example of exercising dynamic flexibility: the right to acquire (that is, to expand the investment) if the operation looked promising was built into the design of the venture. The venture failed, but the experiment succeeded.

Many joint ventures are established as trial investments in new markets for the purpose of learning, or establishing a foothold in, a technology or market. Often, a right-to-buy clause is attached, with the timing of a firm's decision to exercise the option influenced by changes in the market (Kogut 1991). Particularly during the early stages of a joint venture, short-term financial measures will fail to capture the value that the venture provides in terms of increased capabilities and the flexibility to move into new technologies and markets. In many ways, joint ventures, like many strategic investments, are similar to R&D projects in that seemingly unsuccessful investments can contribute to the achievement of corporate strategies through the learning and capabilities that the venture contributes. Consequently, their performance should be measured based, at least in part, on their contribution to the acquisition of the desired capabilities.

Erin Anderson uses the framework in Figure 7.1 to guide the evaluation of joint venture performance. Many ventures in basic research and experimental technologies fall in the upper left cell, where knowledge of the appropriate actions to take and the ability to judge outputs and inputs of the joint venture are both low. In these cases, evaluations should be less formal with a greater emphasis on qualitative assessments of progress and learning, including such factors as harmony among partners, morale, adaptiveness, innovativeness, and the acquisition of resources. At the other extreme are joint ventures that can be effectively evaluated using output measures, such as profitability. These ventures tend to be older, in familiar markets and products, and in mature industries. Between these extremes lie the joint ventures that are designed for a specific purpose, such as acquiring knowledge in a new product or market. In the early stages of these ventures, outputs are not good indicators of performance; output measures such as profitability and cash flow provide no information on whether the learning and capabilities required for long-term success are being built. However, since these ventures exist for definable reason (for example, knowledge acquisition, footholds in emerging markets, and so forth), certain activities or inputs can be prescribed. To the extent that organizations can identify the capabilities that are desired from a joint venture, the appropriate measures, which will typically be nonfinancial, can be implemented to direct managers toward the achievement of these goals.

Metrics and Incentives

Our recommendation that companies place greater emphasis on nonfinancial measures when evaluating flexibility stands in opposition to the view that if managers are to do the right thing, they must be under the appropriate financial incentives. Unless they bear risk, they will not be motivated to capitalize on flexibility.

A number of corporations, including one of our Japanese research sites, are rethinking their compensation package with an eye on promoting greater attention to financial returns. The proposals to use financial measures to motivate managers' incentive raise an intriguing issue: can control systems promote the development of flexibility through the creation of optionlike incentives? An optionlike incentive pays a manager more if the business does well but limits the penalty if it does badly, thereby eliminating any disincentive to invest in the development of flexible capabilities that are potentially risky. Moreover, if you cannot determine the potential uses of flexibility ahead of time, should not incentives be created to motivate managers to find them?

One of the common threads in our interviews was the belief that individual rewards should be tied to the fulfillment of the original capital plan. As one manager stated, "Capital is a sunk but not forgotten cost." A few companies that we interviewed for comparison purposes are adopting various techniques to transform accounting numbers into "economic values" in order to tie managerial pay to the economic value created by using an organization's capital and human resources.

For example, a number of the U.S. firms are experimenting with new bonus plans.[10] These proposals establish a pseudomarket price for divisions using techniques similar to those used to value acquisitions. Managers receive part of their compensation in the form of "stock" options on their divisions, with the exercise price set at a few percentage points higher than the division's current "market" price.[11] An increase in the division's value should be reflected in an increase in the "market price", thereby linking compensation to the achievement of the capital plan's financial objectives.

The advantage of this type of proposal is that managers bear no downside risk. The minimum value of the stock option is zero, no matter how badly the division performs. At the same time, because managers directly bear the upside risk (that is, their pay increases if the "stock price" rises), they are provided with strong incentives to develop the capabilities needed to capitalize rapidly on emerging market opportunities.

These advantages suggest that optionlike incentives are the ideal solution to the problem of designing a control system that supports flexibility. However, research on the risk-taking behavior of managers suggests otherwise. There is strong evidence that managers tend to take risks when in a *losing* situation but are averse to risk in situations where the choice is between two *winning* alternatives (Kahneman and Tversky 1979). There is also reasonable evidence that people prefer compensation to be "equitable" or "fair" (Bazerman 1992).

What does this mean? Well, it means that giving optionlike incentives to encourage taking risks and flexibility may not be successful, and surely will be resented. It will not be successful because managers will start to worry about maintaining the value of their options once they are "in the money," reducing their motivation to undertake higher risk and potentially higher reward investments. Moreover, when options are "out of the money," managers may be encouraged to take unacceptable risks since they bear no downside.

Studies of the use of performance measures and options in executive compensation by Surya Janakiraman, Richard Lambert, David Larcker, and Robert Verrecchia of the Wharton School shed some light on the use of option-like incentives (Janakiraman, Lambert, and Larcker 1992; Lambert, Larcker, and Verrecchia 1991). As discussed in chapter two of this book, it makes sense to hold executives responsible for corporate results, and it is relatively straightforward since stock prices already exist in the market. Conventional performance measurement theory also states that a good incentive system rewards managers for the actions they control. Consequently, a bonus plan using options should "filter" out the changes in performance that are due to external factors, such as overall increases in market prices or industry-wide downturns due to regulatory changes. In other words, what should matter is performance relative to executives in competing firms.

The results of the executive compensation studies are surprising. First, there is no correction for market or industry effects that are outside of managers' control; these effects are simply passed into the bonus. Second, compensation plans that use options are poorly designed. As options become valuable, managers treat them as part of their wealth. Their actions, consequently, become more conservative in order to preserve the value of this wealth. This contradicts the needs of many organizations to provide incentives that encourage managers to make potentially risky investments in the development of flexible capabilities.

If effective measurements and incentives for top executives are hard to design when stock prices already exist, imagine the problem for lower levels of management. In some businesses, the separation of environmental influence and individual performance can be sorted out. There is a logic, after all, to the statistical interests of baseball fans because players bat individually and in fairly homogeneous circumstances. It is not surprising that optionlike incentives are common in these cases.

But in most businesses, individuals not only work in groups but also face very different competitive markets that differ in risk. Tying pay to economic value added generates large discrepancies in employee rewards as the variability in risk among businesses increases. These discrepancies may be attributable to risk differences or to simple luck, either of which creates the perception that the compensation system is not "equitable".

Optionlike incentives inside the corporation aggravate a tendency of people to believe that risk can be controlled. In a survey of corporate managers, James March and Zur Shapira (1986) found that managers see risk taking as good when the outcome is positive, but as a "foolish gamble" when the project fails, even though earlier it was recognized to be a bet. The fundamental quality of risk is that there will be winners and losers regardless of difference in ability or effort. Managers, and people in general, have a hard time acknowledging luck retrospectively.

The problem with optionlike financial incentives is not that it is wrong to tie payment to results. The problem is believing that a single output measure, no matter how sophisticated, can provide the incentives to develop the flexible capabilities required to achieve competitive success in today's increasingly volatile marketplace. As we noted at the start, the value of flexibility lies in increasing an organization's ability to respond to changing and, therefore, uncertain, environments. Developing an organization that does not shield itself from risk requires more than a new financial measurement system. It requires a commitment to experimentation that may not be captured in financial output measures. This, in turn, means that companies must implement control systems that promote the capabilities that are needed to achieve strategic objectives. In most cases, these control systems will emphasize nonfinancial input measures that more closely reflect the development of longer term organizational capabilities.

Conclusions

We began by asking why firms are less flexible than their potential. The simple answer, we suggested, is that organizational actions are based on rules—both formal and informal. Given the constraints of these rules, it is not surprising that the use of flexible capabilities falls short of their theoretic possibility. But the wide variance in corporate practices suggests that some firms are much more flexible that others. Part of the explanation for this difference rests on the extent to which these firms have created control systems to support flexibility.

There is an interesting difference of opinion on whether financial measures should play any role in providing incentives to develop organizational capabilities. One camp clearly believes that the necessary tonic lies in improving financial methodologies and tying performance measures to these numbers. Another camp, often more operations-oriented, is clearly skeptical of the value of financial measures. An extreme view is that the "new technology . . . will relegate accountants and finance staffs . . . to a minor role in the organization . . . New operating measures will be needed . . . (Kaplan and Atkinson 1989). A more moderate view reflects a displeasure with financial criteria, proposing that, in addition to new measures, financial measures will remain important in evaluating heavy capital investments, despite their "many drawbacks" (Bennet et al 1987).

As in all debates of this nature, there is a middle ground. The findings in this chapter indicate that wisdom depends not only on where you sit, but also in what hole you have dug for yourself. For example, many of the Japanese corporations appear to be overcapitalized. This, coupled with the rising cost of capital, is awaking an interest in the cost of capital estimations. Including capital charges in managers' measurements provides a strong signal to avoid the tendency to overinvest and to introduce new generations of products too rapidly, problems that have been ascribed to Japanese companies. U.S. and European firms seem divided in their attitudes, with a number of firms increasing their reliance on financial measures, while others resist the use of financial methodologies.

What we have suggested is that the control system should be treated as a tool to guide the evolution of the corporation; performance measurement should be subsidiary to long-term objectives. The case of the pharmaceutical R&D laboratory may be the right vision for a corporation seeking to develop new organizational capabilities. The focus is on building capabilities in certain chemical compounds by investing in a portfolio of related experiment projects; expert scientists make informed judgements to continue or to abandon, to invest more or to withdraw. The philosophy is evolutionary and the emphasis is placed on broad strategic objectives; individual failures, although inevitable, contribute to the buildup of knowledge in the desired area of competence.

Of course, pharmaceutical R&D is unusually risky. Many businesses enjoy substantially more tranquil markets and technologies. If environments are stationary, then financial measures probably work well for companies at the frontier of best practice. For the majority of firms that operate in a less than stationary world, however, control systems should be seen as a powerful way to direct the attention of managers toward experimentation and the building of the long-term organizational flexibilities that are necessary to compete in today's increasingly uncertain marketplaces.

Notes

We would like to acknowledge the comments of Jim Allison and Blaine Davis of AT&T, Ned Bowman, and two reviewers on earlier drafts, as well as the excellent research assistance of Vipin Gupta. The research has been supported by funding from KPMG Peat Marwick and the Reginald H. Jones Center.

1. One of the foundational texts in economic risk, Frank Knight's (1921) *Risk, Uncertainty, and Profit,* devotes a chapter to how firms organize to reduce risk. The classic text in organizational theory, Richard Cyert's and James March's (1963) *A behavioral theory of the firm,* regards "uncertainty avoidance" as one of the hallmark features of an organization. James Thompson's (1967) *Organizations in Action* describes the various ways "organizations seek to buffer environmental influences" by maintaining inventories, using joint ventures, or acquiring competitors.

2. We did not interview a Japanese pharmaceutical company.

3. Increasing emphasis on financial results has already forced some Japanese companies to change their decision rules. Nissan, for example, proliferated products during the 1980s in an attempt to gain market share. The decision cue produced by the control system was that market share was desired regardless of cost. As a result, model variations exploded to more than 2,200. Poor financial results have now forced Nissan to shift its emphasis to cost control, leading to reductions in the number of models offered and greater use of common parts. See Chandler and Williams (1993) for details.

4. Anderson's (1990) framework is adapted from Ouchi (1979).

5. Similar distinctions between static and dynamic flexibility are made in Carlsson (1988) and Cohendet and Llerena (1990). De Groot (forthcoming) shows why flexibility requires jointly understanding the technology and environmental diversity. We have cut our discussion showing how flexibility can be modeled and financially evaluated as an option. See Brealey and Myers (1991) for a general discussion, especially in reference to R&D; Kogut and Kulatilaka (1994) and Kogut (1991) show applications to manufacturing and joint ventures, respectively.

6. The study is under the joint coordination of Christopher Ittner and Marshall Fisher.

7. These observations would also apply to the measurement of flexibility achieved by coordination among global manufacturing plants. A multinational corporation has the potential to shift production among sites located in different countries, depending on exchange rates or changes in wages. See Kogut and Kulatilaka (1994) and Cohen and Huchzermeier (1991). This kind of flexibility can be measured ex post by looking at variances derived from a flexible budget. But these variances do not measure the extent to which the potential is realized.

8. Although the need to use different performance measures for traditional and flexible manufacturing operations may seem self-evident, studies indicate that many American firms have not done so. A study by Howell and his colleagues (1987), for example, found that 82 percent of U.S. manufacturers used the same performance measurement and control systems for both automated and nonautomated processes, despite the wide differences in the processes' capabilities.

9. The field study was aided by the ongoing research of Randy Case and by a preliminary summary of his extensive interviews prepared for his dissertation.

10. Two firms were trying out the proposal of Bennett Stewart and Joel Stern. See Stewart (1990).

11. Since no market prices or stock options actually exist for these divisions, the companies are developing proxies for these financial instruments.

References

Anderson, Erin. 1990. Two firms, one frontier: On assessing joint venture performance. *Sloan Management Review* 31:19–30.

Bennett, Robert E., James A. Hendricks, D. E. Keys, and E. J. Rudnicki. 1987. *Cost accounting for factory automation*. N.J.; National Association of Accountants.

Berry, M. 1983. *Une Technologies Invisible? l'impact des instruments de gestion sur l'evolution des systemes humains*. Paris: Centre de Recherche en Gestion, Ecole Polytechnique.

Bowman, Edward. 1963. Consistency and optimality in managerial decision making. *Management Science* 9:310–21.

Brealey, Richard, and Stewart Myers. 1991 *Modern principles of corporate finance*. 3rd. ed. New York: McGraw Hill.

Brown, Warren and David Gobeli. 1992. Observations on the measurement of R&D productivity: A case study. *IEEE Transactions on Engineering Management* 39:325–31.

Carlsson, Bo. 1988. Flexibility and the theory of the firm. *International Journal of Industrial Organization* 7:179–203.

Chandler, C., and M. Williams. 1993. A slump in car sales forces Nissan to start cutting swollen costs. *The Wall Street Journal*, March 3:A1, A6.

Cohen Morris, and Arnd Huchzermeier. 1991. Global manufacturing under fluctuating exchange rates. Thesis, University of Pennsylvania.

Cohendet, Patrick and Patrick Llerena. 1990. Flexibilité et evaluation des systèmes de production. Gestion industrielle et mesure économique. Approches et applications nouvelles. Paris: Economica.

Cyert, Richard, and James March. 1963 A behavioral theory of the firm. N.J.: Prentice-Hall.

de Groote, Xavier. The flexibility of production processes: A general framework. Management Science (forthcoming).

de Pouvourville, Gerard. 1981. Volonté de changement et coherence organisationelle. Peut-on changer les politiques d'achat des grandes entreprises. Annales des Mines, July–August.

Dixon, J. Robb, Alfred J. Nanni, and Thomas E. Vollmann. 1990. The new performance challenge: Measuring operations for world-class competition. Homewood, Ill. Business One Irwin.

Hiromoto, Toshiro. 1988. Another hidden edge—Japanese management accounting. Harvard Business Review 66:22–26.

Howell, Robert A., J. D. Brown, S. R. Soucy, and A. H. Seed. 1987. Management accounting in the new manufacturing environment. Montvale, N.J.: National Association of Accountants.

Jaikumar, Ramchandran 1986. Postindustrial manufacturing. Harvard Business Review 64:69-76.

Johnson, H. Thomas, and Robert S. Kaplan. 1987. Relevance lost. The rise and fall of management accounting. Boston: Harvard Business School Press.

Joyce, William, and Lawrence Hrebeniak. 1984. Implementing strategy. New York: Macmillan.

Janakiraman, Surya, Richard Lambert, and David Larcker. 1992. An empirical investigation of the relative performance evaluation hypothesis. Journal of Accounting Research 30:53–69.

Kagono, Tadas, I. Nonaka, K. Sakakibara, and A. Okumura. 1985. Strategic versus evolutionary management: A U.S.–Japan comparision of strategy and organization. Amsterdam: North Holland Press.

Kahneman, Daniel, and Amos Tversky. 1979. Prospect theory: An analysis of decision under risk. Econometrica 47:263–91.

Kaplan, Robert S., and A. Atkinson. 1989. Advanced Management Accounting. Englewood Cliffs, N.J.: Prentice Hall.

Knight, Frank 1921. Risk, uncertainty, and profit. Boston: Houghton Mifflin; Chicago: University of Chicago Press, 1971.

Kogut, Bruce. 1991. Joint ventures and the option to acquire and expand. Management Science 37:19–33.

Kogut, Bruce, and Nalin Kulatilaka. 1994. Operating flexibility, global manufacturing, and the option value of a multinational network. Management Science 40:123–39.

Lambert, Richard, David Larcker, and Robert E. Verrecchia. 1991. Portfolio considerations in valuing executive compensation. Journal of Accounting Research, 29:129–49.

Lim, S. H. 1988. Flexible manufacturing systems and manufacturing flexibility in the United Kingdom. *International Journal of Operations and Production Management* 7:44–54.

March, James G.,and Zur Shapira. 1986. Managerial perspectives on risk and risk taking. *Management Science* 33:1404–18.

Ouchi, William. 1979. A conceptual framework for the design of organization control mechanisms. *Management Science* 25:833–48.

Stewart, G. Bennett. 1990. Remaking the public corporation from within. *Harvard Business Review* 68: 26–37

Thompson, James D. 1967. *Organization in action. Social science bases of administrative behavior.* New York: McGraw Hill.

Tversky, Amos, and Daniel Kahneman. 1973. Availability: A Heuristic for Judging Frequency and Probability. *Cognitive Psychology* 4:207–32.

Voss, Christopher P. 1988. Implementing manufacturing technology: A manufacturing strategy approach. *International Journal of Operations and Production Management* 7:17–26

III

Form, Space, and Time

8

The Design and Redesign of Organizational Form

FRANKLIN ALLEN AND PETER D. SHERER

There exists a whole spectrum of organizational forms ranging from "mom and pop" grocery stores to large conglomerates, from financial mutuals, such as insurance companies and mutual funds, to nonprofits, such as hospitals and universities. The three most typical organizational forms used in the business sector are proprietorships, partnerships, and corporations.[1]

Surprisingly little attention outside of legal arguments has been given to the type of organizational form a firm should adopt. In recent years, however, firms in a number of industries have redesigned their form. Twenty-five years ago most major investment banks were partnerships. Now, with the exception of Goldman Sachs, they are all corporations or divisions of corporations. Highly visible legal suits against law and accounting partnerships have called into question whether their current organizational form is best. This concern was highlighted by the recent bankruptcy of the accounting partnership Laventhol and Horwath and the requirements for partners to meet liability payments. For many other service industries, organizational form is an important issue.

Even among manufacturing firms, the type of organizational form is a design and redesign issue. It would be surprising if General Motors became a partnership, even though this form would save the firm several billion dollars a year in taxes. In Japan, though, the automobile industry is structured very differently with a considerable amount of outsourcing to firms that are proprietorships and partnerships rather than corporations.

We therefore propose a theory that offers a framework for guiding senior executives in making strategic decisions on the design and redesign of organizational form. We argue that organizational form determines the capabilities and capacities of a firm to compete in the marketplace. Proprietorships foster quality; corporations foster efficiency; partnerships do some of both. In a proprietorship, the owner's human and financial resources are *dedicated* to the firm in the sense that they cannot be easily removed without dissolving the firm. This provides strong incentives to provide quality. The owner will directly suffer the future consequences if poor quality is provided today. In a corporation this is not the case. Top managers are not tied to a firm nor are financial resources. The advantage of the corporate form is precisely this *Fluidity* or mobility of resources. Production can be organized efficiently because of the lack of ties between the organization and resources.

Our theory predicts that corporations will be the predominant organizational form when quality can be guaranteed in a specific way, such as an explicit warranty. Proprietorships and partnerships will exist where explicit warranties or some other way of guaranteeing quality are not feasible.

An interesting illustration of our thesis is provided by the restaurant industry where explicit guarantees are difficult if not impossible to provide. Forty years ago relatively inexpensive restaurant meals were provided by diners, which were mostly proprietorships. Quality was guaranteed because the owners' resources were dedicated. One important innovation provided by the fast-food chains was to guarantee quality by providing raw materials and standardization. The efficiencies associated with the corporate form allowed them to dominate the market, and now diners are relegated to the fringe of the industry.

Our theory builds on the work in many fields of academicians who have sought to explain organizational form—accounting, finance and economics (Fama and Jansen, 1983a 1983 b; Williamson 1985; Scholes and Wolfson 1992), law (Klein and Coffee 1983), and organization theory and human resources (Hannan and Freeman 1983; Salancik and Leblebici 1988; Sherer 1993). Much of this literature focuses either on finances or on human resources.

Fama and Jensen (1983a, 1983b), in a series of influential papers, argued that firms determine their organizational form by trading off the benefits and risks of financial and decision making responsibility. As organizations become larger and their operations become more complex, proprietorship no longer remains an attractive and efficient organizational form. The owner must be wealthy enough to finance the operation and bear all the financial risk, as well as possess all the necessary expertise to run the firm. However, the benefits of separating these functions must be weighed against the risk that management may pursue their own interest rather than the interests of the owners. For Fama and Jensen, the ideal organizational form for a company is the one that insures that the interests of management are aligned with the interests of the principals.

None of these theories adequately explains the choice of organizational form, however. Neither human nor financial resources alone is a sufficient explanation of organizational form. Fama and Jensen do well to discuss the principal-agent problem in the context of organizational form. Unfortunately, their explanation does not recognize the role organizational form has in a firm's ability to supply its products and services to customers. A better theory must account for all of these factors.

Every firm—no matter how it is organized—needs to obtain certain capabilities if it is to meet the most important goals it has chosen. It may desire to expand and seek new customers, or it may focus its efforts on maintaining long-term relationships with existing customers. It may attempt to enter new markets or concentrate on the markets in which it already competes.

Firms use their human and financial resources to generate the capabilities required to meet their goals. Firms may differ in their financial requirements and the degree of risk they are willing to accept. But they all must possess the ability to obtain financing, manage resources in a way that maximizes return while minimizing risk, and meet their responsibilities to creditors. The same is true for a firm's human resources. Firms must obtain and retain people capable of successfully running the business and insure that they further the interests of the firm.

It is our view that a firm chooses a particular organizational form or ownership structure in the belief that it will best help it obtain and maintain the capabilities it seeks in terms of providing quality and operating efficiently. Marshalling the human and financial resources required to achieve these capabilities requires striking a difficult balancing act between having access to those resources and dedicating them to the interests of the firm. Organizational form is an important part of finding that balance.

Differentiating among the Three Organizational Forms

To understand how organizational form affects a firm's capabilities, and its implications for managing financial and human assets, it is important to consider the differences between the three basic organizational forms. Proprietorships, partnerships, and corporations are fundamentally defined by ownership and control, liability, and claimants.

A proprietorship is owned and controlled by one person, often with the help of family members. The owner is the manager. The proprietor has unlimited liability for his or her debts and is the sole residual claimant (that is, an individual or individuals with rights to the balance of revenues less costs).

Partnerships have two or more joint owners. Partners are liable to an unlimited degree for their debts, just as proprietors are. But partnerships allow expertise and risks to be pooled, and tasks, including the task of day-to-day management, to be divided among the partners according to their skills. In larger partnerships, an executive committee composed of only a subset of partners may run the firm.

In its purest form, partnerships equally divide profit and losses, the right to make decisions and control the firm, and to contribute to and control the firm's capital. The best-known variation of this pure form is the limited partnership where "active" or "general" partners have responsibility for running the firm and unlimited liability for the partnership's debts, while "silent" or "limited" partners simply provide financial capital and have neither responsibility for running the firm nor any financial risk beyond the amount they invest.

Corporations have their origins in Roman law. Because of its vast empire and trade, the Romans found they needed to define a body or a whole (the corpus) that had legal rights separate from its individual members. Modern corporations can own property in their own right, issue transferable shares, and live indefinitely. Corporations have unlimited liability for their debts, but shareholders are only liable for the equity they have invested.

In corporations, the role of ownership and control are separated. Shareholders own the corporation, but corporations are controlled by a board of directors and officers who, while obliged to act on behalf of the shareholders, are not necessarily shareholders. Shares are not necessarily traded freely. In publicly held corporations, shares are held by a relatively large number of people (Hamilton, 1991) and are traded on the securities exchange. Closely held corporations involve relatively few shareholders and are not traded on the outside market, as the transferability of shares is restricted. Most of these shareholders participate in running the firm, similar to owners in a partnership.

As summarized in Table 8.1, these differences in control and ownership, claimants and liabilities result in other distinguishing characteristics that affect a company's capabilities:

Compensation

In a proprietorship the risks and rewards are borne by the owner who also supplies the skills needed to run the company. The proprietor is the residual claimant. In a partnership, the general partners supply most of the entrepreneurial, professional, and managerial skills; if there are limited partners, they provide financial capital. In this case, the risks and rewards are shared and partners are the sole residual claimants. In a corporation the risks and rewards are borne by the shareholders and the managers bear a relatively small amount

TABLE 8.1.   Characteristics of Pure Organizational Forms

	Proprietorship	*Partnership*	*Corporation*
Ownership/control	Owner manager	Partners managers	Ownership management separated
Compensation	Owner claims residual	Partners claim residual	Shareholders claim most of residual
Access to human capital: selecting managers	Owner usually selects self	Partners select themselves	Board of directors selects managers
Access to financial capital	Very limited access	Limited access	Ready access
Monitoring management	Rudimentary	Mutual monitoring	Elaborate internal and market systems

of the risk. They thus typically receive a significant portion of their compensation as a guaranteed salary, and they are, consequently fixed claimants.

Selection of Managers

In a proprietorship, the selection of managers is not an issue: the owner selects him or herself on the basis of having the capital for forming the business. In a partnership, new partners must be approved by the existing partners. partners are required to pay capital into the firm as a basis for entry into the firm. While this often takes the form of equity capital, in professional partnerships in particular but also in many other partnerships, an individual must also possess or "pay in" particular human capital such as a law degree in order to gain entry into the firm. Such skills, though of importance to the firm's operation, do not necessarily relate to managing it. In a corporation the top managers are selected, presumably for their expertise as managers, by the board of directors acting on behalf of owners of shares; the shareholders can simply buy votes in the marketplace.

Access to Financing

Proprietorships, particularly small ones, have limited access to capital markets. They primarily rely on the funds generated by the business to finance new investments. To the extent outside funds are needed, they are borrowed from banks, family, or friends. Once committed, funds are illiquid. Owners must either sell the business in its entirety or go public. Lenders such as banks can either wait for their funds to be paid back or force bankruptcy and acquire the assets of the firm.

Partnerships also have limited access to capital. Most of their funds are raised from partners. Banks, family, or friends are the most usual sources of outside funds. Some partnerships do have access to the public capital markets, but this is fairly rare. As in proprietorships, capital is illiquid. Usually partners can only withdraw their ownership interest when they retire. Other lenders must wait for their loans to be repaid over time or force bankruptcy.

Corporations have the best access to capital markets. They can issue both equity and debt in the public markets and they can also borrow from banks. Lenders of both equity and debt capital can sell their interest quickly with little effect on price.

Monitoring Management

In a proprietorship there is no mechanism for monitoring management: the owner is the manager and makes all the decisions in his or her own interest.

In a partnership, mutual monitoring is operative. Each partner is expected to expend effort and exercise judgment in overseeing what the other partners are doing.

When the partnership involves co-ownership, and the parties share the profits relatively equally, there is a great deal of mutual monitoring, consultation, and internal information. Partnerships may divide the organization into units, such as divisions or departments, where to a large extent partners are rewarded for the performance of that unit.

In a corporation, there is separation of ownership from management. Typically, there is a hierarchical structure with the board of directors at the top of the pyramid. Legally, managers of the corporation are employees who are responsible to the Board. This means that extensive information is required. Extensive accounting information helps shareholders verify that managers are not defrauding them, making unnecessary expenditures, or taking unwarranted risks.

The differences in monitoring and information flows thus lead to a difference in the centralization of management. In the proprietorship, all decisions go to the proprietor. In a partnership, the structure is more diffuse; many decisions are made by the individual partner, by the team, or department. In the corporation, there is much greater centralization, so that virtually all important decisions must go through major committees, the CEO, and the Board. The need to report encourages a hierarchical structure, which simplifies information flows; each level is able to report only the important information to the next level.

However, the most critical difference between proprietorships, partnerships, and corporations is the extent to which both human *and* financial resources are committed solely to the firm, or are free to be invested, or work in other ventures. The degree to which these resources are fluid or dedicated to the firm affects both the firm's capacity to provide goods and services, and its ability to generate the capabilities required to meet its goals. The mobility of a company's human and financial resources may be the fundamental factor determining compensation, the selection of managers, how management is monitored, and access to financing.

A proprietorship is an extreme example of *dedicated* resources. The owner cannot be fired; he or she is an integral part of the organization. It is usually not possible to withdraw either the human or financial capital without terminating the organization in its current form. For example, when the proprietors of a "mom and pop" grocery store wish to retire, the business often closes. One way to provide continuity is to pass the business on to the next generation, keeping the firm attached to the family. Nevertheless, the resources remain dedicated since they cannot be easily withdrawn.

A corporation, in contrast, is an extreme example of *fluid* resources. In general, human and financial resources are highly mobile; employees can be hired and fired with few restrictions; financial resources can be readily obtained from the outside. The information flows, which are an integral part of the corporate organizational form, allow this mobility of resources to be well utilized. When a profitable opportunity appears, this fluidity allows the firm to exploit it. It can raise capital and hire people with relative ease. Similarly, resources can be withdrawn or disposed of readily. If a person's skills are no longer needed, the person can be dismissed. Shareholders and managers may change frequently, but the corporation continues indefinitely.

A partnership combines dedicated and fluid resources. It is dedicated in the sense that partners are tied to the firm and are guaranteed significant tenure. It is fluid in the sense that access to capital markets is better than in a comparable proprietorship. New partners can be added with only some difficulties, and existing partners can only be removed with great difficulty. In many partnerships, the expectation is that once a person has obtained the rank of partner, he or she will not move to another firm; it is usually not possible to leave before retirement without forfeiting human and equity capital. The fact that the partners are tied to the firm means that mutual monitoring can be effective without sophisticated information systems or great cost. If a partner wastes the firm's resources or takes unwarranted risks, they are the first to bear the costs. They need to take a long-term view when they make decisions and take actions bearing in mind the consequences to themselves. The unlimited liability feature means they may be called to account for their actions even after they have retired. The main disadvantage partnerships have relative to corporations is that they are not very fluid. It is very difficult, for example, to fire partners if their skills are no longer needed. In comparison to corporations, their access to capital markets is limited.

The Significance of Organizational Forms for Capabilities

Differences in the mobility of human and financial resources mean that different organizational forms have distinct capabilities.[2] The dedicated nature of proprietorships suggests that they are well equipped to deal with situations where long-term horizons and relationships with customers are important. They provide assurance against opportunistic behavior because of the attachment of the proprietor to the firm. This form will be used in situations where the objective observation of the quality of a product or service is difficult. If the firm provides a bad product or service, it is the proprietor who will suffer the penalty. To the extent the horizon of the firm can be increased by making it a family concern, the incentives will be improved.

Partnerships are similar to proprietorships in that the top people are dedicated to the firm. This means they have the capability of allowing long-term relationships and providing some protection against opportunistic behavior. The advantage partnerships have over proprietorships is that they allow a combination of a range of skills and access to greater financial resources. This means that they tend to have more sophisticated capabilities than proprietorships. In comparison to corporations, they have limited access to capital markets so that raising large amounts of capital in a short period is difficult.

Our theory suggests that partnerships should be used where long-term relationships are important and customers are susceptible to opportunistic behavior. They are also likely to be used where a range of services or products is needed, but the ability to raise large quantities of capital quickly is unnecessary. Partnerships are almost universal in the accounting and legal firms where these capabilities are important. These professional partnerships typically offer a range of services, which would be difficult for a proprietorship to provide. Law and accounting firms do not need to raise capital quickly; therefore, access to capital markets is relatively unimportant to them.

Corporations have the advantage of being able to raise large amounts of capital quickly and hire and fire their top employees easily. Their disadvantage is that the top employees are not as dedicated to the firm as those in proprietorships or partnerships. The fact that capital is supplied by other people means that their interests are not fully aligned with those of the firm. As a result, corporations will be most effective where opportunistic behavior is not a major problem and the quality of products and services can be contractually guaranteed. Their main capability is therefore to undertake well-specified tasks where the production processes can be readily controlled and where large amounts of capital are required. It is in large-scale manufacturing industries that these conditions are best satisfied. Long-term relationships are relatively less important, products are usually guaranteed, and capital needs are high.

Table 8.2 illustrates our theory. In manufacturing, where fluidity is important, the number of businesses that are proprietorships or partnerships is small relative to other industries. Corporations are the predominant organizational form by a very large margin. In contrast, in services where dedication is important, proprietorships and partnerships are much more prevalent. The number of businesses that are proprietorships is much larger relatively than in other industries and partnerships are also significant.

The history of the investment banking industry provides a good illustration of the relationship between organizational form and firm capabilities. In the eighteenth and nineteenth centuries the industry was dominated by family-based firms, such as Rothschilds and Baring Brothers. During this era, the prime considerations were the establishment of long-term relationships and the

TABLE 8.2.   Number of Returns and Business Receipts by Organizational Form and by Industry for the United States in 1988

Industry	Number of Tax Returns (Thousands)			Business Receipts ($ Billions)		
	Prop.	Part.	Corp.	Prop.	Part.	Corp.
Agriculture, forest., and fishing	351	122	120	15	9	81
Mining	140	48	41	7	16	87
Construction	1,696	75	381	97	31	486
Manufacturing	355	25	300	20	44	3,118
Transportation and utilities	599	20	149	30	22	780
Wholesale and retail trade	2,414	179	985	230	84	2,891
Finance, insur. and real estate	1,233	868	572	46	115	1,714
Services	6,457	296	995	212	142	644

Source: U.S. Bureau of the Census, 1992, Table 827, p. 519.

Notes: Proprietorships only include nonfarm proprietorships. Corporations include both privately held firms and publicly traded corporations.

maintenance of an impeccable reputation. As the needs of the firms expanded, they were unable to fill all the positions with family members and the firms became partnerships. They were still able to maintain the advantages associated with dedication, namely long-term relationships and incentives against opportunistic behavior, but they gained some fluidity of resources.

When the investment banks were organized as partnerships, each partner had his or her own team, which, to a large extent, operated as an autonomous unit. From a human resources perspective, this arrangement worked well. Unfortunately, the access of partnerships to financial capital was limited. They could only borrow a limited amount using debt because of the high risk of bankruptcy. Their access to equity capital was restricted by the wealth of the partners. Limited partners were a possibility but there was little scope for mutual monitoring, and without this or hierarchical monitoring their capital was at risk. As a result of these factors, the overall size of the partnership was limited.

In 1971 Merrill Lynch was the first investment bank to go public and become a corporation. In the 1980s, nearly all the other investment banks followed suit. By becoming corporations they gained access to equity capital, and the size of their assests grew substantially. On the other hand, the supervision required by the suppliers of equity capital meant that from a human resources point of view very different types of organization and compensation schemes were necessary. In exchange for the fluidity of resources associated with a corporate form, the banks gave up the advantages of dedicated resources. In particular, the people who were previously partners now became employees and were no longer as closely tied to the firm. Motivating these people to act in the interests of the firm has been a significant problem. Whereas partners have incentives to avoid unnecessary costs and unwarranted risks, employees are essentially using the shareholders' money and controls on their actions must be more direct. If employees are given the possibility of earning large amounts when investments are successful, they may be too willing to take risks. If they are successful, they make a fortune; if they are unsuccessful, they do not lose money and, at worst, may have to change jobs. In a partnership their own money would be at risk.

The difficulties of switching from a partnership to a corporate form are well illustrated by some of the problems Salomon Brothers, Inc. has had in recent years (Management Brief, *The Economist*, September 5, 1992). Under their old system, partners' earnings largely remained in the firm and the amount of cash they received in the short run was relatively small. When it switched to being a corporation, there was no longer the same security of tenure; as a result, deferred payments became problematic because employees could be fired. There was therefore a switch to shorter-term incentive schemes, which involved higher cash payments. For example, Salomon introduced a "phantom share" system where employees received a bonus related to the share price, provided they stayed with the firm for five years. This was a much shorter period than partners had previously been expected to wait. Cash bonuses also increased substantially. In 1990, for example, one trader earned a $23 million bonus. *The Economist* suggested that the payment system used to supplant the old partnership profit sharing system "proved disastrous." In contrast, Goldman Sachs has thrived; in the period from 1986-1991, it has outperformed its major rivals, Morgan Stanley & Company Inc., Salomon and Merrill Lynch in terms of pretax earnings (*The Wall Street Journal*, September 22, 1991).

Other industries—in particular the restaurant industry—offer interesting examples of the significance of organizational form for capabilities. The service provided at quality restaurants is difficult to guarantee. Each meal is unique, and specifying a standard procedure is almost impossible; a dedication to traditions and standards for quality is, however, a must. In this sector, proprietorships are almost universal. Owners know that if they fail to deliver quality, the restaurant will go bankrupt and they will lose their investment. In contrast, in the fast-food end of the market, the product is much more standardized. The menu remains largely unchanged and ensuring quality is much easier than at the top end of the market. In this sector, large corporations such as McDonalds and Burger King dominate. The fluidity of resources that corporations have means that they can invest heavily and bring a wide range of advertising and marketing skills to bear.

Grain trading has traditionally been dominated by five major companies. All of these are privately owned. Cargill, the largest grain trading company and the largest proprietorship in the United States, is entirely owned and run by the Cargill and Macmillan families. To a surprising extent, the grain trade is relationship-based. The transaction costs of measuring the quality of all the grain are high, and trust between farmer and purchaser plays an important role. The dedicated nature of a family firm such as Cargill fosters this trust.

Concluding Remarks

In sum, we argue that a critical reason in firms' selection of one organizational form over another is the capabilities of each to provide goods and services to the firms' external clients. Each organizational form strikes a different balance between access to human and financial resources, and their continuing dedication to the firm. A firm that finds itself in, or looking to enter a product or service market where there is greater demand for fluid or dedicated capabilities will need to design or redesign its organizational form accordingly.

We do not think, however, that capabilities is the only determinant of the choice of organizational form. Another factor that has received much attention in the literature is taxes. Scholes and Wolfson (1992) have provided an extensive analysis of the incentives provided by the tax system (See, in particular, chap. 4, Mackie-Mason and Gordon 1991). The corporate income tax distorts the incentives to choose a particular organizational form by taxing corporations more than other organizational forms. Nor is organizational form the only explanation for the troubles that befell Salomon Brothers and other Wall Street firms that became corporations during the 1980s.

Our analysis of firm capabilities and organizational form, however, has implications for a comparison of institutional structures in different countries. A chief criticism levelled against U.S. firms in recent years has been that their time horizon is much shorter than in firms in other countries, such as Japan. Our analysis suggests that this difference might be explained by the fact that large Japanese corporations appear to mix the corporate and partnership models. R. Dore (1992) has argued that the equity suppliers to Japanese corporations operate more like partners or stakeholders than stockholders:

> The main distinctive features of the Japanese situation are as follows: (1) A heavy, though in the last decade rapidly diminishing, reliance on bank loans rather than equity capital; (2) One of the banks is generally considered a firm's lead bank. It may provide only marginally more loan capital than other banks, but it will own more of the firm's equity, it will put forth more effort into monitoring the company's performance, and it will be the prime mover in any brink-bankruptcy reconstructions; (3) A large part of the equity is in the hands of friendly, corporate stock-holders: the suppliers, banks, insurers, trading companies, dealers it does business with. . . . For most firms, the percentage [of floating stock holdings] is relatively small. (P. 9)

Paralleling the financial aspect of the firm, the large Japanese firm views its top managers as key "stakeholders," who operate almost like general partners. These managers have been carefully selected, enjoy long-term employment in their firms, have developed a great deal of firm-specific human capital, and see reward and sacrifice in the firm's fate. Given that the organizational form of the Japanese corporation is a mix or hybrid of the partnership and corporate form, it is not surprising that Japanese corporations appear to be able to have some dedicated capabilities while still having some fluid capabilities.

Japanese firms suggest the wealth of possible choices of organizational form that are available to organizations. Complex attachments of forms may occur through pooling arrangements like franchising, where a parent corporation is linked with a proprietorship. The corporation provides the fluid resources and capabilities; the proprietorship provides the dedicated link to the client.

Such pooling arrangements are the focus of a growing literature that has caught the attention of business practitioners and students of organizations alike. In practice, there is an almost infinite number of configurations. Existing forms in organizations are constantly changing in an attempt to have a form that has more of the advantages of fluidity, as well as dedication. These changes reflect the very significant role for organizational form in the design and re-design of firms.

Notes

We thank our discussants David Pierson of Towers and Perin, Ned Bowman, Bruce Kogut, and Jeffrey Trester for helpful comments and suggestions. Franklin Allen is grateful for financial support from the NSF.

1. The term organizational form is used in a number of ways. One common use of it is for distinguishing among various organizational structures (Daft, 1986; Williamson, 1985), such as the large functional or unitary form (U-form) versus the multi-divisional form (M-form). We use the term in a more fundamental way to refer to the basic choice between proprietorships, partnerships and corporations. Our use of the term corresponds to its legal meaning.
2. For further development of how human resources links to organizational capabilities, see Sherer (1993).

References

Daft, Richard L. 1986. *Organization theory and design,* 2nd ed. St. Paul, Minn.: West Publishing Company.

Dore, Ronald. 1992. Japan's version of managerial capitalism. In *Transforming organizations,* edited by T. A. Kochan and M. Useem 17–27. New York: Oxford University Press.

Fama Eugene, and Jensen, Michael. 1983a. Separation of ownership and control. *Journal of Law and Economics* 26:301–26.

Fama Eugene, and Jensen, Michael. 1983b. Agency problems and residual claims. *Journal of Law and Economics* 26:327–49.

Hamilton, Robert W. 1991 *The law of corporations,* 3rd ed. St Paul, Minn.: West Publishing Co.

Klein, William, and John Coffee. 1983. *Business organization and finance: Legal and economic principles.* Westbury, N.Y.: Foundation Press.

MacKie-Mason, Jeffrey K., and R. H. Gordon. 1991. Taxes and the choice of organizational form. Working Paper, University of Michigan.

Scholes, Myron S., and Mark A. Wolfson 1992. *Taxes and business strategy: A planning approach.* Englewood Cliffs, N.J.: Prentice Hall.

Sherer, Peter D. 1993. Variety and selection in organization-labor relationships: A macro organizational and strategic framework for human resource management. Working Paper, University of Pennsylvania.

U.S. Bureau of the Census. 1992. *Statistical abstract of the United States*, 112th ed. Washington, D.C.

Williamson, Oliver. 1985. *The economic institutions of capitalism.* New York: The Free Press.

9

Organizing the Global Multinational Firm

JOHN FARLEY AND STEPHEN KOBRIN

Organizing multinational firms to capture the advantages of global competition is one of the most difficult problems facing international business managers today. Top managers of multinationals have an intuitive sense that "organization matters" and that the proper fit between organizations, strategy, and environment will lead to better financial performance. Beyond that basic premise, both practitioners and academics agree that adapting a firm to the rigors of global competition is a daunting task—one often arrived at through a process of trial and error.

In this chapter, we analyze the question of the linkage between structure and performance in the global multinational firm. First, we examine the idea of the integrated global firm and explore the paradox posed by the need to fashion a global multinational firm out of local materials. Second, we specifically examine the empirical evidence for the relationship between multinational organization and financial performance. Third, we ask the questions: "What kinds of macro-structures are suitable for this task? and "Is there a logical progression in the evolution of the multinational firm toward global status?" Fourth and finally, we discuss the implications of our inquiry and try to come up with a set of practical guidelines for managers of global multinational firms.

We come to a startling conclusion that experiments in the organizational structure of the multinational corporation may well have come to a logical end. What matters in the design of the global corporation of today is the architecture of process, of measurement, and of coordination. Organizing the multinational firm for performance means the proper design of operating systems more than simply the artwork of an organizational chart.

The Global Firm

What do we mean by a global firm? Although *global* is used frequently in both academic publications and the business press, it typically is not meant to convey its 1992 *American Heritage Dictionary* definition: "Of, relating to, or involving the entire earth; worldwide." We suggest that *global* has three basic firm-specific connotations:

> *Scope:* A global firm has extensive geographic coverage with significant operations in all three legs of the "triad" (that is, North America, Europe, and Asia) and most probably in other major regions of the world as well.
>
> *Cognitive orientation:* In his seminal article, Howard Perlmutter (1969, 11) defined global in terms of managers' mind-sets," . . . the way executives think about doing business around the world." He defined *geocentrism* in terms of managers' mindsets, a global systems approach to decision making where both the headquarters and the subsidiaries see themselves as part of an organic world-wide entity (Heenan and Perlmutter 1979).
>
> *Strategy:* Porter (1986, 19) argues that, "In a global industry, a firm must in some way integrate its activities on a worldwide basis to capture the linkages among countries." (p. 19). A useful and widely accepted concept in the literature is that of multinational strategy as a continuum, anchored at one end by firms whose strategy is multidomestic or nationally responsive and, at the other end, by firms that are integrated transnationally (Bartlett and Ghoshal 1989; Fayerweather 1982; Kogut 1985a; Porter 1986; Prahalad and Doz 1987).

We are concerned with firms that are relatively global in both scope and mindset. They have broad geographic coverage and a management that regards the world as its market and believes that, "Superiority is not equated with nationality . . . (that) good ideas come from any country and to any country" (Heenan and Perlmutter 1979, 21).

Although we have used a definition of strategy that is anchored by both the multidomestic and the globally integrated firm, a global strategy should be conceptualized as a continuum of choices balancing pressures to respond locally with pressures to integrate across borders. Multidomestic firms (consumer products or processed food, for example) face relatively few pressures to integrate across borders and strong pressures to respond to local market differences. On the other hand, globally integrated firms (computers and aerospace) must deal with either the cost of technology or high fixed costs and scale requirements of manufacture by integrating operations across borders. It is important to note that in reality most multinational firms respond to both sets of pressures simultaneously; it is their relative intensity that varies. The critical strategic problem facing managers in the multinational firm is balancing or trading-off pressures to respond to local differences with those to integrate across borders; to deal with the costs and risks of technology, for example, by selling relatively standardized products in a large number of markets while responding adequately to differences in national regulation or standards.

Global multinational firms are those that have global scope and whose top management has a global mindset. They may be found *anyplace* along the strategic continuum discussed above; global firms may compete through transnational integration or by responding to market differences. We often take "global" to mean an integrated global firm that sells similar products worldwide that are characterized either by technological intensity or high fixed costs of manufacture. However, a multidomestic firm—in consumer products or processed foods—may operate in virtually every country with a clear geocentric mind-set. It is *global* in the sense that word is used in this paper.

How Do Global Firms Compete?

All of the costs in managing large, diverse, geographically disparate organizations are exacerbated in the multinational. First, the multinational must operate in a large number of different legal, political, economic, and social environments that magnify problems of strategy setting, implementation, and control. Second, dealing cross-culturally entails significant problems of communication and understanding—of both external events and intraorganizational processes. These problems transcend those of dealing with cultural diversity in the domestic context. Last, anyone who has ever been part of an organization with broad global scope would not underestimate the seemingly mundane problems of dealing with vast geographic differences and multiple time zones.

Why do it? The answer has to be that the firm gains significant competitive advantages from multinational operations. The role of these competitive advantages varies depending upon the firm's position on the multinational strategic continuum. In the case of the globally integrated firm—for example, a semiconductor manufacturer—global scope and integration may be an *absolute* requisite of continued competitiveness in the industry. The development costs of 256K dram chips, for example, are estimated at close to $1 billion. The ability to integrate markets may provide a critical competitive advantage vis-à-vis a firm that operates in just one country. The latter simply cannot afford the research and development necessary to continue to compete—or their associated risks—based on operations and sales in a single country.

The multidomestic firm may find that the advantages of global competition are *relative* to competitors it faces in different markets. A consumer products firm, for example, faces disadvantages vs. local or regional firms in terms of market knowledge, established distribution systems, cultural understanding, and government relations in a context where local responsiveness dominates. The advantages of global competition can help to offset these disadvantages of being an alien in a local environment. In either case, the multinational firm *must* exploit the competitive advantages of competing globally to survive.

We are certainly not the first to argue that the competitive advantages of a global firm flow from its ability to exploit differences in country characteristics or comparative advantages; a multinational network of operations (Kogut 1985b), and/or transnational integration or cross-border scale economies. The global multinational firm exploits one or preferably more of these advantages to survive.

First, the firm exploits differences in country characteristics. It can source labor-intensive components in countries where labor is relatively cheap and productive (for example, Malaysia or Mexico), place energy-intensive operations in an area where hydroelectric power is relatively abundant, or locate research and development facilities where there is a plentiful supply of engineers and scientists. One of the motivations for direct investment in the United States, for example, is to gain access to technological developments in that country.

Second, the firms gain competitive advantages from exploitation of their global (or transnational) network of operations. Kogut (1985b) argues that an important competitive advantage of the multinational is its ability to use its network of operations to take advantage of uncertainty, for example, fluctuations in exchange rates; others (Hamel and Prahalad 1985) posit that cross-border cross-subsidization is the critical competitive advantage. Multinationals with operations in a large number of countries have an ability to scan markets and technological developments—new processes, materials, needs, and the like—and transfer that knowledge rapidly throughout the system. Last, an "exchange of threat" (Graham 1978)—cross-investment by two firms in each other's home market—may be necessary to reduce the risk of foreign competitors competing too aggressively in the home market.[1]

Third, in many industries the increased scale resulting from transnational integration is necessary either to afford competitive technological budgets or to manufacture efficiently. As noted above, the competitive advantages of multinational operations are absolute in this case.

We have seen how the global multinational firm sees itself as a single worldwide organization; how it competes strategically is a function of the relative importance of local responsiveness and transnational integration. In discussing global strategy we have been using terms such as "mindset" and "orientation." Strategy involves mental processes and cognitive orientation.

Organization structure, however, involves tangible or physical reality. Does it matter for performance? We turn to this question now.

Organizing the Multinational Firm for Profitability

We take a broad view of organization, which is itself a much broader phenomenon than it may appear on the surface. At its most general level, organization is concerned with issues of responsibility, authority, communication, coordination, and control. In more concrete terms, organization involves macro issues like departmentalization (functional, divisional, hybrid, and matrix structures), as well as vertical and horizontal coordination mechanisms (formal rules and procedures, spans of control, number of levels, centralization vs. decentralization, or the use of liaisons or project teams). It also deals more with the microlevel issues of job design, planning, designing incentives, controlling, and selecting and training human capital. Besides these concrete macro- and micro-level issues, organization also encompasses the more amorphous but equally powerful factors of firm climate and culture—relatively enduring qualities of the internal environment of the organization, including shared attitudes, values, beliefs, and norms.

Multinational firms are organized in a wide variety of forms. (See the appendix for an extensive review.) Given the complexity of these organizational forms, it is not surprising that the pinning down of superior profitability to any one kind of organizing has proved elusive. Part of the problem seems to be that the best structure does not seem to be the same for all countries.

Take, for example, the divisional form. Many heads of globally dispersed multinationals would certainly find it hard to imagine organizing their operations in any way but by divisions. Yet, studies done in domestic settings provide only mixed evidence that large multidivisional firms are more efficient ("more profitable") than functional firms. (Here we need to be cautious because domestic and multinational settings can be quite different from each other—the apples and oranges problem.) For example, Armour and Teece (1978) examined twenty-eight U.S. petroleum companies from 1955 to 1973 and found that up until 1968, the multidivisional firms had an average profit performance about two percentage points higher than those with a functional form. However, from 1969 to 1973, that performance differential disappeared. Steer and Cable (1978) looked at cross-sectional data from eighty-two large companies in the United Kingdom from 1967 to 1971 and again found a performance spread of around two to three percent. However, similar studies in Japan (Cable and Yasuki, 1985) and in Germany (Cable and Dirrheimer, 1983) found no performance advantage in the divisional form over alternative forms. In fact, in the case of the German study, the firms on average did much worse for several years after the reorganization.

Of course, it is not surprising that there is no one best way of organizing for all countries. Let us examine a few studies that have analyzed different ways of organizing a global firm and their performance implications.

Searching for an Organization–Performance Link

Before proceeding to the empirical studies, a comment is in order regarding causal research on organizations in field settings. Much of what we know about the relationship of organization to performance comes from correlational cross-section studies (that is, they occur at one point in time) or "quasi-experiments" that examine firms in their natural settings over several points in time.[2] Consequently, we depend on changes in the environment (more or less uncontrolled by the firm) or changes in controllable characteristics of strategy or organization to help us characterize "good" firms on the basis of their subsequent performance. The variable to be explained is usually performance and is generally measured with return on capital or equity, but literally dozens of other measures—both accounting and market-based—are used. We usually sample on different industries in various time periods to generate our explanatory variables. Because these research designs occur in a natural setting lacking strict causal controls, it becomes especially necessary to generate reliable data and replicate results with additional studies.

We find relatively little in the economics/industrial organization literature and general management literature linking organizational factors to financial performance, where "performance" is defined as profitability, growth, or reduced variability. One of the authors has done two studies of this linkage.

THE STUDY ON PUBLISHED
PERFORMANCE RESEARCH

The first study is an in-depth analysis of how nearly 300 factors (including measurements of organization and corporate culture) related to the performance and survival of 113 large U.S. manufacturers with a significant part of their revenues generated outside North America (Capon, Farley, and Hoenig 1992). There is no doubt that the most profitable third of these firms (reporting a return on capital of 17 percent) are more international, as they have three times the fraction of revenues generated outside of North America as the least profitable third (reporting a return on capital of 7 percent). The profitable firms had significantly more direct investments, production, and revenues generated in a broad set of geographic areas of the world than their less profitable colleagues.[3] Again, organizational differences between profitable and unprofitable firms were minor and found principally on "softer" rather than structural issues: better access to talented personnel in general and scientific personnel in particular, more confidence in internal communications systems, human resource systems, and marketing systems than competitors, and cultures toward achieving or exceeding performance goals.

THE SECOND STUDY TOUCHED AT MATRIX VS. NON MATRIX FIRMS

As large multinational business networks have grown, so has attention to the "best" way to organize them. For example, businesses that expand by taking a relatively narrow and dominant business abroad tend to develop a geographic type of international organization. Firms developing markets for relatively broad and diffuse product lines tend toward an international product division structure. In either case, the complexity of markets and/or products often cause these organizations to tend to some sort of grid or matrix structure.

The international matrix has drawn particular attention as a way to handle the diversity and complexity that might overwhelm the information-processing capacity of more traditional structures. It is especially appropriate when (1) the environment requires focus on two potentially conflicting dimensions—for example, product and geography; (2) uncertainty and complexity require high information gathering, storage, and dissemination capacity; (3) capital and human resources are widely shared, as are production capacity and product management in international firms. All three of these conditions were met by matrix-organized firms in our sample of U.S. manufacturers (Capon, Farley, and Hubert 1988) where matrix firms: faced more changeable and hostile environments; had more explicit strategies on share and growth; shared resources to a greater degree and were more participative than nonmatrix firms. Further, firms that tempered a strong geographic organization with a matrix structure succeeded in developing more worldwide-oriented sourcing and production strategies. Despite the apparent successes of the matrix in these cases, the matrix and nonmatrix firm earned about the same return on capital (Capon, Farley, Hubert, and Lei 1989).

Explaining the Puzzle: The Process-Performance Link

The failure to find a connection between organizational form and performance is surprising, to say the least. It flies against intuition and against the considerable effort expended by managers to reorganize their operations in the belief that performance will improve.

What is to be made, then, of the above results? First of all, it suggests that firms over time tend to find suitable ways by which to organize their companies. In a competitive environment, performance differences cannot be traced to organizational structures when managers have succeeded in finding the "right" way to organize their operations.

But a more appealing, and complementary, interpretation is that structure is just one aspect of design. What may well matter are the hidden operating systems of measurement, process, and coordination. Being global is above all the coordination of dispersed activities, and coordination demands the appropriate operating and control systems.

GHOSHAL AND NOHRIA'S STUDY

A recent work by Ghoshal and Nohria (1993) provides support for the importance of process over structure. It goes beyond the original classification of firms by structural forms (functional, divisional product, and so forth) and proposes a classification based on a company's "internal pattern of headquarters-subsidiary relations" p. 24. The study proposes in a multinational context the idea that environment-organization fit can result in higher performance.

The structure typology was reconceptualized in terms of headquarters subsidiary relations through three separate governance dimensions. *Centralization* describes the extent to which power and authority are retained at the top organizational levels. *Formalization* describes the degree to which written rules, procedures, and policies dictate what actions should be taken in specific situations. *Normative integration* describes how much control is achieved through socializing managers into a set of norms, values, and beliefs as opposed to bureaucratic controls. Using these three dimensions, they came up with the following classification scheme:

- *Structural uniformity* in which the different subsidiaries are managed in the same way; in other words, there is the same degree of centralization, formalization, and normative integration used in all settings.
- *Differentiated fit* in which the three governance dimensions are changed to fit the local context, where local context is defined as "environmental complexity" and the "amount of local resources available to the subsidiary."
- *Integrated variety* in which a firm uses a differentiated fit but with an "overlay" of a single dominant governance dimension.
- *Ad hoc variation* in which there is neither a dominant governance dimension nor an explicit pattern of differentiation based on local context.

These different ways by which subsidiaries are managed, when matched to the appropriate environments, were found to carry important performance consequences. Structure may not be what gives an advantage to firms, but how subsidiaries and headquarters assign and share authority and worldwide responsibilities does matter for achieving higher performance.

MALNIGHT'S STUDY

These observations lead to an interesting issue. How does a firm get to the position of being a well-performing multinational-corporation? The conventional advice was: adopt a structure appropriate to the strategy. We do not claim this advice is wrong. However, given increasingly complex strategic challenges facing firms, an important issue has become the insufficiency of simple structural changes.

We suggest that the issue of understanding how to become a global firm requires knowledge of how to manage the evolution from where a company is today to what it wants to become. Specifically, most firms' international operations have traditionally been characterized by either highly centralized or decentralized structures. Moving toward a network structure, if it is the desired goal of the company, involves fundamental shifts in a firm's operations. An important issue is the problem of evolutionary design, identifying the sequence of processes required to move toward and ultimately install the desired structure and operating systems.

The importance of an evolutionary perspective is highlighted in the study by Malnight (forthcoming) contrasting the evolutionary process for one traditionally centralized firm (the pharmaceutical company Eli Lilly and Company) and one decentralized firm (Citibank). Malnight's research showed that globalization does not involve discrete and massive changes within a firm, but rather a series of incremental adjustments over time, and that the process differs depending on the organizational and strategic history from which a company begins.

At Lilly, whose traditional operations were highly oriented toward its domestic U.S. market, changes occurred gradually as individual functions moved from being appendages of powerful domestic units to fully integrated components of a single worldwide organization. Initially change focused on building up worldwide resources and capabilities for performing an expanding array of activities to meet first local market requirements before subsequently leveraging such resources to global requirements. The latter stage involved gradually integrating these international operations with domestic ones into a single worldwide organization. At Citibank, with a history of independent affiliates in all major markets operating as "independent kingdoms," globalization involved a

different series of challenges. Their initial adjustments involved building linkages between affiliates to both gather information on opportunities for sharing
resources and to alter the bank's power structure based on autonomous affiliates. The establishment of linkages involved establishing communication to
facilitate coordination of activities before eventually integrating such operations.

Thus, the study suggests that the globalization process involves two inter-
related adjustment processes, affecting where activities are located and how
they are linked. An important factor for a firm in moving toward a network
structure is how it manages each of these processes individually and collectively. For traditionally centralized firms, initial challenges may emphasize
adjustments in locations of activities, while subsequent challenges may emphasize integrating newly installed worldwide operations. For traditionally decentralized firms with extensive, but independent, worldwide resources in place,
initial challenges may involve creating linkages between operations to generate
information on opportunities for cross-border cooperation. As an "independent
kingdom" mentality is overcome, these operations are only then integrated into
a network structure.

How a firm manages these two processes is not only a question of reporting
structures. To the contrary, Malnight argues that globalization means gradual,
but fundamental, adjustments in both where a firm operates and how it structures and manages such operations. It is ultimately changes in both dimensions
that makes a firm global in its behavior. When worldwide operations are integrated and no longer dominated by a single country, then a firm can be described
as a multinational network.

Conclusions

Guidelines for Multinational Managers

Even though the research is far from conclusive, it seems that there are enough
indicators of success factors to make a good "first cut" at some prescriptive
guidelines. Here is a short list of some of the things we have learned.

1. *Organization does matter, but it needs to be seen as contingent on strategy.*
   High-performing organizational forms and processes depend on goals
   and strategies, environment, technology, size, and culture. A summary
   of some of the collective wisdom on these contingencies:
   • If foreign sales are low, then an international division prevails.
   • If foreign sales are large and product diversity is high, then a world
     product division is used for high-technology and standardized mar-

kets. International divisons seem, however, to be sometimes better at more rapid product introduction than global production organizations.
- If foreign sales are large and a relatively narrow product line is tailored for regional differences, then a world area division is used for high-advertising-intensive markets.

But

- If foreign businesses must achieve global efficiency while being nationally responsive, world area or production organizations become increasingly less satisfactory. A matrix organization is used as a solution when the home headquarters wishes to maintain central authority.
- As foreign operations grow in size and in competence, more responsibilities are delegated to subsidiaries. A network (or heterarchy) or lead country design is used when world strategic authority is assigned to the most capable subsidiaries. The emphasis shifts from how to structure activities to how to build in the operating and control systems for achieving flexibility in the network.
- Although we have not emphasized technology that much in our discussion, the new technologies employing "lean" or "flexible" production techniques have far reaching structural consequences (See Womack, Jones, and Roos 1990). Manufacturing firms employing these new approaches will perform best by developing *local or regional core networks* of suppliers and *highly integrated customer information systems* to drive the design and manufacturing process.

2. *Work to locate, train, and keep highly talented, knowledgeable, and competent people.* Skilled human capital is a resource that competitors can find difficult to duplicate, which can lead to a competitive advantage. For multinational networks, it is especially important that young managers be properly selected and trained, and then given assignments around the world. They should be given difficult and challenging assignments that allow them to prove themselves, become more competent, and gain perspective. However, because research shows that the failure rate of expatriate managers is anywhere from 25 to 40 percent (Mendenhall and Oddou 1985), it is especially important that new personnel get trained not only with technical skills but also *relational skills and knowledge of local cultures.*

3. *Establish a high-performance goal setting program.* Challenging goals seem to be part of any high-performance organizational system. Goals need to be challenging, specific, and accepted by the performance team. Goals are especially helpful if the tasks are meaningful and "growth facilitating." Global managers need to be aware of the moderating effects of employee ability, commitment, feedback, task complexity, and situational constraints. To reinforce the high performance goal system, re-

wards need to be seen as equitable and consistent. (See Locke and Latham 1990, 253)

4. *As firms become global and dispersed while simultaneously becoming more locally differentiated, it becomes important to use corporate culture—vision, values, beliefs, attitudes, and norms—to coordinate and control employees.* Bureaucratic controls need to be de-emphasized in favor of "clan control" (Ouchi 1980) in order to deal with the problems of coordination and control in large, globally dispersed heterarchy-type organizations. This advice seems to be contrary to the conventional wisdom that stresses clan control for small groups. It is said of the Unilever management that their first task with new managers is to set up both formal and informal training sessions to "Unileverize" them. As operational units become more differentiated to respond to local conditions, it becomes more important to integrate them with a common corporate culture (Maljers 1992). Jack Welch of General Electric has spent years trying to build up a consistent corporate vision *("Be customer driven." "Be number 1 or number 2 or get out." "Work on speed and agility." "Quality." "Ownership." "Continual change." "Respect for others." and "Boundarylessness.")*[4] These messages are so ingrained in G.E. management around the world that there is no need to do fine-grained monitoring of their activities; they just act on the vision.

Concluding Comments

On the basis of the large-scale studies cited here, it is difficult to find a consistent pattern that shows a causally strong organization/performance connection between organization and performance for either domestic or multinational firms. This finding is in sharp contrast to the evidence that environmental and strategic factors are consistently related to current and future performance and firm survival. It appears likely that ready access to good resources and organizational practices that encourage innovation (including challenging goal setting and high-quality vertical and horizontal communications) contributes to short- and long-term performance.

Our best guess at this point is that managements of large multinationals have been more successful at putting workable organizational structures in place than they have been in dealing with the vagaries of competitors and customers in the marketplace. Thus, it pays to watch organizational developments in successful innovative firms, as they probably lead the way in this process. The constant organizational changes or at least tinkering that seems to characterize many multinationals indicates that functional managers keep the firm more or less on track. Process, not structure, is the central factor in influencing international corporate performance.

Appendix: The Varieties of
Multinational Firm Structures
by Mark Hanna

Multinational firms can take on many kinds of structures. We will review here the kinds of structures typically seen in United States multinationals and make a brief note of some different forms found in European and Japanese firms. Following the example of Stopford and Wells (1972) and Malnight (1994), we take a "life cycle" or "evolutionary" approach to these forms. We say "almost" because real organizations do not always follow textbook prescriptions of what "ought" to happen to them.

The course of organizational evolution can vary with culture and geographical location. Sometimes organizations skip over certain stages or regress back— usually because of some unforeseen contingency factor. Our discussion covers the following U.S. multinational forms, which (roughly) increase in complexity of coordination and control: small enterprise, holding company, worldwide functional, divisional, (which can include international division, worldwide product, worldwide area), worldwide mixed, and worldwide matrix. We also make brief mention of some alternative structures: network structures, the European mother-daughter structure, the Japanese trading company, and the heterarchy.

Organizational Forms with Simple Structures

Organizational structures that can have very limited strategic planning, coordination, and control capability include the entrepreneurial form, the domestic holding company, and the functional firm.

SMALL ENTERPRISE

In the early part of an organization's life cycle, the firm is both created and then run by one person with the help of a small but dedicated group of employees. A small exporting company might have this form as it first starts out. The organization might be characterized as having a "simple structure" (Mintzberg 1979). There are usually very few support or staff persons. Coordination and control mechanisms are minimal.

THE FUNCTIONAL FORM

The *functional form* is often an appropriate structure early in the organization's life cycle. The functional form is where activities are grouped into functionally specialized areas like marketing, accounting, finance, production, and so forth. They might also be found grouped by work process or by knowledge, skills, or discipline. A functional firm that conducts international business might take the form of a domestic firm with an export office, or it might take the form of a worldwide functional, where every function gets scaled up to the global level. Another possibility, one that U.S. manufacturers often took advantage of, was to *establish an autonomous subsidiary*. Stopford and Wells, in their study of 170 U.S. manufacturing multinationals, note that many of these firms "stumbled into manufacturing abroad without much design." They go on to say that:

> The threat of losing an export market to a competitor often leads managers to decide that the firm should build its own plant abroad to maintain its competitive position. The firm has taken the first step towards becoming multinational without having had an explicit plan for doing so. . . . Purely non economic reasoning sometimes influences managers. The rush to invest in Europe during the late 1950s undoubtedly induced some managers to follow suit because they did not want to be judged old-fashioned (Stopford and Wells 1972, 19–20).[5]

It is also possible for a domestic functional form to turn into a *worldwide functional* form if the company needs to expand into the international arena, and its supplies and environment are sufficiently stable. For example, in a study conducted by Daniels, Pitts, and Tretter (1984), ten out of ninety-two large U.S. multinationals had a worldwide functional form. The authors note that all were raw materials extractors and eight of them involved energy or where characterized by high capital intensity.

More Complex Coordination and Control Structures

Some of the more complex organization structures include the multidivisional, the mixed structure, and the matrix firm.

HOLDING COMPANY

The holding company is a divisionalized firm in which the necessary internal controls are missing—or virtually so. Thus, a moderately successful businessperson might decide to set up a loose collection of businesses—a small vineyard in southern France, a furniture factory in Spain, a travel agency in Germany—each of which might have its own president. In continental Europe, these firms are often in closely related businesses.

MULTIDIVISONALS

As the firm grows in volume and product diversity or in geographical dispersion, the firm often reorganizes itself into a *multidivisional* form (also called *divisional*). Each division is a semiautonomous profit center and usually has a functional organizational structure. Multidivisional firms that have an unrelated product strategy (one division handles defense hardware, another is in hotel services, and yet another handles agricultural products) are called *conglomerates*.

The divisional form separates operating from strategic decision making and relies on an internal control apparatus that is systematically employed. Thus, the headquarters engages in both strategic planning and monitoring activities while the divisions carry out the actual day-to-day operations. Each division is examined through internal audits and compensation is awarded based on performance. Most importantly, the headquarters allocates cash to each division based on their ability to yield further profits.

There are numerous advantages to the divisional form besides issues of pure efficiency. The form decentralizes decision making, which allows for adaptability in a quickly changing environment. Coordination across functions within the division is made easier by having a product or geographic perspective; people get focused on the major strategic or tactical issues at hand instead of getting embroiled in functional turf battles. But the redundancy of functions within each department is costly and eliminates any economies of scale of the functional departments. (Apple Computer, Inc. at one point switched from a divisional form to a functional one in order to save money. It is now back to a divisional form.) Another disadvantage is that there tends to be poor coordination between divisions without the provision of liaisons or cross-divisional teams. Yet another problem is that in diversifying, it may get outside its area of expertise.

Multinational divisional structures. Given this background on multidivisionals, we can go on to specify international evolution. While the firm exists with a simpler control structure, it may start engaging in foreign trade or acquire foreign subsidiaries. To deal with this increased coordinating activity, the firm may decide to establish an *international division* alongside its, say, product divisional structure. Under this arrangement, the head of the international division is a vice president who reports directly to the CEO and has equal footing with the other vice presidents. In many cases, the CEOs feel pressure to reorganize when they start acquiring foreign subsidiaries. For example, the Harvard Multinational Project studied 170 companies and found that usually after only the fourth acquisition, many—but not all—firms moved to an international division form. But they also report that about 14 percent of the firms simply skipped the international division form to go to a worldwide structure. (In these cases, there was usually some kind of merger and acquisition activity going on.)

As activity increases and the information-processing capacity of top management gets strained, firms often resort to a worldwide structure. The "trip wire" for such a decision occurs when the international division becomes at least as large as the largest domestic division. The new structures can be organized along one of several lines: by product, area, or business line, mixed, and matrix. We will quickly review several of these options.

The *worldwide area* option is often chosen when the product line is narrow and markets seem to naturally divide up due to legal, political, cultural, or distance considerations. Although the Europeans tend to use this option frequently due to their fragmented and diverse markets, the study by Daniels, Pitts, and Tretter (1984) indicated that only 12 percent of their sample of U.S. multinationals had this structure. Firms that did adopt this form almost always had a high proportion of foreign sales. Of the firms with a *worldwide product structure,* about 85 percent had medium-to-high product diversity (although there were situations where low diversity companies had a worldwide product structure and those with high diversity did not.)

THE HYBRID

The *hybrid form* occurs when a firm has both functional and multidivisional components. Thus, functions that are important to a product or market are put into a decentralized division, whereas other functions that are important due to economies of scale or specialization are centralized to the central headquarters. The *mixed form* occurs when a multidivisional firm mixes two or more division types. For example, a mixed form might include an international division alongside several worldwide product divisions. Kramer and Freudmann (1981) observe that mixed forms may occur because the firm might be in a transitional stage between a domestic structure with an international division and a type of worldwide structure (p. 6).

The matrix. The *matrix,* also called a *grid,* is a special organizational structure where two reporting relationships—one "vertical" and one "horizontal"— are simultaneously imposed on an individual or other organizational unit. Thus, we might see a functional structure and product (or area or business line) structure implemented simultaneously. Sometimes matrix structures are designated with the terms *permanent* or *shifting.* A permanent matrix has a relatively stable structure, whereas the shifting matrix changes when the projects, markets, or people change around (Mintzberg 1979).

When they were first developed back in the 1960s, matrix organizations were immediately hailed as an organizational form that increased flexibility and innovation. In a sense, that is true. But the experience with matrix organizations in general and international matrix firms in particular have dampened some of the enthusiasm. On the positive side, they achieve the kind of organization necessary to meet the dual demands from the environment. They seem to work best with firms that are medium sized or have medium product diversity. On the negative side, they can be frustrating to the people who report to two bosses because there are two inputs, which may conflict.

Some Alternative Structures: A Brief Overview

There are some structures which do not fit into the typical (U.S.) organization theory of structural forms. These include the mother-daughter structures, Japanese trading companies, and networks and heterarchies.

MOTHER-DAUGHTER STRUCTURES

Mother-daughter structures are a hybrid between a domestic functional form and an international holding company. Many of these structures had so many companies associated with them that they almost resembled internal markets. The thing that is so unusual about these organizations is that (1) they seem to have been found primarily outside the United States and had prevailed in Europe and (2) they usually had every head of every functional department plus every subsidiary head report to the president (spans of control of up to seventy were not unheard of); (3) they had virtually no internal controls as a multidivisional would; and (4) they have been in rapid decline during the 1960s and 1970s. According to Franko (1976), the number of mother-daughter structures dropped to sixty-one from seventy in 1961. By 1971, that figure had dropped to only twenty-five. Most of those that switched (about forty four) actually adopted the multidivisional form, most of which were worldwide product forms. (Galbraith and Nathanson 1978, 41–44).

JAPANESE TRADING FIRMS AND KEIRETSU

Known as *sogo shosha*, these are not quite like anything else in the world. According to Kraemer and Freudmann (1981), there are literally thousands of these in Japan, but only about fifty are large enough to do their trading on a global basis. These trading firms include such names as Mitsubishi, C. Itoh, and Sumitomo. The best way to describe these firms is that they are part of a sourcing, marketing, financing, and information grid. These organizations are frequently only the trading arm of an industrial group, or the so-called *keiretsu*.

Indeed, as the individual industrial firms belonging to a keiretsu developed their own international expertise, the sogo shosha has come to play a smaller role in the overall Japanese foreign trade. Increasingly, they have focused their efforts on commodity trade, including that between other countries.

The keiretsu represents a distinctive alternative to Western models of organization, though it is in some ways similar to the holding company structure found in France, Germany, and other continental European countries. Mitsubishi is an example of a keiretsu. Distinct companies specializing in chemicals, electronics, autos, and trade (for example, Mitsubishi's sogo shosha) are part of the group, and are held together by the role played by the main Mitsubishi bank and various cross-holdings.

In some cases, Japanese industrial groups do not consist of diversified companies, but of vertically related suppliers and buyers. Toyota is an example of such an organiztion. Compared to General Motors, Toyota is rather small. (See chapter 1 in this book.)

NETWORKS AND HETERARCHIES

The Japanese keiretsu is, in many ways, a network of industrial enterprises. There is a fairly wide conviction that the traditional classification of categorizing firms by their structure (for example, functional or divisional) is less useful for understanding trends in the design of multinational and other complex organizations. Instead, the design of complex firms operating in today's volatile environments is much closer to that of the Japanese network.

A network form of design appears as a better way to handle the uncertainty of the market and to profit by the coordination of activities among business units and countries. Whereas there is agreement that coordination of a network is valuable (Kogut, 1985b), there are different views regarding the overall trends. Bartlett and Ghoshal (1990) suggest that multinational networks are characterized by assigning different functions to country subsidiaries depending on the resources of the location and their own competence. Prahalad and Doz (1987) have advocated more strongly the notion of a "lead country" subsidiary, whereby the subsidiary that has developed specialized competence in an important market takes on global responsibilities. In fact, many firms, such as Asea Brown Boverie, IBM, and Proctor and Gamble, have moved some or many global product responsibilities to diverse country locations. The advantage of this lead country form is that it gives initiative to so-called foreign subsidiaries to build on what they do best for the benefit of the global corporation.

An extreme argument is that the structural hierarchy of the firm is giving way to what Gunnar Hedlund (1986) has called a "heterarchy." Unlike the traditional form, a heterarchy consists of multiple centers. Coordination and control relies heavily on long-term careers and shared values rather than on financial yardsticks of performance. The price of this kind of organization is redundancy; the benefit is the encouragement placed on flexibility and exploration of new markets and ideas. Hedlund distinguishes the structural hardware from the psychological software of the heterarchy. The heterarchy is unlike the matrix in that it has more mixed and flexible dimensions and does not end in an apex "top manager." Conflicts are resolved with arms-length bargaining or conflict resolution techniques based on shared perspectives. The human resource aspects of heterarchies include rotating personnel, developing the capacity for strategic thinking among a broader range of people, and encouraging the willingness to take risks and experiment. It is interesting that there has been a change in the conventional wisdom regarding the backwardness of the European form of organization. In fact, the mother-daughter form appears to be well suited as a platform from which to develop a network organization. Perhaps because the structure is more fluid, there is a need to develop operating systems by which to support coordination and flexibility. It may well be no coincidence that European firms, such Asea Brown Boverie, are often held up as the current standard of what constitutes the future design of multinational firms.

Notes

We would like to acknowledge the editorial assistance of Bruce Kogut, Ned Bowman, and Vipin Gupta, comments by Howard Perlmutter and the background research and appendix by Mark Hanna.

1. If a British firm has operations in its rival's U.S. home market, it may cut prices at a very low cost to itself but a very high cost to its competitor. To match the price cut would be disastrous for the U.S. competitor. (It may have only a small percentage of its worldwide business in its competitor's home market and be able to afford a loss for a significant period that would be disastrous for the competitor to attempt to match.)
2. These studies are not true experiments because they do not involve random sampling or stringent control of all relevant variables. Drawing valid inferences becomes more complicated, though certainly not impossible.
3. There is some ambiguity about the direction of causation of internationalization and performance; histories of companies such as those in the sample generally show that expansion abroad is purposive (seeking new sources of raw materials and later expanding markets). There are, of course, a number of other environmental and strategic differences between the most profitable and least profitable thirds. (See Capon, Farley, and Hubert 1988, chp. 9). However, the only variable that has the discriminating power is a firm's commitment of a higher fraction of revenue to research and development.

4. For a fascinating portrait of Jack Welch, the CEO of one of the largest multinationals in the world, see Tichy and Sherman (1993).

5. In other words, the momentous decision to go abroad and make a huge investment in plant and equipment can be explained in terms of game theory or institutional theory!

References

American Heritage Dictionary of the English Language, 3rd. ed. 1992. Boston: Houghton Mifflin Company.

Armour, Henry O., and David J. Teece. 1978. Organizational structure and economic performance: A test of the M-form hypothesis. *Bell Journal of Economics* 9:106–22.

Bartlett, Christopher A., and Sumantra Ghoshal. 1989. Matrix management: Not a structure, a frame of mind. *Harvard Business Review* 68:138–45.

Bartlett, Christopher A., and Sumantra Ghoshal. 1990. *Managing across borders: The transnational solution.* Boston: Harvard Business School Press, 1989.

Cable, John, and Hiro Yasuki. 1985. International organization, business groups, and corporate performance. *International Journal of Industrial Organization* 3:401–20.

Cable, John, and Manfred J. Dirrheimer. 1983. Markets and hierarchies: An empirical test of the multidivisional hypothesis in West Germany. *International Journal of Industrial Organization* 3:43–62.

Capon, Noel, John U. Farley, and James M. Hubert. 1988. *Corporate strategic planning.* New York: Columbia University Press.

Capon, Noel, and John U. Farley. 1993. Strategic planning and financial performance: More evidence. Working Paper, Columbia University.

Capon, Noel, and John U. Farley, and Sumantra Hoenig. 1992. Why some firms perform better than others. Manuscript, Columbia University.

Daniels, J. D., R. D. Pitts, and M. J. Tretter. 1984. Strategy and structure of U.S. multinationals: An exploratory study. *Academy of Management Journal* 27(2):292–307.

Fayerweather, John. 1982. *International business strategy and operations* (2nd ed.). Cambridge, Mass.: Ballinger.

Franko, Lawrence G. 1976. *The European multinationals: A renewed challenge to American and British big business.* Stamford, Conn.: Greylock.

Galbraith, Jay R., and Daniel A. Nathanson. 1978. *Strategy implementation: The role of structure and process.* Saint Paul, Minn.: West Publishing Company.

Ghoshal, Sumantra, and Nitin Nohria. 1993. Horses for courses: Organizational forms for multinational corporations. *Sloan Management Journal* 34:23–25.

Graham, Edward M. 1978. Transatlantic investment by multinational firms: A rivalistic phenomenon? *Journal of Post-Keynesian Economics* 63:82–99

Hamel, Gary, and C. K. Prahalad. 1985. Do you really have a global strategy? *Harvard Business Review* July–Aug.:139–48.

Hedlund, Gunnar. 1986. The hypermodern MNC: A hierarchy? *Human Resource Management* spring:9–35.

Heenan, David A., and Howard Perlmutter. 1979. *Multinational organizational development: a social architectural perspective.* Reading, Mass.: Addison-Wesley.

Kogut, Bruce. 1985a. Designing global strategies: Comparative and competitive value-added chains. *Sloan Management Review* 26:15–28.

Kogut, Bruce. 1985b. Designing global strategies: Profiting from operational flexibility. *Sloan Management Review* 27:27–38.

Kraemer, Robert J., and Aviva V. Fruedmann. 1981. *New directions in multinational corporate organization.* New York: Business International Corporation.

Locke, Edwin A., and Gary P. Latham. 1990. *A theory of goal setting and task performance.* Englewood Cliffs, N.J.: Prentice-Hall, Inc.

Maljers, Florrs A. 1992. Inside Unilever: The evolving transnational company. *Harvard Business Review* 70(5):46–52.

Malnight, Thomas W. 1994. Globalization of a polycentric firm: An evolutionary perspective. *Working Papers for the Huntsman Center for Global Competition and Innovation.* Philadelphia: Wharton School.

Malnight, Thomas W. 1995. Globalization of an ethnocentric firm: An evolutionary perspective. *Strategic Management Journal* 16(2):119–41.

Mendenhall, Mark, and Gary Oddou. 1985. The dimensions of expatriate acculturation: A review. *Academy of Management Review* 10:39–47.

Mintzberg, Henry. 1979. *The structuring of organizations.* Englewood Cliffs, N.J.: Prentice-Hall, Inc.

Ouchi, William. 1980. Markets, bureaucracies, and clans. *Administrative Science Quarterly* 25:129–41.

Perlmutter, Howard. 1969. The tortuous evolution of the multinational corporation. *Columbia Journal of World Business.* Jan.–Feb.:121–32.

Porter, Michael E. 1986. Competition in global industries: A conceptual framework. In *Competition in global industries,* edited by Michael E. Porter, pp. 15–60. Boston: Harvard Business School Press.

Prahalad, C. K., and Yves L. Doz. 1987. *The multinational mission: Balancing local demands and global vision.* New York: The Free Press.

Steer, P., and John Cable. 1978. Internal organization and profit: An empirical analysis of large U.K. companies. *Journal of Industrial Economics* 27:13–30.

Stopford, John M., and Louis T. Wells, Jr. 1972. *Managing the multinational enterprise: Organization of the firm and ownership of the subsidiaries.* New York: Basic Books.

Tichy, Noel M., and Stratford Sherman. 1993. *Control your destiny or someone else will.* New York: Currency Doubleday.

Womack, James P., Daniel T. Jones, and Daniel Roos. 1990. *The machine that changed the world.* New York: Macmillan Publishing Company.

10

How Firms Adapt to
Evolving Markets

GEORGE S. DAY

AND JOHN R. KIMBERLY

Managers contemplating entry into an emerging market, or assessing their prospects in a high-growth market they already serve, cannot avoid the following persistent questions:

- How much does the timing of entry and initial choice of strategy matter? In particular, will the rewards of early entry compensate for the extra risks, and are there entry strategies that can overcome the penalty of later entry?

- As the market evolves toward maturity, what new capabilities must the firm acquire, and how should the strategy be adjusted to ensure long-run success?

- What are the odds of a major shakeout in the numbers of competitors as the market matures? How many firms are likely to exit, and why will they exit? What will be required to survive and what advantage can be gleaned from the shakeout?

These questions are becoming more pressing as the rate of technological change accelerates, product life cycles shorten, customers become better informed and more demanding, markets globalize and introduce formidable new competitors, and once homogeneous markets become increasingly fragmented. Theories of strategic management and innovation need to speak clearly to these questions even as management practice is being influenced by them.

Conventional wisdom and facile theorizing offer some ready answers.

These answers, however, are often either wrong or of such restricted applicability as to be seriously misleading. For example, a large body of empirical research shows that market pioneers tend to enjoy a persistent advantage over followers. However, this work has mainly studied surviving pioneers and fails to reveal the downside risks that pioneers have to overcome. Also the rewards of pioneering are unevenly distributed (Lambkin 1992). Only those that invested heavily from the outset to build capacity and organizational capabilities, secure distribution, and improve their offering are likely to achieve superior profitability.

As research on these questions has progressed, insights that challenge conventional wisdom have begun to emerge. The general pattern of these insights is that while circumstances matter greatly, the impact of these circumstances can be avoided, minimized, or exploited, depending on the strategic choices and the capabilities that permit firms to anticipate and adapt to rapidly changing, multifaceted, uncertain markets—in short, to redesign themselves continuously.

This chapter assesses what is presently known about (1) the influences that shape the initial strategic choices of time of entry, market coverage, product line breadth, and choice of technology, and (2) the process of adjustment of this initial strategy as uncertainty is reduced, a dominant design emerges, and new key success factors are dictated by the evolution of the market toward maturity. Our emphasis is on the interplay of market forces with the firm capabilities. Capabilities can be both constraining and enabling. Unless the pioneer aggressively builds new capabilities and adjusts the initial strategy to keep it in line with the changing market situation, the odds of failure are high when the industry structure undergoes the inevitable consolidation to bring industry capacity in line with market requirements. Later entrants, on the other hand, may be able to exploit the pioneer's vulnerabilities, capitalize on market evolution, and/or introduce a new basis of competition.

These ideas are explored in a context featuring high growth, rapid technological change, uncertainty about competition, market demand, and regulatory actions, and considerable diversity in strategies, performance, and survival prospects of the competitors. This is an apt description of the market for magnetic resonance imaging (MRI) equipment. This context is well suited to our purposes because it brings many features of emerging high-technology markets into bold relief. There is little room for error on either the *supply side*—as global firms struggle to master and integrate many complex technologies—or on the *demand side* as customers make capital commitments of between $1 million and $2.5 million to purchase and install a machine in a hospital or outpatient facility.

Every market evolves toward maturity at its own pace, which is set by the complex interplay of technological development, competitive moves and reactions, and changing customer behavior. Nonetheless, we find the same recurring events in the life history of most markets. These are shown schematically in Figure 10.1. The timing and duration of these events, and the strength of their facilitating or inhibiting force on the pace of growth are difficult to predict. Usually, however, the impact of each event is most sharply felt in one of the defining stages of market evolution—emergence, rapid growth, slowing growth, consolidation, and maturity—or causes a transition from one stage to its next. Managers with the ability to anticipate these events, or whose scanning gives them an earlier warning than their competitors, are much better equipped to position their firms to succeed in the long run.

Market Emergence and Growth

To understand what happens during the early stages of a market, we need to know what led to its emergence in the first place. As venture capitalists know all too well, promising markets may be stillborn or emerge very slowly and sorely disappoint investors. So, what causes a market to take off? These are the issues in this section. Once we review what is known, the lessons will be tested in the specific case of MRI.

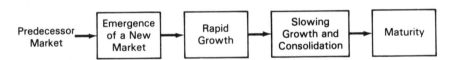

- Technological disruption
  - Pioneering entrants
    - Development of enabling resources and infrastructures
      - Emergence of dominant design
        - Adoption and diffusion of innovation
          - Substitution possibilities
            - Increasing competitive entry rate ⟶ strategic variation
              - Emergence of distinct segments
                - Market nearing saturation ⟶ increasing probability of competitor shakeout

Figure 10.1. Events on the Path of Market Evolution.

Market Emergence

An emergent market can be viewed as a major disruption in a period of relative stability of an established market. To be sure, few managers in intensely competitive markets will concede they have calm periods. Yet, the normal turmoil and uncertainty they have in mind is quite different from the discontinuity resulting from the introduction of new technologies that force the industry down new paths, perhaps even to the creation of a new industry structure serving previously unsatisfied customer needs. During the period of dramatic change and adjustment, competition is between the old technology and a variety of new technologies that have different limitations and capabilities. Eventually, one technology prevails; and the industry begins a period of convergence where the emphasis is on incremental improvements and cost reductions to better meet market needs (Tushman and Romanelli 1985). As uncertainty abates and large commitments are made to plant, equipment, and knowledge, the emergent structure becomes increasingly resistant to dramatic technological changes that could devalue these investments. The result is a period of relative stability.

While the notion of disruption has descriptive appeal, it is unsatisfying as an explanation of market emergence. For instance, it is unclear that the emergence of a new technology with new functions is always the initiating event. Many markets appear to be initiated by small, start-up firms that take existing technologies and knowledge and combine them in novel ways in response to a market need (Utterback 1974). A further problem is that some markets never approach stability, being continuously buffeted by rapid change in the technological base and subject to high levels of uncertainty from market, regulatory, and other factors. In such environments the premium is on flexibility, continuous innovation, and the pursuit of discontinuous changes (Foster 1986, Eisenhardt and Bourgeois 1988, and Page and Wiersema 1992).

SOCIAL SYSTEMS PERSPECTIVES

An appealing alternative explanation for the emergence of an industry is the accumulation theory of change proposed by Van de Ven and Garud (1989). Here the focus is on the interaction of individual entrepreneurs with the enabling conditions that provide the infrastructure (ranging from component and software developers to channels of distribution) and the resources, knowledge, and activities for transforming concepts into viable businesses. Eventually, these elements coalesce into a social system, with three defining elements. One is the *competitive* subsystem that includes all the direct rivals offering competing products to the emerging market. The second subsystem provides the *enabling re-*

sources, including the basic scientific and technological research, financing via venture capital, and a pool of competent human resources. Third, there is an *institutional* subsystem that comprises government regulations and policies, quality and performance standards, patent protection, endorsements by trusted institutions, trade associations and other organizations that lobby on behalf of the members of the industry.

Each of these elements of the social system is necessary for the emergence of a new industry. Over time, these elements become more closely coupled, interdependent, and committed to the new technology. Their increasing isolation from traditional industries signals the full emergence of a new industry able to serve a new market.

Market Growth

New entrants are attracted to an emerging opportunity by the potential size of the market, and prospects for significant growth. In turn their entry—and the subsequent jockeying for advantage and investment in market positions— further stimulates growth. But what made the growth prospects attractive in the first place? Some markets born of the convergence of a market need and technological solution grow rapidly, while others penetrate the potential market very slowly and exhibit a virtually flat sales curve for many years. One explanation for this observed diversity in patterns of growth comes from research on the diffusion of innovations (Rogers 1983). According to this work, the factors that explain why some innovations spread more quickly than others include:

- The perceived advantage of the new product relative to the best available alternative.
- The risk perceived by prospective buyers because of their uncertainty about performance.
- Barriers to adoption (such as a commitment to existing facilities or investments in the previous generation of technology) will slow acceptance.
- Information and availability. Not only must the product be readily available (for purchase and servicing), but also the buyer must also be informed of the benefits.

Facilitating the Diffusion Process

The ability of a new product to quickly penetrate a potential market is improved by (1) enhancements in performance that increase the relative advantage over the alternatives, (2) reductions in the uncertainty perceived by both prospective buyers and potential entrants, and (3) the expansion of the market itself, which creates new possibilities for segmentation and the adaption of the product to better fit the needs of customer groups whose needs were previously too modest to be served. Thus, with the advent of new competitors and increased experience with the product, the growth process gains an increased capacity to sustain itself.

Initial acceptance of a product is often slowed by lack of buyer experience and information that results in tentative behavior for coping with uncertainty. Buying patterns are marked by experimental purchases, pilot tests, and delays in commitments. The usage of the product is also tentative. The new product is frequently underutilized, or confined to lead users who may or may not share their experiences (Von Hippel 1988). Meanwhile, there is very little reliable information to help discriminate among vendors, so buyers wait for the picture to clear. As experience accumulates, usage becomes more informed and broader diffusion then follows.

A significant milestone—usually reached early in the rapid growth stage—is the emergence of a dominant design (Abernathy and Utterback 1978; Anderson and Tushman 1990). This milestone has two consequences. First, it enforces standardization so production economies can be realized. Second, it reduces uncertainty for both manufacturers and buyers and speeds the diffusion process.

Often a dominant design emerges when a leading firm decides there is more to be gained by concentrating on one design and starting down the cost experience curve at a faster rate than could be achieved with continued experimentation. The experience curve of a dominant design may also have a steeper slope because both learning and scale effects are more focused.

As uncertainty wanes there is a concurrent improvement in the relative advantages of the product. Manufacturers invest in promotion and distribution coverage to increase awareness, expand sales activities to induce trial, provide service and warranties to reduce risk, and introduce new features that increase performance. Meanwhile, experience effects operate to reduce delivered costs, which permit lowered prices. This effect is highly interactive, for an increased relative advantage should accelerate the rate of acceptance and hence the rate of accumulation of experience.

The early history of many new products is also shaped by outside factors, such as changes in government regulations, changes in the position of complementary products, or shifts in the availability and cost of input materials that improve the appeal of the finished product. For example, the demand for electronic home entertainment products or computers was and still is dependent on the availability of supporting software and programming.

How useful are these perspectives on market emergence and growth? What are their limitations? And how do they illuminate the strategic questions posed at the beginning of this paper? We attempt to answer these questions in the context of the emergence of the market for MRI.

The Emergence of the Market for MRI

Magnetic resonance imaging technology enables the user—generally a radiologist—to create images of internal body tissue noninvasively and without radiation. As such, it is a subfield of the diagnostic imaging industry. This industry emerged at the turn of the century with the commercialization of x-ray equipment that could produce dim images of bones and organs. New subfields emerged in the 1950s when the ultrasound and nuclear medical modalities became available to radiologists and other medical specialists. These were followed in the early 1970s by the introduction of computed tomography (CAT) scanners that used computers to record and interpret the pattern of absorption of x-rays after they passed through the body. Each of these modalities was a partial substitute for previous ones.

The CAT scanner represented a major advance in imaging quality, but had the drawback of using invasive x-rays. When MRI was introduced, in 1978 in the United Kingdom and in 1981 in the United States, it was welcomed as a major improvement because it was noninvasive. An image produced by an MRI procedure is based on an analysis of the minute radio frequency signals given off by the hydrogen atoms in the human body. An MRI machine employs a huge magnet, which surrounds a patient with a magnetic field in one direction. This field is disturbed by bursts of radio frequency energy, which cause the nuclei in the body tissue and bone structure to line up in the opposite orientation to the magnetic field. After the radio pulse, the nuclei "flip" back and emit distinctive signals that can be plotted by a high-speed computer to form an image.

This technology was introduced into the market for diagnostic imaging equipment, which was dominated in the early 1980s by hospitals and radiologists as purchasers and users, and by x-ray and CAT scanners as competing technologies. The emergence of the MRI market was clearly a technological discontinuity that satisfied a well-known customer need. However, a more compelling explanation for the emergence of MRI comes from an analysis of the enabling conditions. Here we find a convergence of supportive factors that made commercialization possible by the late 1970s:

- Availability of powerful superconducting magnets, with the associated power supplies. Even in 1978, it was apparent that permanent ferrite core magnets were inadequate. It is believed that the independent development of powerful magnets for other purposes brought forward the emergence of the MRI technology by three-to-eight years.

- Patient-handling devices and computer systems for data manipulation could be adapted from CAT scanners.

- The radio frequency generator and receiver had to be developed by each of the entrants, but benefited from recent military advances.

- The ability of radiologists to interpret the MRI scans was well advanced by clinicians who had learned how to read the similar CAT scans.

- Direct sales coverage and service facilities (including siting, installation, and after-sales service) were already available from established companies serving the diagnostic imaging market.

Clearly the incumbents in the diagnostic imaging industry benefited by having specialized assets and capabilities that could be transferred to the new market (Mitchell 1991). However, as we will see when we analyze the strategic choices of the eventual entrants, the first movers were not entrenched incumbents.

Sources of Uncertainty and Risk

Any new technology with the potential to open new markets or to penetrate existing markets more deeply carries certain risks for its producers and prospective customers. These risks are born of the uncertainty that is inevitably associated with newness—how well will the technology perform? How great an improvement over existing alternatives does it represent? How big is the potential market? What kind of distribution network does it require? How should it be priced? And, of course, how are other producers likely to respond to these same questions?

When MRI was initially introduced, uncertainty was particularly intense in three areas—regulation, technology, and demand. The *regulatory environment* for MRI manufacturers was a source of uncertainty due to major changes in the hospital payment system, state certificate-of-need (CON) regulations, and the federal tax code (Kimberly et al 1990). Most significantly, in 1983 the federal government established a new system of payment for inpatient services provided to Medicare beneficiaries. Prior to 1983, most expensive medical technologies were purchased by hospitals, as costs could be "passed through" to the customer. For the hospital, financial risk associated with the investment were initially unclear. But since no basic changes were made in reimbursement policies for care provided on an outpatient basis, a new market (or at least a new set of buyers) for the technology was created, and a large number of new entities providing MRI services independent of hospitals sprang up (Kimberly et al., 1990).

Significantly, too, at the time MRI became commercially available, federal statute required all states to have CON programs to regulate the diffusion of new technology to hospitals. Designed to eliminate costly duplication of services of the review process and in the stringency of enforcement, the regulation created uncertainty for the producers as well as for potential purchasers of MRI.

Finally, MRI was the first major equipment-embodied technology subject to a new Federal Drug Administration regulation requiring manufacturers to obtain premarket approval (PMA) prior to commercial sale. The effect of this regulation at the time was unknown. One consequence of these three regulatory initiatives was to create incentives for new location and ownership arrangements for MRI. Whereas previous incentives encouraged hospital ownership, the new incentives, as noted above, encouraged ownership and location outside the hospital, thus confronting manufacturers with a "new" market with markedly different purchaser characteristics. And until the capital investment questions were resolved and until Medicare announced its policy on payment for MRI scans (under what conditions, if any, will Medicare pay for scans and what price will Medicare pay?), manufacturers faced a situation in which their potential customers could not readily assess the economics of the investment.

Technological uncertainty was high as well. There were questions initially about magnet type (permanent, resistive, or superconductive) and magnet size. Although the market moved rather quickly toward superconductive magnets, the debate about the relationship between magnet size and both image quality and potential applications (for example, spectroscopy) persisted. Determination of optimal product configurations was clouded by questions about the clinical efficacy of alternatives and the needs of buyers. And the development of mobile MRI units, that could be moved from one location to another, contributed further to the matrix of considerations that manufacturers needed to take into account in formulating their strategies and developing their capabilities.

Not surprisingly, the regulatory and technological uncertainty described above resulted in considerable *demand uncertainty*. Prospective buyers had questions about clinical efficacy (what the technology was good for), product obsolescence (how soon it would have to be replaced), and the cost of after-sale service. Both the potential size of the market and the needs and nature of the purchasers were unclear as the market began to evolve, and, as will be shown later, different firms mounted quite different strategic responses in the face of this ambiguity.

Market Evolution and Strategic Response

How has the market for MRI evolved in the United States, and how have competing firms approached this evolving market? Despite the initial uncertainty and associated risk on both the supply and the demand side, the market has evolved rapidly. Between 1981 and 1983 twenty-seven units were installed, mainly in large teaching hospitals and research centers and frequently on very attractive financial terms with the manufacturers. One early strategy of the manufacturers was to place the equipment in prestigious, influential hospitals—because they were both opinion leaders and sources of potential research-based information on applications of MRI. By 1985, sales jumped to 144 units, as both medium-sized hospitals (300–500 beds) and free-standing imaging facilities became buyers (or leasers) of the equipment. Since then, U.S. sales have grown steadily, reaching 550 units per year by 1991, with the expectation in some quarters that eventual sales might reach the 2,000 units per year achieved by CAT scanners. Furthermore, as early machines become outmoded and inefficient, replacement sales will be contributing to volume, as will multiple purchases by single sites.

The growth in the market followed a typical sequential segmentation pattern as new segments were successively opened up. This is shown schematically in Figure 10.2. The first adopting segment was large prestigious teaching hospitals, a largely price insensitive segment. Next were the revenue-generating centers (in both hospitals and free-standing imaging facilities), which sought high patient throughput and the assurance of a good return on investment. More recently, sales have grown rapidly at the low end of the market—small hospitals and small machines. Indeed, nearly 45 percent of the machines sold in 1991 were

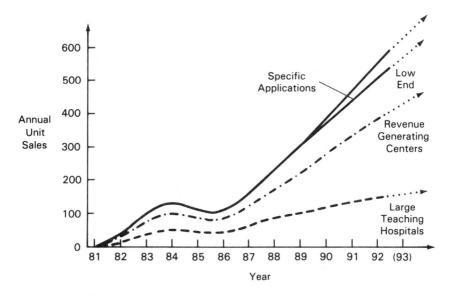

Figure 10.2. Sequential Evolution of the MRI Market.

small, with magnets of 0.5 Tesla or less, and segments for machines tailored to specific niche applications, such as orthopedics, are currently emerging.

The takeoff in sales that began most noticeably in 1986 was due to a combination of reductions in customer uncertainty, as operating experience mounted and regulatory uncertainty abated, and major improvements in relative value. For example, the real cost of a machine dropped by 50 percent, siting costs were reduced with improvements in shielding, and scan time dropped steadily from 45 minutes per scan per patient in 1982 to 10 minutes by 1992. These improvements continue to open up new markets, and new applications are continually being developed.

Competitive Entry, Adaptation and Survival

The evolution of a market involves two reciprocal processes—the demand-side diffusion process and the supply-side production process. The former has to do with why and when buyers adopt a new product. The latter defines industry structure. New competitors enter, the search for advantage continually improves the relative attractiveness of the product, competition increases in intensity, and consolidation inevitably follows as weaker players are forced to exit, merge, or radically transform their strategies. The relationship between demand- and supply-side processes defines the rate of market growth.

To understand these supply-side processes, we need to understand (1) the rate of entry of competitors, (2) the rate of subsequent exit, and (3) the attributes of the winners and losers during this consolidation. Population ecology theory, as adapted to the study of organizations by a number of theorists (Hannan and Freeman 1977, 1982; Carroll 1981; Freeman and Boecker 1984; Wholey and Brittain 1986), has three elements that serve these purposes well:

- A *population growth process* that accounts for the rate of change in the number of competitors as a logistic function of the natural rate of increase and an upper limit of carrying capacity;

- A *typology of strategies* for competing in new markets that recognizes the diversity of resources and capabilities among the entrants, as well as differences in their order of entry; and

- A *process of natural selection* for predicting which strategies are most likely to succeed under various types of environmental conditions—notably, the intensity and frequency of change

By combining these three elements, it is possible to draw a number of implications for rates and strategies of entry and survival (Lambkin and Day 1987). A key factor is the density of competition, which depends on the number of organizations competing for available resources—especially customers. In a new population with few members, the competition is likely to be indirect and diffuse, since the relative abundance of resources means one competitor does not have to grow at the expense of another. As population density increases, competitive activity intensifies, to the point where the size of the population exceeds the carrying capacity of the environment. This seems analogous to the consolidation or shakeout stage of the product life cycle, during which over-capacity is reduced due to business failures or merges.

Because the density of the developing population is continuously changing, the resources available to prospective entrants and the nature of prevailing competitive conditions stay in flux. Hence, each competitor entering a market at a given point faces a different resource situation and makes different choices of degree of *generalism* or *specialism*. Some will choose to spread their resources across a broad spectrum of the environment, to spread their risks, while others will concentrate resources on a narrow, protected segment in hopes of earning a high return.

Emerging Markets

Pioneers are expected to be mainly small new organizations set up specifically to exploit first-mover advantages. They may be "spin-offs" from established organizations led by individuals who have the skills and sufficient resources to exploit a perceived new opportunity but are impatient with the slowness of response of their current employers.[1] Because their resources are limited, they tend to concentrate on activities needing relatively low levels of investment and simple structures.

The eventual number of competitors depends on the size of the potential market, the perceived ease of imitating the new product innovation, and the level of profits being earned by the incumbents (Gort and Klepper 1982). The influence of these variables varies with the source of the innovation; if it arises within the industry, it will act as a barrier to entry, whereas if it comes from outside the set of existing producers of related products, entry will be encouraged. Other barriers to entry include requirements for large capital investments to obtain regulatory approval, build facilities, develop the market, or launch the product.

Developing Markets

As sales gain momentum, the potential of the market becomes clearer and the initial uncertainties are gradually resolved. These conditions make it more feasible to design a large-scale generalist organization that can achieve adequate performance by exploiting a wide range of environmental opportunities. Thus, the early followers into a rapidly growing market are most likely to be subsidiaries or divisions of large, integrated firms that have specialized assets and capabilities that can be transferred to the new market. These businesses are likely to enter on a relatively large scale in comparison with pioneers, with a broader product range, and to market the product more intensively. This strategy, when backed by extensive resources and the advantage of a strong brand name inherited from the parent, enables these businesses to become the long-term market leaders and achieve strong financial performance. These generalists, in a few cases, may have evolved from specialists who exploited their first-mover advantages and acquired sufficient resources to undertake a large expansion in scale. However, it is predicted that such transformations will be very difficult to achieve because of the intrinsic inefficiencies of new organizations and because structural inertia acts as an inhibitor to timely adaptation.

Some large followers will be subsidiaries of large, diversified firms with extensive resources but few market-specific capabilities. This disadvantage restricts them to a relatively low share and correspondingly weak financial performance. In an effort to overcome these deficiencies and still participate in a rapidly growing market, these entrants may acquire early specialist firms.

Maturing Markets

As growth slows and the size of the population approaches the carrying capacity (which, of course, may be expanding if performance improvements increase the market potential), there is increasing certainty. Where economies of scale or scope are influential, there is a growing tendency toward concentration, with a small number of firms coming to dominate the market. These long-run leaders are most likely to be large, long-established firms selling closely related products. Nonetheless, these leaders will not usually control all of the resource spaces. The cost advantages of a strategy appealing broadly across the market may be offset by an inability to cater to small segments with distinctive needs. The areas of the market that are either overserved (at high cost to the customer) or underserved by the market leader are attractive and available to specialist firms offering tailor-made products. These untapped niche opportunities are most readily identified as the market approaches maturity. By this time also, knowledge about the relevant technologies and marketing methods is likely to be more widely available and no longer as significant a barrier to a new group of small, independent entrants. These late arrivals may be captive producers, or compete on the basis of lower overhead costs, exceptional quality, or performance for unique customer requirements.

Consolidating Markets

As population density reaches and exceeds the carrying capacity of the market, two classes of competitors are especially vulnerable. The most likely failures are the small-scale subunits of large diversified companies. They are trapped between two sets of competitors better-suited to a more predictable, albeit more intensely competitive market. On one side are the generalists with scale and efficiency advantages, and, on the other, are the more recent entrants attracted to emerging segmentation possibilities whose overhead costs are often lower than incumbents.

Additional dropouts are likely among the earlier specialists, who did not or could not change their strategy of concentration on a narrow range of the environment. They have little slack in resources to withstand any unexpected shocks in an overcrowded market.

As important as who will exit is the question of how many will exit, for this influences the risk of entry. Certainly the risks can be sizable. One study of twenty-one mature industries found a net decrease of 52 percent in the peak number of participants (Klepper and Graddy 1990). In some cases, fully 87 percent of the peak number exited before relative stability in industry structure was reached. This study actually understated the rate of exits, since it only began counting after a peak was reached and the exits began outnumbering the entries. Many exits would have also occurred prior to this, when entries were greater than exits.

How firms exit also matters.[2] Some may declare bankruptcy and cease production. Others may be acquired by existing domestic firms in a bid to expand quickly or cheaply, or to gain access to previously unserved markets. In the latter case, there may be no diminution in the intensity of competition. Some acquisitions may actually intensify competition if they are takeovers by foreign firms seeking to enter and expand sales of imported products while enhancing the capabilities of the acquired firm.

Of particular interest is the consolidation through a wrenching shakeout, in which a significant number of competitors depart in a relatively short period of time. High rates of entry followed by a significant shakeout are most likely when:

1. The industry and its high-rate of growth has high visibility, so strategists in related industries feel compelled to pursue the opportunity;
2. The threats to the growth rate are not considered or are discounted; enthusiasm is particularly contagious when the venture capitalists and stock analysts become advocates;
3. There are few initial barriers to entry and, in particular, the product employs an existing technology; and

4. Some potential entrants have low visibility and their intentions are unknown or uncertain; thus, the quantity and commitment of competitors is likely to be underestimated (Aaker and Day 1986).

There is a further question of what would trigger the shakeout itself. No doubt a slowdown in market growth below expectations plays an important role, as does aggressive share-building moves by either attackers or defenders.

The complexity of the consolidation process makes it difficult to predict how firms will adapt their strategies and capabilities to evolving markets or which firm will prosper and which will fail in any particular emerging market. By returning to the case of MRI and examining how firm-level strategies were initially defined and subsequently evolved, we may develop some deeper insights into the relationship between market evolution and firm response.

The Evolution of Firm-level Strategies and Capabilities in the MRI Market

Firms entering new markets must take decisions about the nature and extent of commitments to particular product configurations, to particular market segments, and to particular pricing strategies. Furthermore, these firms must make decisions about timing and scope of entry. And finally, they must be prepared to modify these commitments very quickly, as feedback is received from the market and technical advances create new possibilities.

Competing firms within the MRI market followed a variety of entry strategies, each representing different tradeoffs between risks and levels of anticipated return. Each alternative requires tradeoffs among resource requirements, market coverage, and capital risks on the one hand and the possibility of preemption by a competitor and the potential loss of a business opportunity on the other (Teplensky et al 1993). For descriptive purposes the three basic alternative are called *niche, portfolio,* and *generalist* strategies, and, in principle, each may be used by an entrant at any time in the evolution of the market.

A niche or specialist strategy is an emphasis on a particular need, or geographic, demographic, or product segment. It represents a much narrower strategic focus than the others detailed below. In the extreme case, it may consist of only one product or service being offered to one customer group to satisfy one particular need. Or, a firm may focus on only one technology to satisfy a specific need, but may offer it to a wide array of customer groups. This would represent a less extreme variant of a niche strategy.

By focusing on only one primary segment, the firm can develop specialized expertise or knowledge that enables it to serve this narrow market better than firms which compete more broadly, enabling it to earn higher returns (Porter

1980). Attention to only one niche may also reduce the risk of a competitive response by market leaders. Nevertheless, a niche strategy has its risks. There may not be enough of a cost differential or basis of differentiation between a focused and a broad-line firm to make focusing more profitable. Second, the segment may not be clearly enough separated from the rest of the market to protect the firm from a strong competitive response by larger firms, or to allow it to clearly establish a basis for differentiaton or cost leadership. Finally, by focusing on only one segment, the firm must be vigilant with respect to changes in technology or buyer tastes, as these could easily eliminate its market or competitive advantage.

Portfolio strategy is well recognized in the strategy literature, though it has been used primarily to understand diversification at the corporate level. In contrast, the marketing literature has long utilized the concepts of portfolio theory to balance product lines (Day 1977) and to understand behavior at the business level. Portfolio theory states that it is possible to diversify away unsystematic (that is, alternative-specific) risk. For example, a portfolio of strategic alternatives can be constructed so that expected returns will be constant, given a level of risk. Thus, the characteristics of the portfolio can be very different from the characteristics of the strategies that make up the portfolio.

An optimal portfolio is comprised of market segments that are expected to be perfectly negatively correlated with each other, given changes in the environment. When two alternatives are perfectly negatively correlated, it is always possible to find some combination of these two alternatives that has zero risk. To the extent that alternatives are independent, it is possible to construct a portfolio with less risk than the weighted average of the risks associated with the individual alternatives. This means that to the extent a manufacturer can find a variety of customer groups, needs, or technologies that negatively correlate with one another, both the risks of resource commitment and competitive preemption can be reduced. What differentiates a portfolio strategy from a niche strategy that addresses several technologies, need, or customer groups is that the goal is to create a portfolio that consists of customer groups, needs, or technologies that are negatively correlated in order to maintain a given level of risk and return.

A generalist strategy is most investment intensive since it requires that the firm serve the whole market. Possible benefits include recognition as a category leader, competitive advantage based on being able to meet all needs, and economies of scale in R&D, manufacturing, and advertising. However, firms may fail to achieve competitive advantage across many segments, unable to satisfy simultaneously a broad set of demands due to the extensive resource requirements associated with generalist strategies. Moreover, by addressing multiple segments early on, new firms may find it difficult to establish a consistent or memorable image.

In principle, a firm may enter the market with any of these strategies. Over time, the firm may modify the entry strategy, resulting in a need to modify firm capabilities. In practice, however, these options are constrained by a combination of existing capabilities, firm culture, and learning capacity.

In the case of MRI, twenty-eight manufacturers entered the market between 1981 and 1992. Of these, some were single product (MRI) firms, some were smaller medical and diagnostic equipment firms in which MRI was one of the several different kinds of diagnostic and imaging equipment produced, and some were divisions of larger diversified firms in which MRI was one of a broad array of products and services. At the end of 1986, the MRI market was served by one single-product firm, six medical or diagnostic equipment firms, and four division of larger firms, with two divisions of larger firms having been acquired by a larger diversified firm. As noted in Teplensky et al (1993), the strategies pursued by the manufacturers were related to their corporate structure; those that were part of larger diversified firms tended to focus on high-end products and on large- and moderate-size hospitals, whereas those in the medical or diagnostic equipment exclusively focused on smaller magnets and on freestanding imaging facilities and smaller hospitals.

In the first five years of the market's evolution, all manufacturers increased installations in smaller hospitals and broadened their scope to include both hospitals and nonhospital sites and both fixed and mobile units. However, there was a striking difference in the speed with which they moved. Furthermore, technology strategy and market strategy were tightly coupled; firms that installed units in hospitals had a high proportion of superconductive large magnets; those installing relatively large numbers of their units in freestanding imaging facilities tended to install units with smaller magnets. As the market has evolved subsequently, however, the forms of segmentation has become less firm specific.

The observed pattern of competitive entry and consolidation is generally consistent with our expectations. The most interesting departures are traceable to the growing necessity for competitors to have a global strategy and presence. So, while the U.S. market continues to have distinct requirements, it is increasingly being served by global competitors with considerable staying power.

When the U.S. market emerged in 1981, it was being served by three U.S.-based pioneers. Each was a specialist with limited prior sales to the medical diagnostic imaging market, who entered with small (less than 0.5 Tesla) machines. As expected, none has survived, two were acquired by larger firms as a way of speeding entry. The third was unable to compete on cost or performance and failed.

By the end of 1983, seven more firms had entered. Most of these early followers were incumbents of other parts of the industry. They were led by General Electric (GE), who dramatically changed the industry by introducing the largest possible (1.5 Tesla) field strength magnet. They had announced their intentions in 1981 and were able to persuade many hospitals to wait for the promised higher resolution and faster throughput.

Four more firms entered the market between 1984 and 1986. Modest consolidation was experienced during this time because of abrupt slowing of sales in 1986, and two players that were divisions of large firms were acquired by other participants. In general, these later entrants were not diagnostic imaging companies, which conforms to expectations.

Between 1986 and 1992, another nine firms entered the U.S. market. Many were Japanese or European firms seeking to expand their scope beyond their home markets. Although these firms had secure positions in their home markets, because hospitals tend to buy domestically, they needed a broader base of sales to fund R&D investments, as well as the benefits from being exposed to emerging market requirements. The entry was typically by acquisition or joint venture.

By 1992, twenty of the original twenty-eight aspirants were still active in the market, even though it was widely believed that only two were showing profitability. This pattern of gradual consolidation without a distinct shakeout was largely explainable by the continued prospects for growth (since sales were running at half of long-run potential) and service revenue. Once an MRI unit is installed, it is virtually impossible to replace, so the incumbent gets a steady stream of service revenue. By 1995, the average firm was expected to get 80 percent of its MRI profit contribution from service. More fundamentally, there was widespread belief that a firm could not be a future player in medical diagnostic imaging without offering MRI. The MRI market continues to expand, and MRI will substitute for other modalities. Optimism about future prospects will continue to justify substantial losses and will slow consolidation.

Conclusions

In this chapter, we have considered what is known about how firms adapt to evolving markets in general and have examined the case of the emergence of the market for magnetic resonance imaging (MRI) equipment to "test" the applicability of this knowledge to a context characterized by sophisticated technology, rapid growth, and high uncertainty in many domains. Overall, we have found that whereas many of the dynamics anticipated by available research characterized the evolution of the MRI market and the behavior of firms in that market, some differences appeared as well. The principal points of convergence and divergence are summarized in the following paragraphs.

The debate about first-mover advantages in general is fueled further by the case of MRI. Perhaps because of the regulatory, technological, and demand uncertainties described earlier in the chapter, the first-movers did not appear to gain significant competitive advantage. In fact, it might be argued that the strategy of GE to focus on the high end of the market combined with the fact that it entered the market late and has been very successful in building market share, together illustrate the potential advantages to be gained from later entry. In a sense, the market waited to see what GE, already a major player in the diagnostic imaging business, would do.

The willingness of the radiologists to wait illustrates how GE was able to deploy the distinctive capabilities it had previously developed in the imaging business to achieve leadership in the emerging MRI market. Perhaps the most critical capability was the web of close relationships it had formed with influential users of imaging equipment—especially the "luminaries" in research-based hospitals. These relationships were built on high levels of mutual trust and strong communication channels. Thus, GE was able to persuade the radiology community that high field strength was important for potential future applications, such as spectroscopy. In the face of considerable uncertainty, GE—already a respected market leader in medical imaging—was able to offer a compelling vision of what equipment was required to position oneself for the future. GE was also able to leverage its far-reaching and effective service capability—a knowledge network of service people who could quickly diagnose and repair faults. This capability was highly valued by the market because it ensured that expensive downtime would be minimized. This was a major consideration early in the evolution of the market when these capabilities required huge investments of both time and money to develop, and neither could be created overnight. GE could afford to not be a first mover technologically because of the other capabilities required for commercial success in the market to which it had ready access.

In a related vein, the single-product start-up firm has an obviously different capability set and a much more constrained array of strategic options than a large, highly diversified firm. The advantages of the start-up firm are proximity to the market itself and focus. These advantages should allow it to penetrate the market deeply in those segments it chooses. The advantages of the diversified firm are resources (which provide, among other things, staying power) and existing capabilities. As the market evolves, the diversified firm may be able to modify its capabilities in ways that both shape the evolution and capitalize on it, as Microsoft has done in the 1980s and early 1990s. The risk, of course, is that large scale makes modification of capabilities extremely difficult, and where the firm is unable to keep pace with changes in the market, it may run into serious problems, as in the case of IBM. From a design perspective, in the ideal case the firm would like to be able to maintain the advantages of start-up as it grows and becomes involved in multiple products in multiple markets. The question is whether and how this can be achieved.

The case of MRI illustrates how the emergence of a dominant design influences competitive dynamics in an evolving market. Although initial uncertainty about magnet type was resolved reasonably quickly, and the market moved toward superconducting, uncertainty about magnet size persisted. Each of the manufacturers had its own particular strategy based on product configuration and perceptions of market demand. As long as some ambiguity remained with respect to the benefits of different size magnets, no single dominant design could emerge. This enabled a variety of players to maintain segments of the market. As this ambiguity diminishes, one can anticipate consolidation as those who bet on the wrong horse scramble to reposition themselves.

Although MRI in a new technology, demand-side perceptions of advantages and disadvantages are invariably conditioned by experiences with other imaging technologies. In the case of MRI, potential buyers were initially very wary because of their experiences with CAT scanners; generational improvements in the underlying technology had required purchasers to invest in new machines, often within just two or three years of the original purchase. Given the high cost of MRI equipment, potential buyers were unenthusiastic about the prospect of similar patterns and behaved accordingly. *All* sellers of this equipment were faced with the consequences. The early experience in any evolving market, we posit, is bound to be conditioned by the previous experiences of *both* buyers and sellers in related markets.

Interestingly and somewhat surprisingly, there has not as yet been a major shakeout among competitors in the MRI market. Some consolidation has taken place, but the niche players have exhibited considerable staying power and may be evolving toward a strategy of after-sale service as a principal source of revenue. Such an evolution, if successful, implies a significant change in capabilities and, for the smaller firms, obviously depends on their finding protected niches where their intrinsic cost and scale disadvantages are minimized. Whether the firms in question can acquire the capabilities required to be successful in the short run, and whether the strategy itself is viable in the longer run, remain to be seen.

The subject matter of this chapter challenges both the sophisticated researcher and the experienced practitioner. Although our understanding of the evolution markets has advanced to the point where broad patterns can be understood and partially anticipated, it has not advanced to the point where specific normative guidance can be unequivocally provided to the firm that is contemplating market entry. The story of the evolution of the MRI market, which itself continues to unfold, illustrates both the broad patterns and the idiosyncratic dimensions. The tension between the general and the specific goes to the heart of the work of the manager. The message for the researcher is: continue to accumulate cases, to monitor and describe patterns of adaptation, and to distill commonalities. For the manager, the message is that the design of the firm must be built on sufficient flexibility in capabilities to permit reorientation in anticipation of shifts in market requirements and competitive initiatives. The half-life of effective organizational arrangements is, if anything, shorter than the half-life of new technologies.

Notes

Financial support from the Huntsman Center for Global Competition and Innovation of the Wharton School, comments by Arthur L. Glenn of GE Aerospace, and the research assistance of Marjorie Adams are gratefully acknowledged.

1. This proposition is also supported by Rumelt's (1987) economic theory of entrepreneurship that provides for institutional myopia, even though all the participants behave rationally, and explains exits and spin-offs in terms of incentive failure rather than as intellectual theft.
2. If the rate and type of exits is primarily due to declining expectations of profits (in the face of dropping prices), it is also likely that the incumbents who do not exit will cut back on their planned capacity expansions. The net result is a rapid slowdown in the rate of increase in output (Klepper and Graddy 1990).

References

Aaker, David A., and George S. Day. 1986. The perils of high growth markets. *Strategic Management Journal* 7:409–21.

Abernathy, William J., and James M. Utterback. 1978. Patterns of industrial innovation. *Technology Review* 80:2–9.

Anderson, Phillip, and Michael L. Tushman. 1990. Technological discontinuities and dominant designs: A cyclical model of technological change. *Administrative Science Quarterly* 53: 604–33.

Carrol, Glenn. 1981. Organizational ecology. *Annual Review of Sociology* 10:71–93.

Day, George S. 1977. Diagnosing the product portfolio. *Journal of Marketing.*

Eisenhardt, Kathleen M., and L. Jay Bourgeois. 1988. Politics of strategic decision making in high-velocity environments: Toward a mid-range theory. *Academy of Management Review* 31:737–70.

Foster, Richard N., 1986. *Innovation: The attacker's advantage.* New York: Summit Books.

Freeman, John and Warren Boecker. 1984. The ecological analysis of business strategy. *California Management Review* 26:73–86.

Gort, Michael, and Steven Klepper. 1982. Time paths in the diffusion of product innovations. *The Economic Journal* 92: 630–53.

Hannan, Michael T., and John Freeman. 1977. The population ecology of organizations. *American Journal of Sociology* 82: 929–64.

Kimberly, John R., Lauren R. Renshaw, J. Sanford Schwartz, Alan L. Hillman, M. V. Pauly, and Jill D. Teplensky. 1990. Rethinking organizational innovation. In *Innovation and creativity at work*, edited by James L. Farr and Michael West. New York: John Wiley & Sons.

Klepper, Steven, and G. Graddy. 1990. The evolution of new industries and the determinants of market structure. *Rand Journal of Economics* 21:27–44.

Lambkin, Mary. 1992. Pioneering new markets: A comparison of market share winners and losers. *International Journal of Research in Marketing* 9:5–22.

Lambkin, Mary, and George S. Day. 1987. Evolutionary processes in competitive markets: Beyond the product life cycle. *Journal of Marketing* 53:4–20.

Mitchell, Will. 1991. Dual clocks: Entry order influences on incumbent and newcomer market share and survival when specialized assets retain their value. *Strategic Management Journal* 12:85–100.

Page, R. A., and M. F. Wiersema. 1992. Entrepreneurial strategies and radical innovations: A punctuated equilibrium approach. *The Journal of High Technology Management Research* 3:65–81.

Rogers, Edward M. 1983. *Diffusion of innovations.* New York: The Free Press.

Rumelt, Richard P. 1984. Towards a strategic theory of the firm. In *Competitive strategic management*, edited by R. B. Lamb, 566–70. Englewood Cliffs, N.J.: Prentice-Hall.

————. 1987 Theory, strategy, and entrepreneurship. In *The competitive challenge: Strategies for industrial innovation and renewal*, edited by D. Teece. Cambridge, Mass.: Ballinger.

Teplensky, Jill D., John R. Kimberly, Alan L. Hillman and J. Sanford Schwartz. 1993. Scope, timing and strategic adjustment in emerging markets: Manufacturer strategies and the case of MRI. Working Paper, Leonard Davis Institute of Health Economics, University of Pennsylvania 1992.

Tushman, Michael L., and Elaine Romanelli. 1985. Organizational evolution: A metamorphosis model of convergence and reorientation. *Research in Organizational Behavior* 7:171–82.

Utterback, James M. 1974. Innovation in industry and the diffusion of technology. *Science* 183:620–26.

Van der Ven, Andrew H. and R. Garud. 1989. A framework for understanding the emergence of New Industries. *Research in Technological Innovation and Policy* 4:192–225.

von Hippel, Eric. 1988. *The Sources of innovation*. New York: Oxford University Press.

Wholey, Douglas R., and Jack W. Brittain. 1986. Organizational ecology: Finding and implications. *Academy of Management Review* 11:513–33.

IV

Summary

11

Modularity and Permeability as Principles of Design

BRUCE KOGUT AND EDWARD H. BOWMAN

Amid the burst of new thinking on how to design the firm, there is, surprisingly, a consistency in themes. In this final chapter, we develop twin ideas, those of modularity and permeability, that represent two of the most important new principles of design. Modularity is a structural design concept to increase flexibility and experimentation; permeability is a procedural principle to amplify the flow of information and the coordination of action across functional and ownership boundaries. In our discussion, we seek to develop the human side of the efforts to increase flexibility through a discussion of the challenges posed to notions of fairness, equity, and loyalty. We lay out, in conclusion, the implications for the design of corporate governance, lateral coordination, and the (declining) hierarchy of authority.

The question of organizing has been a cornerstone of the inherited wisdom regarding the explosive growth in the quality of life over the past few hundred years. In his treatise on the wealth of nations, Adam Smith begins with the division of labor. "It is the great multiplication of the productions of all the different arts," he writes, "in consequence of the division of labor, which occasions, in a well-governed society, that universal opulence which extends itself to the lowest ranks of the people." The sources of this wealth lie in the productivity gains due to specialization and automation of work.

The chapters in this book are an assemblage of perspectives on the division of labor at the turn of the twenty-first century. They share Smith's great enthusiasm for the benefits of the design of specialized tasks. If Smith's famous example of the gains to specialization in a pin-making industry seems antiquated, the overall message remains very modern: productivity accrues to specialization.

Or does it? An important theme in this book is the importance of multifunctional teams, whether it be in product design, variety, or strategic alliances. Indeed, the proposals of Bowman and Useem lead to a board of directors that seeks multiplicity in competence and in perspectives for its members.

Yet, there is a widespread recognition that the weakness of the corporation is a failure to focus on a specialized capability. Nishiguchi's and Anderson's comparative study of supplier relations of the British and Japanese system points to the more enduring character of cooperation among Japanese firms. More radically, their description emphasizes the smaller size of Japanese firms and the willingness to source key components from the outside.

There is a paradox in these observations. There are simultaneous calls for a greater emphasis on multifunctional teams within the corporation and on more specialization among firms. Firms should be more specialized but more cooperative.

Unlike Smith, the contributors to this book emphasize cooperation as the basis of coordination. To Smith, the pursuit of self-interested profit making was the engine that encouraged specialization and, consequently, trade among specialists. The social glue of society rested in the belief that the gains to specialization through trade would encourage coordination among individuals and firms. However, the gains to this trade is realized through competition among self-interested agents. To Smith, specialization and competition are companions in motivating economic growth and wealth.

The stress on cooperation in this book is, in part, due to the inherent problem of redesign. Hackman and Oldham (1980) in their influential book on work redesign note that most change is accomplished either by consultation or collaboration. Of course, change is also effected sometimes by conflict. It makes sense that the redesign of corporations confronts management, employees, and external constituencies with the choice between conflict or cooperation.

So why is conflict not recommended as a method of reform? To a certain extent, the belief in the persuasion of competitive markets is a statement that simple cooperation is not enough. People and companies not only improve their performance by competing, but they also recognize the need for change by the force of competition. There is considerable empirical support for the idea that crisis and change go hand in hand.

But conflict is a poor medium for change among people or firms who need to coordinate their activities over a long history. For some firms, the concept of continual improvement is embodied in continual downsizing. Not surprising, the evidence on the benefits of downsizing is mixed.[1]

There is no easy reconciliation between the incentives associated with competition and the facility of change among cooperative parties. Yet, the reason that the weight appears to be shifting toward cooperation is that change is no longer discrete, but is a permanent feature of competition in many industries. Flexibility, variety, speed—these capabilities are the foundation of current competition because change and uncertainty characterize so many markets.

The joint emphasis on specialization and cooperation is not a contradiction, because the pressures of competition to specialize generates two compensating tendencies. The first is that the risk of specializing in the wrong activity suggests that collaboration is often desirable. Many of the alliances that Bailey and Shan review in their analysis of "Schumpeterian" industries are outcomes of the mutual recognition among firms to share the risk of joint development.

The second tendency, we believe, is the more intriguing, namely, the pressure to specialize in uncertain environments pushes firms towards rapid learning and improvement. Sometimes, this learning takes place among teams on the shop floor or in the work place. Other times, the learning occurs in the joint problem solving among firms, as when a larger buyer places its own engineers at a supplier's facility in order to transfer new methods or technologies.

The paradox of specialization and cooperation is keenly felt in the design of control systems, for example, how to determine the compensation for managers. Ittner's and Kogut's recommendation to use measures to signal the direction toward which capabilities should be developed does not deny the importance of acquisition of specialized competence. To the contrary, it places the acquisition of new skills and capabilities at the heart of the redesign of any accounting and control system.

Cooperation is important particularly during periods of change, especially when the direction of change is not certain. Redesign would be a simpler task, though still a difficult one, if the vision of the final design could be put down on paper as if it were a blueprint. Such a hope is certainly ill-founded, for the very lesson of design in unstable environments is—back away from a permanent solution toward a condition of flexibility in organizational structure.

We propose that an appropriate philosophy of redesign is evolutionary in emphasis and perceived as fair and equitable in process. When sufficient knowledge of the "optimal" structure is lacking, the principle of design should be to choose an organizational platform that experiments with a wide range of evolutionary paths. A firm should not emphasize the working out of its destiny, but rather to what family of possibilities it wishes to belong. A forward-looking principle of design should permit experimentation and subsequent redesigning as markets and capabilities evolve.

In addition to an evolutionary approach to redesign, another principle is cooperative and equity-based. It is hard to expect fluid redesign if norms of cooperation and equity are not respected. One of the most pressing challenges is to maintain cooperation through equity and fairness among managers and workers while encouraging performance by appropriate incentives. The dilemma, we feel, is an artificial one: short-term performance can easily drown out long-term learning.

Monitoring behavior for reasons of evaluation compensation is not, obviously, the only role of top management. Motivating learning is all too quickly underemphasized in the bulging legal tracts on corporate governance and shareholder value. Design is far more than monitoring performance or guaranteeing that contracts are performed; design is the creation of evolving systems, which encourage mutual learning and improvement.

The implications of this evolutionary philosophy, we argue below, are best captured in two principles of design: modularity and permeability. Modularity permits flexibility; permeability assures that adaptive learning is promoted among the units.

Modularity

Modularity is a design principle that appears well-suited to encompassing the joint needs of specialization and learning by experiments. In the popular press, modularity has often been interpreted as a policy of outsourcing in order to concentrate on core competences (Tully 1993). An example of modularity in design in this sense is the common practice of outsourcing disk drives in the computer industry, whereby the drive component can be fitted into (and out of) place in the overall product architecture.

There is, clearly, an obvious parallel in the modularity of product design and of organizational structure. In this volume, Nishiguchi and Anderson have described the Toyota production system as consisting of a core focal assembler (Toyota) supported by a three-level hierarchy of suppliers. The first tier of these suppliers often design components as "black boxes," namely, modular components, which Toyota then assembles into a final product (Clark and Fujimoto 1991). In this example, the modularity of the auto product design has a mirror reflection in the modularity of the organization of production.

Black-box designs are examples of a principle of modularity. Such a design is frequently applied in military equipment. The well-known image of GI Joe from World War II trying to fix the jeep in a remote jungle is a memorable illustration of the dilemma of nonmodular design. In the battlefield, a more effective design permits the scrapping of defective components and their replacement by a black-box module.

Of course, there is waste in this design. Since each module must "interface" with each other, they frequently are designed with redundancy to allow for a mixing and matching with a variety of other components. Flexibility comes at a cost of building an excess of functional specifications. In this regard, it is easy to understand the importance of cross-functional product teams in determining the set of potential product functions that are required to meet customer demand.

In the discussion above, we have made three observations. First, the design of the product and the design of the organization are related. Second, the costs of modularity compared to an "integral" design is the investment in redundancy.[2] Third, the benefits of modularity are best exploited when time is short (for example, the battlefield condition) and the "optimal" design is not known.

Let us examine this third point a bit more closely. Modularity is desirable because it permits improvement over time.[3] We are never sure how well the product design team is going to perform, to what extent customers will be satisfied, and what steps the competition will take next. The quality uncertainty of each module is like tossing a die, with numbers one to six on each side. The design team might follow a particular rule, such as, if the number three or a higher one appears, accept the module and proceed with assembly.

This simple example has a number of surprising implications. Clearly, a product design team might want to run a number of parallel experiments, as it is never sure which one might be best. Each experiment is a separate module and, as a result, modularity of experimentation leads to modularity in organization.

Because we are not sure ahead of time which module will be chosen, there is considerable uncertainty in the interface among the components. It is the problem of coordination that drives up costs in modular organizations. Solving the problem that components may not be complements, that is, they may not fit each other, leads to the redundancy we described earlier.

Consider what this means for a firm. There are now multiple product design teams, some of which may be located among suppliers but whose costs in any event are passed through in the final price. Each team innovates a modular solution, but we do not know ahead of time what it will be. To guarantee that the assembled product works, we specify a list of functional requirements. Yet, we also know that the "best" modular part might be ruled out because it fails these functional requirements; it does not provide a good interface with the other modules.

It is easy to see that integral solutions, especially if based on mass production, are not so bad after all. Designing a computer as an integrated system leads to a product blueprint that can be encapsulated "in silicon". Integrated circuits (which are etched in silicon wafers) are then produced in mass volume; design and production costs can clearly be lower for mass-production, integrated products. No wonder Henry Ford swept away his craft-based competitors at the turn of the last century.

The omission in the above analysis is the failure to understand the benefits of modularity as an evolutionary process. The great advantage of modularity is that there is no "final" design. Nor do improvements have to be coordinated among modules. To return to our earlier example, if a module is accepted today as satisfying a certain minimum, continuous improvement can subsequently further enhance its performance.

The critical element is that improvements are not locked into an integral design. Imagine how much slower the improvement in computers would be if all components were tightly coupled; change in processing time would certainly be impeded if every component necessitated a corresponding change. (Of course, the interface technology most likely would be altered to adjust for changes in functional specifications.)

Since modules can be replaced by improvements, the quality and performance of the overall product advances incrementally by evolutionary steps. Through adaptations made by a design team, the twin forces of the marketplace test and engineering know-how act to "select" the better performing modules and improve upon the less satisfactory ones. In this sense, modularity is the foundation of an evolutionary approach to design.

We have illustrated modularity in reference to manufacturing. Yet, the implications may be greatest for service industries. A MacDonald operation is modular, whereby "components" are outsourced and can be recombined for many different products. Customized banking is based on the ability to offer different modular services to customers, depending on their needs; some of these services, such as mutual funds, are frequently managed by an outside company.

Improvement in product performance in this evolutionary perspective is achieved through new combinations of modules (Kogut and Zander 1992). By a process of trial and testing, inferior modules are eliminated, and the product or service, as a package of modular features, improves over time. The cost of redundancy is potentially offset by these evolutionary improvements in customer value. No wonder that the notion of a life cycle is so complex; models of cars, copiers, and many other products live on, though their modular components evolve dramatically.

What works for an efficient evolutionary design of a product should also work for an organization. As customer demand changes, or higher-quality modules are found, components come in and out of the final product. Can we not accomplish the same flexibility in the design of human systems?

Consider an example of a hypothetical supplier network built on modular principles. (We will withhold our criticism of the human consequences of such a system until later.) In this network, suppliers can be changed depending on the whim of the marketplace, or the success of a competing company in offering a better-"black-box" solution. Failed product design teams can be, at least in the United States, dismissed, as can be entire divisions. The large corporation, as we showed in the opening chapter of this book, is stagnating in sales and asset growth in the United States, partly because more value-added outside the firm is shifted to contractors.

These trends are picked up in a few studies. A 1989 study of 25 companies (eleven U.S., four Canadian and ten European) comprising 105 organizational units showed a rapid increase in the layers of hierarchy as firms got bigger (Janger 1989). (Figure 11.1) Yet, in the late 1980s, between one and two million middle managers lost their jobs; nearly a million U.S. managers with salaries of more than $40,000 were laid off in 1990. (Overman 1991). Clearly, hierarchy still exists, but it is also the object of change.

There are two interpretations of this trend. In one view, the new flexible work force is often based on a contractual agreement giving them far less redress to legal protection. This pattern is not unique to the United States; in Japan, contract and part-time workers, who are more likely to be female or older workers, provide a variable work pool, which bears the brunt of cyclical changes in demand.[4] In effect, contract work is exacerbating a situation of a "dual labor force," comprising a tier of well-paid and full-time workers and a second tier of contingent contractors. Indeed, recent studies of American companies show that while the percentage of part-time and self-employed workers rose only from 26 percent to 27 percent of total employment between 1983 and 1994, there has been a steady increase in the number of part-time workers who would rather have full-time jobs. (Doeringer 1991, Fierman 1994; Pfeffer and Barin 1988).

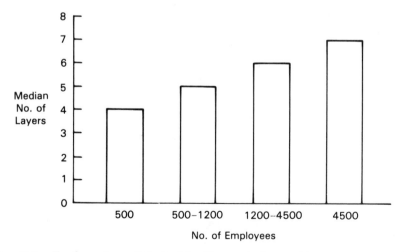

Figure 11.1. Employee–Layer Relationship. (*Source:* A. Janger. Measuring managerial layers and spans. New York: Conference Board, 1989.)

A second interpretation is that the growing number of highly skilled workers has created new labor forms (Sherer 1993). In return for bearing greater risk, these workers provide highly skilled services at high pay. To use the terminology of Allen and Sherer, employee contracts resemble more closely the partnership structure than either the owner or corporate model. Contrary to past U.S. practice where work was "internalized" through vertical integration, the current move, argue Jeffrey Pfeffer and James Baron, is towards the "externalization" of work and workers.

The increasing prevalence of contingent workers, coupled with the evidence on the stagnating large corporation, points to a need for a modularity in design of organization. More work is being delegated to outside firms, or contractors. It is easy to understand why Bailey and Shan propose that the competitive focus must be often shifted from an individual company to the network alliance of many firms.

Permeability

But the analogy between modularity in product and organizational design is somehow not right. The implications are simply too ruthless, and the data do not indicate a widespread policy of contracting and recontracting as economic conditions change. What we have is a greater use of external sourcing and contractors, but without the exercise of flexibility. Why?

An important observation, picked up widely in the notion of a "boundaryless" corporation, is that human systems are rarely rigidly modular as are product designs. A fundamental conflict is between the stress on flexibility and the procedures that bind employees together in large concerns. In a statement to shareholders in the 1988 Annual Report, Jack Welch, the CEO of General Electric, noted: "In addition to the strength, resources and reach of a big company, which we have already built, we are committed to developing the sensitivity, the leanness, the simplicity and the agility of a small company. We want the best of both."

Permeability among units in a firm, and between firms is, we propose, a central principle in combining the efficiency of standardized operating procedures associated with the large firm and the flexibility inherent in a small company. Permeability is characterized by greater communication flows and cooperation among people who are nominally separated by boundaries of function, division, or ownership. Yet, the idea of permeability flies in the face of other well-known principles of design. Herbert Simon, winner of the Nobel Prize in economics, noted that organizational design can be seen as the decomposition of activities into modules (Simon 1969). In this view, managers who frequently interact with each other should be grouped together; those who do not interact should be assigned to different groups. The role of top management is to coordinate these modules.

As fruitful as this analysis is for understanding organizational design, it underestimates the important role of strategy and cooperative learning. Much as Dougherty and Cohen describe, divisions within corporations have an inherent tendency to follow natural cognitive propensities along functional lines, for example, marketing people think marketing. The challenge of a multifunctional design has been to break down these cognitive orientations in creating cohesive and market-oriented project teams. Strategy means that the design should structure the interactions rather than passively reflect them.

Another way that firms are not rigidly modular is that, as human systems, they have the potential for guided learning, for working out ways to improve performance. In the cybernetic literature on organizational design, this potential is called "dual loop" learning; human systems have the ability to be designed for "learning to learn."[5] In a product design, it is nonsensical to think of one module "teaching" another. Teaching, cooperation, and joint problem solving are distinctively human activities.

A case in point is the Toyota supply system, as described earlier. A failure to meet a delivery does not simply result in a shift from one supplier to another. In practice, such shifting is not possible, since the first-tier suppliers tend to be "single sources", that is, the only supplier of particular components. But more important, failures in quality or delivery would lead to joint efforts to solve the underlying problems. Engineers from Toyota are permanently assigned to suppliers, and learning between the various firms belonging to the supply network is rapidly shared.[6] The wall between firms belonging to the network is a highly permeable boundary.

To take a polar example, learning is an important feature of multinational networks, as sketched by Farley and Kobrin. Subsidiaries in different countries have vastly various experiences. These diverse country settings provide, in some sense, opportunities for "natural experiments." Increasingly, international firms are investing in procedures by which learning in one country is transferred from a subsidiary to another. A striking example is the transfer by General Motors of know-how from its joint venture with Toyota in California to its operations in Eisenach in eastern Germany. Nor does this learning remain within General Motors; the knowledge is also shared among suppliers in both the United States and eastern Germany.

It is an important feature of human systems that rewards and participation must be perceived as equitable. A strong motivation for investing in experimentation is that the flexibility of a modular system that relies on only shifting among employees is not tolerable. The investment in learning and joint problem solving is a policy that complies with a deep-rooted belief in the importance of equity.

The little we know about performance and employees' perceptions of equity suggests that their relationship is fundamental. In a study by Joe Harder (1992) on basketball teams, it was found that players that were measured as overpaid were more cooperative; underpaid players were not only less cooperative but they were prone to taking excessive shots. Equity is consistent with efficiency; it promotes cooperation and, where such cooperation is desirable, better performance.

Cooperation, equity, and joint problem solving are distinctive human traits in their joint presence. The easy coupling and decoupling of modules in a product design is beneficial as long as the improvement in these modules are roughly independent processes. But independence is, by no means, desirable. What human organizations do better than physical systems is joint improvement by cooperation. Permeability in communication and in coordination is a critical and important feature in how the benefits of modularity can be enhanced.

Future

The twin organizing principles of modularity and permeability provide the capabilities to respond rapidly with variety and quality of goods and services. But principles of design are not adopted overnight, largely because their implications are understood only through experience and experimentation. The principles of mass production required a half-century to be widely diffused in developed countries. Modularity and permeability—to the extent they capture new principles of design—are only gradually being explored.

An informal reading of the popular press and business manager literature clearly indicates that these ideas are in current parlance there. To cite a few examples from well-known commentators on business practices:

> Organizations will have to learn to work simultaneously on productivity and innovation and almost nobody can do that . . . Neither
> things . . . [can] . . . you do from the top down. These are things you do as a whole organization. (Drucker 1993)

> In the emerging organization, managers add value by deal making, by brokering at interfaces, rather than by presiding over their individual empires. (Kanter, 1989)

> A variety of individual groups allied together under a common flag with some shared identity . . . The center, therefore, does not direct or control

so much as coordinate, advise, influence, and suggest . . . The initiative, the drive, and the energy comes mostly from the parts, with the center an influencing force, relatively low in profile. (Handy, 1989)

No doubt, there is an element of fad in this discussion. But we caution against a too skeptical rejection of this wave of interest in flatter, more decentralized structures. The data, some of which we reviewed earlier, regarding the elimination of ranks, the downsizing, and greater reliance on contingent contracting indicate trends that confirm the spirit if not the precise substance of the debate.

Let us take as a starting point that the principles of modularity and permeability are in an early period of diffusion and development. The question that intrigues us is, what should be our anticipations regarding the evolution of these principles. We propose that the following trends, though still nascent, will become more important:

National Boards of Directors and "Non-national Firms"

There is potentially no greater ground of contention with regard to permeability that in the top boards of management. Who belongs on the board has been a perennial issue. Yet, consider the issue in the wide range of different national experiences. In Japan, board members are almost always chosen from the inside. Despite this, the evidence shows that, contrary to belief, top management people are rapidly replaced in response to disappointed stock and profit performance. Clearly, outside voice is being exercised through the web of banking agreements, usually under the auspices of a main bank.

In Germany, the highest board consists largely of outsiders, often with representation from one of the three dominant banks. By law, workers must be represented on the board of stock companies, and all companies with more than five employees must create a work council with veto powers usually reserved for top management in the United States.

It is surprising that so much national diversity remains a characteristic of boards of directors, whereas work practices at lower levels of firms are converging in a number of ways. The resistance to change is due partially to the slow pace by which the body of corporate law is altered. It is also due to the complexity of financial institutions, in which sizeable actors, for example, commercial and investment banks, pension funds, and insurance companies, are unlikely to be displaced as formidable influences on boards.

What puzzles us is how national these boards are in times of growing international interdependence. In corporations of large countries, it is not uncommon that 50 percent of sales and assets are located outside the country of domicile. In Swedish or Swiss firms, this proportion increases dramatically. Nevertheless, boards of directors remain incredibly national in their membership. In a Conference Board study of large U.S. firms, only 17 percent reported more than one director as a citizen of another country; the percentage was double for the subsample of multinational corporations (Bacon 1990). An intriguing number is that 62 percent of these directors were employees, a percentage much greater than average. In effect, the internationalization of boards is occurring through internal promotion rather than through external constituencies, such as foreign shareholders.

It is an intriguing issue whether "non-national" firms are possible in theory. Firms generally evolve from a home market to foreign markets, and they bring their national baggage with them in the form of organizing principles. To a certain extent, the growth of international consortia, such as in telecommunications or airlines, represent a new corporate form, where national origins cannot be said to exist. Only here do we see boards of directors that are truly international in membership.

The most impermeable membrane occurs, in effect, at the heights of corporate control. As stock ownership becomes more nationally diverse, as employees, sales, and assets continue to be dispersed globally, the mechanisms of corporate governance will also be internationalized. We expect rapid and dramatic changes in this regard.

Lateral Cooperation and Loyalty

Throughout our discussion, we have pointed to the factual evidence regarding the smaller and flatter firm, the use of teams inside and outside corporate boundaries, and the increasing specialization of strategic tasks among members in a network. These trends, when coupled with the potential of new information technologies, have led many industry participants to see a new form of organization emerging. John Scully, as CEO of Apple Computer, commented that:

> When we talk about virtual corporations today, we're mainly talking about alliances and outsourcing agreements. Ten or 20 years from now, you'll see an explosion of entrepreneurial industries and companies that will essentially form the real virtual corporations. Tens of thousands of virtual organizations may come out of this (The virtual corporation, *Business Week*, February 8, 1993, 99–102)

We find this trend to be difficult to assess due to two principal issues. First, for all the discussion of potential, the concept of "virtual organizations" poses a tremendous problem for the bearing of risk and job security. It may seem odd, but we believe that the ripest area of change is in the legal and social protection of a more vulnerable work force.

This protection may be private, such as through the provision of greater work-related insurance schemes. It will certainly be partly public, either in the form of safety nets, retraining programs, and a more aggressive stance on protecting the employment contract for contingent workers. As corporate walls are made more permeable and work contracts, more flexible, the pendulum is bound to swing toward greater regulation of extraorganizational labor relations.

The second issue that complicates the forecast is the notion of loyalty to a firm, alliance, or nation. We do not cite the long list of studies on the importance of leadership as a motivating device, other than to note that leadership implies loyalty. We have suggested earlier that people require the organizations to which they belong to be perceived as equitable. Equity itself implies an ideological loyalty, which is somehow circumscribed by the perception of boundaries.

The bias is easy to detect in the language of "others." We believe our firm, our country, our club are equitable. We do not believe that the rest of the world is or should be; indeed, we would doubt those claims that suggest other organizations or countries are more equitable. The logical inconsistency of all national groups believing in these biases does not seem to dampen their prevalence.

We agree with Larry Hirschhorn and Thomas Gilmore (1992) that one of the most difficult boundaries to manage is that of identity, that is, "who is and isn't us?" Chris Argyris (1957), a well-known organizational psychologist, has long noted that a basic human reaction is the defensive routine, where contradictory knowledge, especially when perceived as coming from the outside, is rejected. Lateral communication and cooperation are always threatened when the sense is that boundaries have been crossed.

The fundamental dilemma is the following. Loyalty, leadership, and equity are important elements in the performance of human systems. At the same time, lateral cooperation is especially critical as a way to reduce the brutal reliance on selection of the best modules (or people) and to promote adaptive learning among partners. Firing people, and asking for cooperation, are easily perceived as contradictory by a work force.

The use of project teams, as outlined by Dougherty and Cohen, is one avenue of further development. We imagine that they will be utilized more extensively as a mode of organizing work among firms through long-term alliances. In this regard, managers and workers will hold two primary allegiances, one to their principal firm, the other to the project team. The matrix organization becomes a network in the sense that managers hold dual lines of loyalty.

Hierarchical or Heterarchical Organization

In the debate over lateral cooperation, the easy target has been the hierarchical organization. The following view of D. Quinn Mills, who is a well-known writer on strategy and implementation, is not unusual in the context of the debate:

> The traditional hierarchical structure of our companies is more than just a system that has outlived its usefulness—*it's a clear and present danger to the economic welfare of all of us. (Mills 1991)*

The futurologist Alvin Toffler has a clear vision of the firm as modular with a loose control structure:

> The organization of the future will be more like a Calder mobile, with a thin wire of control, and with modules hanging down of various shapes and colors, each of which is capable of twisting in the wind as the wind changes. And each of which is also capable of being decoupled and disposed of and replaced by some other unit. (Interview with A. J. Vogl, "Breaking with Bureaucracy," *Across the Board*, January/February 1991)

We embrace the vision of Mills and Toffler, but reject the analysis for the reasons adumbrated above: the importance of loyalty and leadership, of consistency in strategy, and of the proper balancing of incentives with cooperation. We do not believe that the practice of "coupling and decoupling" modules is sustainable for the mass of the work force, nor even desirable. Decoupled systems prevent shared learning.

We envision a more nuanced understanding of hierarchy as built around competence and leadership rather than given authority. What we see as no longer viable is the simple acceptance of hierarchy as a unidimensional ranking of authority. Instead, we picture a corporation as existing of multiple hierarchies, nested within a shell of control that delegates ultimate legal and fiduciary responsibility.

The term heterarchy has been suggested in a few contexts as a way to describe the structure of this multiple hierarchic structure. A heterarchy is a particular kind of modular structure. One influential view is that of Gunnar Hedlund, as described in the chapter by Farley and Kobrin, that proposes that the multinational corporation is increasingly heterarchic in its structure and process. A good example of this design is the so-called "lead country" structure, in which a subsidiary that has proven capabilities, or is allocated resources to acquire them, is given worldwide responsibilities for a particular product line. As this design is extended to many products, the multinational corporation

becomes a collection of lead-country subsidiaries, each with strategic responsibilities. There is no center, but centers. Yet, subsidiaries are not decoupled
from the corporation, but the allocation of responsibility is permitted to be
shifted among contending groups.

Contrary to the belief that this heterachical structure is not compatible
with strong leadership, we believe that the fluidity of this structure will require
an increase in the vertical incentives and will put a premium on long-term
employment or affiliation. Without the creation of effective vertical incentives,
modular systems along these lines would be vulnerable to the remarkable fluctuations in national economies, be they economic, political, or technological in
origin. Movements in the value of foreign currencies alone can shift low-cost
sites dramatically among countries. Consider how the rapid depreciation of the
U.S. dollar doubled the dollar wage costs for subsidiaries operating in Germany
or Japan over only a few years!

With so much environmental volatility, human resource management will
be a principal mechanism by which vertical incentives are exercised. The
constant element in the flexibility among projects and the rapid changes by
which groups are reassigned to tasks, is the participation of individuals. The
role of top management to cultivate future leaders is particularly important. As
the operational and strategic responsibilities of headquarters declines, the importance of cultivating leaders is, perhaps contrary to intuition, of central
importance (Bowman 1986).

Conclusions

Adam Smith would not be surprised by the increasing division of labor among
core firms and their contractors, among regions, and nations. His vision was
deficient, however, in his failure to understand the firm and the variety in the
forms of the division of labor. The famous pin example, whereby workers
specialize in various tasks of manufacturing, is silent on the organizational
context. With the multinational corporation involved in roughly half of manufactured trade, the division of labor among countries is often conducted within a
designed system of coordination and cooperation.

Hebert Simon (1969) has noted that "professional schools will reassume
their professional responsibilities just to the degree that they can discover a
science of design." And yet he also observes that "design . . . is the core of all
professional training; it is the principal mark that distinguishes the professions
from the sciences." A science of design and yet not a science—these observations represent well the inherent contradictions in any academic professional

school in its efforts to bridge the "artificial" and "real," what is imaginable and what is out there.[*]

Permeability between the artificial and real is a major source of benefit and concern for a business school. Competition for training business managers is hardly limited to that among academic schools, but has grown to include consulting companies, as well as in-house educational programs. The great strength and vulnerability of professional business schools is its situation between academic centers of research and the practicing community.

In this bridging role, there is a great benefit to professional schools insofar as they can act as laboratories of social experimentation. Diversity of students, by sex, by nationality, by race or ethnicity, provides a dramatic example of the leading role professional schools can and sometimes do play in the advancement of societal progress. That this leading role by business schools as forums of experimentation is not always performed, and when performed, not always admired, is a frequent point of contention among the many stakeholders in its operation.

By design, business schools can provide an opportunity for exchange between the artificial and real. It is surprisingly neglected that the operation of a business school belongs to the "real" by providing a service to students and the business community. The recent introduction of greater modularity in course choice, interdisciplinary projects, and experiential methods is an innovation that has radical implications for those working in business schools.

Yet, these real changes in the organization and content of curricula should not blur the importance of the artificial. Researchers or innovators see no contradiction in speaking of the science of design as an art. Professional schools should not lose sight of the fact that experimentation in artificial worlds is the most unique service provided in education and research.

The chapters in this book are expressions of the importance of experimental design in research and dialogue between academic and managerial communities. They are reflections on practice and experiments in thought. As such, they represent the play between science and craft, and the artificial and real, that pushes professional schools in their research and in their education toward the meaningful frontier where managerial practice and thought mutually inform each other.

---

[*]These are not precisely Simon's concerns. He focused on the tendency of professional schools to move away from the artificial sciences toward natural sciences; his distinction was between the "natural" and "artificial" sciences.

Notes

We thank Bertha Chan for her research assistance and Peter Sherer and Mike Useem for many helpful conversations.

1. O'Shaughnessy (1994) found that downsizing alone has negligible effects on performance; when coupled with the implementation of short-term incentives (for example, cash bonuses), the immediate effect on performance is positive, but these effects turn negative with time.
2. The distinction between "integral" and "modular" design is drawn from Ulrich (1993).
3. The following draws from the intriguing paper by Baldwin and Clark (1992). We thank Per-Göran Persson for suggesting that the problem be recast in terms of dice.
4. Dore's (1986) study on the sources of Japanese flexibility highlights extensively the use of contract workers as a buffer. The early retirement age of full-time workers leads to the rehiring of these workers on a contingent basis when their benefits expire.
5. See Bateson (1972) for the classic and remarkably brief statement; Argyris and Schoen (1978) have developed these ideas substantially further.
6. Moreover, the pricing policy creates an incentive to learn better ways of doing things. Prices are established with the expectation that they will decline with costs; the supplier is permitted to keep most of the gains if costs fall faster than expected. See Nishiguchi (1994) for an explanation.

References

Argyris, Chris. 1957. *Personality and organization.* New York: Harper and Brothers.

Argyris, Chris, and Donald Schoen. 1978. *Organizational learning: A theory of action perspective.* Reading, Mass.: Addison Wesley.

Bacon, Jeremy. 1990. *Membership and organization of corporate boards.* New York: Conference Board.

Baldwin, Carliss, and Kim Clark. 1992. The benefits and costs of modularity in design. Mimeo, Harvard Business School.

Bateson, Gregory. 1972. *Steps to an ecology of mind.* New York: Ballantine.

Bowman, Edward H. 1986. Concerns of the CEO. *Human Resource Management* 25:267–85.

Clark, Kim, and Takahiro Fujimoto. 1991. *Product development performance: Strategy, organization and management in the world auto industry.* Boston: Mass.: Harvard Business School Press.

Doeringer, Peter. 1991. *Turbulence in the American workplace.* New York: Oxford University Press.

Dore, Ronald. 1986. *Flexible Rigidities. industrial policy and structural adjustment in the Japanese economy, 1970–1980.* Stanford: Stanford University.

Drucker, Peter. 1993. SEI center speech to the Warton School. April 7, 1993.

Fierman, Jaclyn. 1994. The contingent work force. *Fortune Magazine,* Jan., 30–36.

Hackman, J. Richard, and Greg Oldham. 1980. *Work redesign.* Reading, Mass.: Addison-Wesley.

Handy, Charles. 1989. *The age of unreason.* Boston, Mass.: Harvard Business School Press.

Harder, Joe. 1992. Play for pay: Effects of inequity in a pay-for performance context. *Administrative Science Quarterly* 37:321–35.

Hirschhorn, Larry, and Thomas Gilmore. 1992. The new boundaries of the boundary-less company. *Harvard Business Review* 70:104–15.

Janger, Allan. 1989. *Measuring managerial layers and spans.* New York: The Conference Board.

Kanter, Rosabeth Moss. 1989. The new managerial work. *Harvard Business Review* 67:85–92.

Kogut, Bruce, and Udo Zander. 1992. Knowledge of the firm, combinative capabilities, and the replication of technology. *Organization Science* 3:383–97.

Mills, D. Quinn. 1991. Breaking out of hierarchy traps. *Executive Excellence* 8:15.

Nishiguchi, Toshihiro. 1994. *Strategic industrial sourcing. The Japanese advantage.* New York: Oxford University Press.

Pfeffer, Jeffrey, and James Baron. 1988. Taking the workers back out: Recent trends in the structuring of employment. In *Research in organizational behavior,* edited by Barry M. Staw and L. L. Cummings. Greenwich, Conn.: JAI Press.

O'Shaughnessy, K. C. 1994. *Downsizing and performance.* Ph.D. dissertation in process (title tentative).

Overman, Stephanie. 1991. The layoff legacy. *HR Magazine* 36:28–32.

Sherer, Peter. 1993. New forms of employment. Mimeo, the Wharton School.

Simon, Herbert. 1969. *The science of the artificial.* Cambridge, Mass.: MIT Press.

Tully, Shawn. 1993. The modular corporation. *Fortune,* Feb. 8, 106–14.

Ulrich, Karl. 1993. The role of product architecture in the manufacturing firm. *Research Policy* (forthcoming).

Index